STEALING
FROM A CHILD

STEALING FROM A CHILD

THE INJUSTICE OF 'MARRIAGE EQUALITY'

David van Gend

CONNOR COURT PUBLISHING

Published in 2016 by Connor Court Publishing Pty Ltd

Copyright © David van Gend 2016

All rights reserved. No part of this book may be reproduced or transmitted in any form or by any means, electronic or mechanical, including photocopying, recording or by any information storage and retrieval system, without prior permission in writing from the publisher.

Connor Court Publishing Pty Ltd
PO Box 7257
Redland Bay QLD 4165
sales@connorcourt.com
www.connorcourt.com
Phone 0497-900-685

Printed in Australia

ISBN 978-1-925501-23-0

Proceeds and royalties go to the Australian Marriage Forum Inc.

Front cover design Maria Giordano

DEDICATION

To the victims of 'marriage equality'

To the future child of same-sex 'marriage',
forced by our law to miss out on her mother or father.

To future children of a 'genderless' culture,
subjected by law to 'genderless' sex-education.

To all husbands and wives,
degraded to 'Partner 1 & 2'.

To all mothers and fathers,
debased to 'Progenitor A & B'.

To conscientious objectors against LGBT dogma,
harassed by anti-discrimination law into silence.

THE CHOICE

Same-sex marriage ... forces us to choose between giving priority to children's rights or to homosexual adults' claims.

Professor Margaret Somerville AM[1]

Contents

INDICTMENT — 9

PART I: STEALING A CHILD'S BIRTHRIGHT
1. Motherless children; fatherless homes — 25
2. Children of homosexual homes speak out — 35
3. Gay men speak out — 49
4. Social science speaks out — 59

PART II: STEALING CHILDHOOD
5. LGBTQ sex-education at your 'safe school' — 89
6. Bullying, blackmail & 'born that way' — 109

PART III: REPEALING NATURE
7. Mutations of marriage — 137
8. The abolition of male & female — 147
9. Children of the State — 181

PART IV: PILLAGING THE VILLAGE
10. The silence of the shepherds — 197
11. Bigots, bakers & the Thought Police — 219

SETTLEMENT — 231

Acknowledgments — 238
Bibliography — 239
Endnotes — 241

INDICTMENT

Coercion is built into gay marriage. They used to say love and marriage went together - in the gay-marriage movement, it's authoritarianism and marriage that are bedfellows.
    Brendan O'Neill[2]

This book is about what happens if we enshrine a lie at the heart of our culture.

If the law says that two men can 'marry', that is an idea with consequences. For if we redefine marriage, we redefine parenting and we redefine family. It is no small matter to revoke the definition of "family" in the Universal Declaration of Human Rights – "the natural and fundamental group unit of society" – and replace it with a genderless fiction.[3]

Lesbian social historian E.J. Graff exults that "same-sex marriage is a breathtakingly subversive idea," but we, the public, are assured that nothing will change.[4] This book takes a hard look at the changes that will come with this subversive idea: how it redefines marriage and family for all of us; how it breaks a child's bonds of kinship and identity; how it usurps parental authority over their child's education; how it eats away at core liberties of speech, conscience and religion; how it serves that century-long ideological quest to deconstruct the natural family and subjugate it to the authority of the State.

Those of us who once thought that 'marriage equality' was just about marriage now realise we were wrong. For the serious lesbian, gay, bisexual, transgender and queer (LGBTQ) activists, it is about capturing the legal high ground from where the entire 'rainbow agenda' can be implemented. This ranges from imposing radical "Safe Schools" gender theory on our kids (Ch.5) to passing laws that let cross-dressing males use girls' bathrooms (Ch.8); from bankrupting bakers who don't want to write a gay 'marriage' slogan on a cake (Ch.11) to prosecuting pastors for teaching traditional values on marriage (Ch.10); from removing 'mother and father' from birth certificates to changing 'husband and wife' into 'partner 1 & 2' (Ch.9). Worst by far, laws for 'marriage equality' force future children to miss out on their mother or father while telling them it doesn't matter (Ch.1).

G.K. Chesterton said, "this triangle of truisms, of father, mother and child, cannot be destroyed; it can only destroy those civilisations that disregard it."[5] I do not want to see our civilisation further decline or our marriage culture further decay because of a "breathtakingly subversive" falsehood at its heart. Hence this book, a defence of the timeless truth of 'father, mother and child'.

I. Same-sex 'marriage': An unjust proposition

Injustice against the child is the central offence of 'marriage equality'. We are guilty of stealing a child's birthright when we institute motherless families and fatherless homes as an ideal in our law.

Why would we do that to a future child? Have we learnt nothing from past government policies that broke bonds of blood and belonging? In 2013 our then Prime Minister, Julia Gillard, gave the National Apology for Forced Adoption of babies from their teenage mothers. In a moving speech she confessed our shame for a policy that broke "the most primal and sacred bond there is, the bond between a mother and her baby".[6] Just three years later we are being asked to support a new policy that will break that primal and sacred bond all over again; for if we institute the 'marriage' of two men, we are instituting motherless families. We are saying that future children do not need a mother; we are legislating to guarantee they will not have a mother. We are shallow fools. Which future Prime Minister will have to deliver our heartfelt National Apology to the "motherless generation"?

The bulk of this book will deal with the multifaceted injustice that comes with 'marriage equality' and with its ideological fellow-travellers who comprise the wedding party. For the purposes of this introductory indictment, there are two further charges that must be laid: that the proposition of same-sex 'marriage' is untrue and unnecessary. Untrue to nature and timeless culture; unnecessary for achieving civil equality between citizens.

II. Same-sex 'marriage': An untrue proposition

If the Labor Party had won the Australian election in July 2016, 'marriage equality' would have been legislated "within 100 days". Since the Liberal National Coalition prevailed, there will be a people's vote, a plebiscite, to decide the future of marriage. A plebiscite is certainly the less bad option, but both are symptoms of advanced social dementia. A sane society would not even think such thoughts; it would know that some things are beyond the authority of any government, any court, any plebiscite to redefine.

Marriage is ultimately defined by nature. Marriage is not a social invention to be cut to shape according to political fad; it is a social recognition of pre-existing biological reality: male, female, offspring. The greatest of modern anthropologists, Claude Levi-Strauss, described marriage as "a social institution with a biological foundation."[7] All of our marriage laws and customs exist to reinforce this biological foundation, helping bind a man to his mate for the sake of social stability and, above all, for the sake of any child they might create.

Not all marriages do create children – but typically they do, and an institution exists for the typical case. Married couples who cannot have children are still fully married because they fulfil the twin criteria of marriage: they bring together the two halves of nature, male and female, in a conjugal union; they are able to give a child, albeit an adopted child, the mother and father relationship a child needs. Same-sex couples obviously do not bring together the two halves of nature in a conjugal union; they cannot give a child, any child, the mother and father relationship a child needs. It is a statement of anthropological fact, not a personal slight, to say that two males cannot marry. Same-sex relationships matter greatly to the individuals involved and demand neighbourly civility, but they are a different kind of thing to the great natural project of marriage and family. They need to find a different word.

This is not a theological argument. The atheist philosopher Bertrand Russell understood the child-centred basis for marriage, writing in his 1929 book *Marriage & Morals*: "It is through children alone that sexual relations become of importance to society, and worthy to be taken cognisance of by a legal institution."[8] Same-sex relationships obviously cannot create children, so society has no institutional interest in regulating such friendships. It is only because the man-woman pair-bond typically results in offspring that every society has needed to put great effort into reinforcing that relationship – striving to keep the feral-by-nature male faithful to the mother of his child, because the alternative is abandoned mothers, fatherless children, poverty and chaos.

Keeping a man with his mate

Another of the great anthropologists of the twentieth century, Kingsley Davis, reflects on the role of marriage in reinforcing these natural bonds:

> While the mother is bound to her offspring by physiological and psychological bonds, the same cannot be said of the father. To be sure, he has a sexual bond of sorts with the mother, but as time goes by he tends to feel more attraction to new or younger females. As a consequence, human societies have evolved strong controls, or incentives, that attach the male to the family. These are particularly evident when a new family is formed, that is, at marriage. At that moment advantage is taken of the youthfulness of the bride and groom to emphasise their togetherness, to impress upon them the importance and social approval of their sexual contact, and to stress the durability of the relationship and its connection with children.[9]

Surveying the same scene, the Chief Justice of the US Supreme Court, John Roberts, recognised the natural structure and purpose of marriage. In his dissenting judgement in the 2015 *Obergefell* case (which legalised same-sex 'marriage') he observed:

> Marriage ... arose in the nature of things to meet a vital need: ensuring that children are conceived by a mother and father committed to raising them in the stable conditions of a lifelong relationship ... The premises supporting this concept of marriage are so fundamental that they rarely require articulation. The human race must procreate to survive. Procreation occurs through sexual relations between a man and a woman. When sexual relations result in the conception of a child, that child's prospects are generally better if the mother and father stay together rather than going their separate ways. Therefore, for the good of children and

society, sexual relations that can lead to procreation should occur only between a man and a woman committed to a lasting bond. Society has recognized that bond as marriage.[10]

So marriage of man and woman is founded on the truth that only a man and woman can create a child; only a man and woman can give that child her own mother and father, her biological identity and ancestry. That is nature's job description for marriage, and two men or two women need not apply. Attempting to give marriage a different meaning – "Best Friends Forever" for any passionately connected adults of any sex – is an adolescent prank, but not a harmless one. It tramples on truths of nature and culture, kinship and creed, and it has consequences.

But hasn't marriage 'evolved'?

Go as far back in written history as it is possible to go and you will find marriage, always and only a man-woman thing, as the necessary basis of family and society. Surveying human culture through the ages, Levi-Strauss concluded that "the family – based on a union, more or less durable but socially approved, of two individuals of opposite sexes who establish a household and bear and raise children – appears to be a practically universal phenomenon, present in every type of society".[11] Even in the most primitive societies, he observed, this timeless, pre-political order is to be found:

> To cite a few examples, the insular Andamanese of the Indian ocean, the Fuegians of the southernmost tip of South America, the Nambikwara of central Brazil, and the Bushmen of South Africa lived in small, semi-nomadic bands; they had little or no political organisation; and their technological level was very low; some of these people had no knowledge of weaving or did not practice pot making or construct permanent dwellings. Among them, however, the only social structure worthy of the name was the family, often even the monogamous family. The fieldworker had no trouble identifying married couples, who were closely united by sentimental bonds, by economic cooperation in every case, and by a common interest in their children.[12]

Even in societies too primitive to have a government, man and woman make their vows to each other and commit to their young. It is misleading (and condescending) to suggest that a "closely united" man and woman with "common interest in their children" is something only found in highly evolved societies; the bond of father, mother and child is a natural nobility in human nature.

It is misleading in a different way to claim that marriage has 'evolved' by citing historical cases of racism where blacks were not allowed to marry whites, or cases of polygamy where a man was allowed to marry several women. Neither of those degraded social situations ever changed the fact that marriage was always and everywhere between male and female. Racist laws existed to keep black and white apart and that included keeping men and women apart, but the banned marriages were still, of course, a man-woman thing. Tribal structures might have allowed a man to have several wives, but each and every sexual relationship within that polygamous marriage was a man-woman thing. Never was the male-female essence of marriage under question.

Ancient legal codes of Hammurabi and King Dadusha in Babylon four thousand years ago specify social conditions for valid marriage similar to our own, including the need for a formal contract, a public ceremony and even obtaining consent from the in-laws. If King Dadusha had been a guest at the Royal Wedding of William and Catherine in 2011 he would have understood the Bishop of London's exposition, from the 1662 *Book of Common Prayer*, as to why we have the institution of marriage:

> First, [marriage] was ordained for the increase of mankind ... Secondly, it was ordained in order that the natural instincts and affections should be hallowed and directed aright ... Thirdly, it was ordained for the mutual society, help, and comfort that the one ought to have of the other.

Note that the Bishop's basic rationale is anthropological, not theological: marriage exists to nurture a new generation; to discipline the sexual energies to constructive ends; and to be what John Locke called "the First Society" of husband and wife, mother, father and child. What King Dadusha would not have understood, nor any other King or philosopher in the last four thousand years, is the warp of public policy that allowed two gentlemen sitting in the pews at the Royal Wedding, Sir Elton John and his partner David Furnish, to have their relationship elevated soon thereafter to "the honourable estate of marriage".

Have there been homosexual 'marriages' in history?

Homosexual and bisexual relationships are recorded, even affirmed, in history but there has never been an institution of homosexual 'marriage', since it could serve no vital social purpose. As a rare aberration that proves the rule, the ancient Romans did record one case of homosexual 'marriage' in the year 64 AD, but that was the Emperor Nero – whom the contemporary historian Tacitus described as "corrupted by every lust, natural and unnatural".[13] Even that historian of decadent Rome had trouble concealing his disgust: "The emperor, in the presence of witnesses, put on the bridal veil. Dowry, marriage bed, wedding torches, all were there. Indeed everything was public which even in a natural union is veiled by night."

I have not seen that historic gay wedding, that imperial affirmation that "love is love", celebrated in any TV ads for Marriage Equality.

The ancient Greeks indulged homosexual relations but never confused that with the necessary life-task of marriage and family. As early as Homer we find the word *gamos* to describe the honoured relationship between man and woman that we recognise as monogamous marriage, centred on the *oikos* or family home. The Romans gave us our word "matrimony", made up of two words: *mater* meaning mother, and *monium* meaning state or condition. Matrimony is the institution built around the condition of motherhood. And mothers are built around babies, for nine intimate months and beyond. And babies are built around the double helix of DNA: one strand from the mother, one strand from the father, interwoven and encoded into a new name; moulded into a unique face that reflects the man and woman who together gave her existence.

That is matrimony. That is marriage and family. That is nature's masterpiece. It can only be a man-woman thing.

III. Same-sex 'marriage': An unnecessary proposition

The Australian Bureau of Statistics tells us that 1% of couples in Australia are same-sex.[14] The Australian Parliament tells us that same-sex couples now have 100% the same legal status and benefits as any other couple in Australia. So where is the inequality? Where is the injustice that 'marriage equality' is meant to address?

All couples have the same status

Since 2008, when eighty-five laws were amended by a bipartisan majority of federal parliament, there has been no unjust discrimination against same sex couples in Australia, whether in taxation, superannuation, Medicare, DVA spouse pension, next of kin status, whatever. As the deputy Labor leader, Tanya Plibersek, confirmed in May 2015, "We changed 85 laws at the time, removed every piece of legal discrimination against gay men, lesbians and same-sex couples on the statute books."[15] Every piece. In the eyes of the law, there is no difference between a same-sex couple and any other de facto or married couple. Your average gay couple has the same legal standing as, for example, our former first couple, the Hon. Julia Gillard and Mr Tim Mathieson. Neither couple has a marriage certificate, nor do they need one to enjoy the same status and benefits as a married couple.

No self-respecting gay couple needs a certificate of their relationship from the government! The daughter of a loving lesbian couple, Katy Faust, emphasised that point on ABC *Lateline* in August 2015. Asked by compere Tony Jones about the dignity that would be conferred on same-sex couples by their inclusion in marriage, Faust replied,

> You don't gain dignity by a government bestowing that on you, you just have it … They have dignity and the question is not even really whether or not they have the capacity to love and commit the way heterosexuals do. They do. They absolutely do. The question is: what is government's interest in marriage? It's really not about affirming the connections that we have with one another. It has to do with the product of those unions and there's something distinct about the product of a union between heterosexuals. What's distinct is that they make babies and those babies have rights.[16]

So while all couples in Australia have full "relationship equality", it is a different situation when a third party, the baby, is brought in. A baby is not related to two men the same way she is related to her mum and dad. Marriage exists primarily to bind children to their mother and father; same-sex couples cannot meet that primary criterion for marriage. To say a same-sex couple cannot marry is like saying a man cannot attend a women's hospital; there is no ill will, no unjust discrimination, just a statement of the biological obvious.

Most gay people don't want to marry

Consider just one more figure: 20%. According to Dutch statistics in 2013, twelve years after gay marriage was introduced, only 20% of same-sex couples were married, compared to 80% of man-woman couples.[17] So where is the great issue of injustice and inequality, one might ask, if same-sex couples already have the same legal status and benefits as any other couple and the vast majority of same-sex couples don't even want to marry?

During a debate on ABC radio in 2015, Rodney Croome, then director of Australian Marriage Equality, put the inequality claim to me this way: "To exclude same-sex couples … from such a core institution … stigmatises same-sex relationships and puts us out in the cold. Marriage equality will bring us in from the cold."[18] But is it really so cold out there? We've just noted that most Dutch same-sex couples prefer to stay out in the cold! And hundreds of thousands of heterosexual de facto couples in Australia also choose to stay out in the cold but they don't seem to mind. So I say to Mr Croome: don't invent injustice where it doesn't exist. Same-sex couples are de facto couples with all the status and benefits of any other couple: there is no unjust discrimination against same-sex couples in Australia. Find another slogan.

Should we change the law as a health initiative for gay adults?

A related argument, although very weak, is that marriage improves the health and wellbeing of partners, so we should let same-sex couples 'marry' as a public health measure. Paul Ritchie, for example, in his recent book makes this the centrepiece of the conservative case for same-sex 'marriage': "The reason why the case for same-sex marriage is compelling is because the case for marriage is compelling. The 'marriage advantage' permeates our health, our relationships, our finances, and our wellbeing."[19]

Ritchie is correct that marriage generally carries these advantages, but so does a happy, stable de facto partnership. It is a leap of faith to claim that same-sex 'marriage' would bring significant health advantages above and beyond the advantages of a happy de facto same-sex partnership. The weakness of this claim becomes clear when we see how Ritchie accounts for the health benefit of marriage:

> Researchers surmise that this is the result of three factors. First, when there is someone else around, they tend to remind us to eat better, sleep more, take care of ourselves or visit a doctor, even if we don't think we need to. There is someone to care for us – to watch out for us. Second, we tend to take better care of ourselves if we feel that our lives matter to others. Third, in ways most of us do not understand, there is a deep interrelationship between our physical health and our emotional wellbeing. Marriage helps us to feel better about ourselves and our lives, and provides comfort and succour when we need it.[20]

So the health benefit comes from companionship and care and feeling good about ourselves. It strikes me as condescending to suggest that stable de facto couples do not provide equally good companionship and care or feel equally good about themselves. Hundreds of thousands of heterosexual de facto couples in Australia would agree: they are not married but they still benefit from mutual companionship and care. Same-sex couples are de facto couples, and they can provide each other with the same loyal companionship and care as any married couple – so where is the compelling health-based reason to change from de facto to 'married'? And is it proportionate to radically redefine the timeless institution of marriage as a dubious public health initiative for gay adults?

Do kids in gay households need 'married' parents?

Far more impressive than the adult-centred argument is the child-centred argument for same-sex 'marriage'. We will hear again and again over the course of the plebiscite that it is necessary to redefine marriage for two reasons: first, to make children of same-sex couples feel normal and included; second, to make gay kids feel normal and included.

In my discussion with Mr Croome he made the first point this way: "Children being raised by same-sex couples should have the affirmation, sense of security, sense of stability that comes with having married parents." Security and stability are good things, but children being raised by same-sex couples already have the same legal security and stability as children in any other household. Where is the deficiency? I doubt Mr Croome was suggesting there is something second-rate about de facto parents that makes their children insecure and unstable. Granted that de facto parents are as good as married parents, and their families as secure in the eyes of the law, who is Mr Croome to suggest that same-sex de facto couples do not offer their children affirmation, security and stability?

Two other considerations are relevant to the claim that we must grant same-sex 'marriage' because kids in gay households want it. First, some don't. Chapter 2 gives examples of children of same-sex households who don't support same-sex 'marriage'. Katy Faust, as mentioned, is one of them; in her *Lateline* interview, she brought it back to the issue of biological bonds and belonging.

The other cautionary consideration is the finding of social science that we *cause* emotional insecurity and instability for children whenever we break their biological kinship bonds. Same-sex parenting is just another way of breaking those biological bonds. If we encourage same-sex parenting through instituting same-sex 'marriage', that destines more kids to suffer the emotional instability that comes with this new form of broken family. How is that a good move for children? Plenty on this in Chapter 4 (Social science speaks out). And a fascinating footnote: contrary to popular opinion, letting same-sex parents 'marry' does not appear to improve children's emotional stability; initial research by Sullins in 2015 indicates a worsening of emotional problems for children in same-sex homes when the parents legally 'marry', and the problems intensify the longer the parents are 'married'.[21] So let's not naively assume that a 'marriage' certificate will benefit kids raised in same-sex households.

Should we change the law as 'therapy' for gay youth?

The second child-centred argument for same-sex 'marriage' – the need to make gay kids feel normal and included – was powerfully expressed by the former Irish President Mary McAleese, mother of a gay man, before the Irish referendum on same-sex 'marriage' in 2015:

> The only children affected by this referendum will be Ireland's gay children … We have to make it happen for them and for all the unborn gay children who are relying on us to end the branding, end the isolation, end the inequality, literally once and for all.[22]

Putting aside the curious notion of "unborn gay children" (see Chapter 6 under 'Born that way'), we can all agree about wanting to ease emotional distress for young people. The question is, does it make sense to overturn the foundational institution of society as a form of psychological therapy for some troubled kids? There are less radical ways to help! There are other ways to make them feel loved and included in our families, schools, churches and clubs.

This second argument gets emotive to the point of blackmail: "Give us marriage equality or you are causing young people to suffer, be bullied, and even commit suicide!" The same ultimatum is used to demand gay-affirming sex-education, and more recently to demand transgender-affirming legislation and sex-change therapy. I deal with the fallacies of such emotional arm-twisting under the heading 'To combat depression' in Chapter 6. This all-purpose ultimatum to comply with LGBT demands on marriage, sex-education and transgender rights – and if we don't, we are culpable for LGBT deaths – reminds us that legalising same-sex 'marriage' is only part of a package deal of demands. It is the most important means to the more ambitious end of normalising everything homosexual/bisexual/transsexual with the force of law. Indeed, after the Irish referendum was over, McAleese confirmed the broader goal: "There is more to be done, for the work of dismantling the entire architecture of homophobia is still not complete. The achievement of marriage equality surely and irrevocably propelled us further along the road…"[23]

"Dismantling the entire architecture of homophobia" is another way of saying, "imposing the entire architecture of homophilia", or coercing society to accept and affirm the entire LGBTQ spectrum of rainbow politics. 'Marriage equality' provides the legal clout to compel such acceptance. For once homosexual/bisexual/transsexual behaviour is normalised in the central institution of marriage, that gives the LGBTQ lobby the big stick of anti-discrimination law to normalise homosexual/

bisexual/transsexual behaviour in the culture, especially in the schools, and to silence conscientious dissenters, especially in the churches. So if you vote Yes at the plebiscite, you will get so much more than just 'marriage equality'; you will get the full rainbow package deal, whether you like it or not.

Putting the child first

This book votes No because it puts the rights of the child ahead of the demands of homosexual adults. It says that our fellow citizens, our friends and family who are same-sex attracted are our equals in every way. The 1% of couples who are 'same-sex' already have the same legal status and benefits as any other couple under Australian law. We say that they are free to live as they choose but:

- they are not free to choose a motherless or fatherless existence for future children;
- they are not free to impose radical LGBTQ sex-education on all of our children;
- they are not free to silence pastors and conscientious objectors with the big stick of anti-discrimination law;
- they are not free to so radically distort the natural truth of marriage and parenting, husband and wife, mother and father, and even male and female that future marriage and society will be unrecognisable.

For daring to indict the subversive idea of genderless 'marriage', for wanting to protect the birthright of future children and protect our own children from the onslaught of gender ideology in schools, we are called bigots. The week I completed this book I read Professor Peter van Onselen in *The Australian* declare, with great moral superiority, "Those who oppose the tsunami for change to the Marriage Act will eventually be left looking every bit as bigoted as southern white Americans who argued that blacks should sit at the back of the bus, long after the rest of society recognised that segregation was morally wrong."[24] As I understand it, a tsunami is something that hurts a lot of people. If there really is a tsunami coming, then this book will serve as a warning for families who want to get to higher ground; another possibility is that this 'tsunami', as often happens, will turn out to be much weaker than we thought.

Part I

Stealing a Child's Birthright

1

MOTHERLESS CHILDREN; FATHERLESS HOMES

> *Redefining marriage redefines parenthood. It moves us well beyond our "live and let live" philosophy into the land where our society promotes a family structure where children will always suffer loss ... Have we really arrived at a time when we are considering institutionalizing the stripping of a child's natural right to a mother and a father in order to validate the emotions of adults?*
> Katy Faust[25]

This is the heart of opposition to same-sex 'marriage': that it means same-sex parenting, and same-sex parenting means that future children must miss out on either their mother or their father.

That's because 'marriage and parenting' is a compound right under Article 16 of the Universal Declaration of Human Rights: "the right to marry and to found a family". Therefore homosexual 'marriage' includes both the legal recognition of an exclusive relationship and the right to form a family by artificial reproduction – such as surrogacy. As the result of a law for 'marriage equality', future children will be deprived of the primal relationship with either their mother or their father – not through tragic circumstance, but by an Act of Parliament.

Of course, there are already tragic situations where a child misses out on her mother or father, such as the death or desertion of a parent – but that is not something we would wish upon a child, and it is not something a government should ever impose upon a child. Legalising same-sex 'marriage' would impose this deprivation in a premeditated way on any child created within that institution.

There are already situations where broken families reform as a homosexual household and nothing can or should be done about that. What we must not allow, however, is the situation where government facilitates the deliberate creation of motherless or fatherless families. There are already situations where single parents have to raise a child on their own, and in my experience as a GP they often do a great job – but I have never met a single parent who *planned* for their child to miss out on the other parent. That is the difference with a law for same-sex 'marriage'.

Some people also raise the scenario of an abusive mother and father and argue that it is better for a child to have two loving same-sex carers than a dysfunctional pair of biological parents. But neither option gives a child what she needs. Just because a child in one house is being mistreated by her father does not make it 'right' that a child in another house should be forced to miss out on her father altogether. We must reject both scenarios, restraining parents who would inflict abuse while also restraining governments who would inflict laws that steal a child's birthright to her own mum and dad.

'But gay couples can already get kids'

Other people, like Labor Senator Penny Wong, insist that because some same-sex couples already obtain children by adoption or surrogacy, nothing is going to change with same-sex 'marriage'. That is not correct. A number of states rightly prohibit same-sex couples (and single people) from adopting or creating a child by surrogacy or IVF since that is not considered to be in the best interests of the child. It is important to understand that the ethical objection applies equally to single people as to same-sex couples, since neither family structure can give a child what she deserves: a father-relationship and a mother-relationship. At the time of writing, June 2016, single people and same-sex couples cannot adopt in Queensland or South Australia.[26] They cannot obtain a child by surrogacy in Western Australia or South Australia. Likewise, a lesbian couple cannot create a child by IVF in South Australia. Present permissive laws are also open to reversal: in Queensland, the opposition LNP has a policy to overturn Labor's surrogacy provisions for single people and same-sex couples.

Surrogacy and adoption are state issues and they will come and go according to the policies of rival parties, but a federal law for same-sex 'marriage' would overrule any state prohibitions on same-sex adoption and surrogacy. Such a law would become the nationwide, permanent violation of a child's right, where possible, to be raised by both mother and father. It is a law with teeth.

Gay men need surrogate wombs

And those teeth will do more than just strip away a child's birthright; they will add, inevitably, to the exploitation of women whose services will be required if rich gay men are to exercise their right "to marry and to found a family". Writing in the *Sydney Morning Herald*, bioethics commentator Michael Cook warned:

> Supporters of same-sex marriage must recognise they face a serious moral dilemma. Cheap wombs might bring gay men the happiness of being the father of a child of their own. But the cost of that happiness is often borne by poor and uneducated women.[27]

Cook quotes the words of a "surrogate-mother broker" telling his gay clients about how they are to view the woman: "She's just like an easy-bake oven except with no legal rights to the cupcake."

> This is a hard-nosed description of the woman's role in gay marriage and child-rearing, but it sums it up accurately. In heterosexual relationships, the birth rate rises when couples are married. One would expect similar dynamics to apply to same-sex couples. For lesbian couples, this is not a huge problem; all they need is a sperm donor. But male couples need surrogate mothers. Where will these women come from? Unless the law of supply and demand is repealed, the answer is: where wombs are cheapest.[28]

In Australia, commercial surrogacy remains prohibited – but how long will that last once 'marriage equality' gives two men the associated right "to found a family" on a par with an infertile man-woman couple? Why should their right be limited by the availability of a sister or friend who is prepared to be an unpaid altruistic surrogate?

In her submission to the Australian Senate enquiry into same-sex marriage in 2012, Margaret Somerville AM, Professor of Law and

Medicine at McGill University, Canada (and from 2016, Professor of Bioethics at Notre Dame University, Sydney) confirmed the logical and legal connection between 'marriage equality' and 'reproductive equality': "If exclusion of same-sex couples from marriage is found to be discrimination by way of comparison with opposite-sex couples, not providing same-sex couples with the means for procreation… is a related discrimination."[29] Progressive judges will be scrambling to prohibit discrimination against the marital rights of gay men and justify their access to surrogacy. Likewise, any prohibition on artificial reproduction for lesbian couples will fall once they have 'marriage equality'.

Then what of the children? Does it matter to them to have their kinship bonds sliced and diced in this way – gestated by an anonymous and impoverished Asian woman whom they will never meet, with whom the maternal bond is denied during pregnancy and disrupted during lactation, delivered to two men as part of a business contract? Or created by an anonymous sperm donor so that two women – or a single woman, which is the same violation – can fulfil their emotional need to mother a child?

Kinship bonds matter to kids

Such a violation does matter to young people – including this young woman, who misses her unknown father but does not want to seem ungrateful to her loving mother:

> Don't get me wrong, I am so grateful to be put on this earth knowing that I was the product of love and effort, but I go to sleep every night and wake up every morning feeling lost. I will never know what it is like to play catch with a father at age 6. I will never know what it is like to bring a boy home, only to have a dad threaten them. I will never know what it is like to wake up on Father's Day morning to anything other than my mom saying we should send a photo to the family to celebrate – only to have me say "there is no father to send this photo to". I will never know what it is like to make eye contact with the man that is responsible for my existence. All I am left with is my unique olive complexion and my small nose. Those are the bits and pieces I can make out to be the pieces of me that have come from him, and while small or

dumb, it all means the world.[30]

It does matter to this sixteen-year-old daughter of a single mother who used donor sperm. She gives simple yet moving reasons for her sense of loss:

> People who are not donor conceived will never truly understand the struggles we go through. I have a boyfriend and it hurts me that I don't feel protected. I never got to introduce my boyfriend to my father and have my father act protective. I won't have a father to walk me down the aisle. I never had a father to get me into sports or help me with my homework or even just to talk to. I crave the attention of a man who truly loves me but not at all in a sexual way. I want to tell him of my achievements and straight A+ GPA and feel his pride.[31]

We cause deep disruption when we cut a girl off from her father. Not just emotionally but physiologically, since social science finds that girls who lack the protection and attachment of their biological father - the one male figure who is close and loving but not sexually – typically experience earlier menstruation, more premature sexual activity and a higher risk of teenage pregnancy.[32] Breaking the father-daughter bond messes with a girl's life in ways we barely understand. The young woman continues,

> I stare in the mirror for hours sometimes wondering what features I got from him because I don't look like my mother at all ... I want to be able to have a face in my head to know simply who the people are that created me. I want to know my biological surname. I want to know my biological grandparents. I want to hug my father more than anything and I want him to know I specifically exist, and I am real, and every human has a father and a mother and I deserve to know both. We all deserve to know where we come from and who we are. I will always feel incomplete. I will never stop searching. I must know before my life is over.

"Every human has a mother and a father and I deserve to know both." Let that be the epitaph on this heartbreaking experiment in genderless 'marriage' and parenting. We understand that indigenous children have a deep need for kinship and belonging, yet we are dismissive of the need that all children have for kinship and belonging. Even some of our politicians seek to dismiss public discussion of the possibility of grief and loss for children of same-sex households. Senator Penny Wong says she opposes holding a national plebiscite on same-sex 'marriage' because, "I don't want my relationship, my family, to be the target of discussion, disrespect and derision."[33] Let's try to understand this position: it is acceptable for the Senator to pose with her lesbian partner's baby to create a useful political image for the LGBT cause, but it is unacceptable for anyone else to discuss what such a family structure might mean to children. I know of no person who is interested in "derision" of any relationship, but we are certainly interested in "discussion" – and a politician should not be trying to silence discussion. Groups like the Australian Marriage Forum hold a different position to the Senator on same-sex family structures, and we will say it now, as we have for years, and will continue to say during the plebiscite: no two women have the right to deliberately deprive a child of his relationship with his dad. To do so is to place the emotional desires of adults above the primal kinship needs of a child. It says a father does not matter to a child. It is, in our view, an abuse of adult power and deserves the strictest social criticism – indeed, we commend the present law of the Senator's home state of South Australia, where a lesbian couple is not allowed to create a child by assisted reproduction. Why such a law? Because the lawmakers consider that it is not in the best interests of a child to be deliberately deprived of her father. The rights of adults end where the birthright of a child begins. That point of view will not be silenced.

Ethics say: put children first

Professor Somerville is one of the most resolute advocates for putting the child first in any policy on marriage or assisted reproduction. She advised the Senate enquiry in 2012,

> Same-sex marriage is symptomatic of adult-centred reproductive decision-making, a stance that our Western democratic societies have largely adopted. But reproductive decision-making should be child-centred … Children also have valid claims, if at all possible, to be reared by their own biological parents within their natural family … And society should not be complicit in intentionally

depriving children of a mother and a father. We must consider the ethics of deliberately creating any situation that is otherwise.[34]

It is important to be clear here: the ethical objection is to the deliberate violation of a child's kinship bonds, not to homosexual marriage *per se*. We are equally culpable of that offence against the child when we allow assisted reproduction for single people. Here, for the record, I have been entirely consistent; for instance, I wrote in *The Australian* in 2011: "Legalising same-sex marriage will inflict that deprivation on a child. That is why it is wrong, and that is why all laws are wrong that permit single people or same-sex couples to obtain a child by IVF, surrogacy or adoption."[35] Any of the reproductive circumstances in which adults fulfil their wishes without regard to the child's rights are unethical.

An adult-centred article on 'marriage equality' by Stephen Keim of Australian Lawyers for Human Rights says, "Equality means the right not to be discriminated against on the basis of sexuality".[36] A child-centred response is to ask why the child should be discriminated against on the basis of the sexuality of two gay men who want to obtain a baby of their own? That is exactly what Elton John and David Furnish did by creating baby Zach, using an anonymous egg donor, a rent-a-womb and a vial of their blended sperm. As the *Daily Mail* noted at the time, "They had previously been turned down for adoption because of Sir Elton's age. And the former drug addict recently said it would not be 'fair' on a child because of his advancing years and the amount of travelling he did."[37] But the 63-year-old rock star's emotional needs won out in the end; too bad about baby Zach's emotional need (and fundamental right) to know the love of his mother.

We are confronted with an unavoidable choice. If you believe that a child should be raised, where possible, by her own mother and father then you cannot vote for the institution of same-sex 'marriage'. I know some people think that they can avoid making this choice. A Galaxy poll commissioned by the Australian Marriage Forum in 2015 asked 1200 Australians to choose between two mutually exclusive options: (1) that two men should have the right to marry and create a family, or (2) that children should have the right to be raised by their own mother and father.[38] By a margin of three to one, Australians chose the rights of the child (48% to 17%) but a full third avoided the choice and said they wanted "both". Logically, that is not an option. Either we defend the rights of tomorrow's children and say no to genderless 'marriage' or we acquiesce to the demands of adults and destine those children to a motherless or fatherless existence.

In the media the demands of homosexual adults always take priority and the child's perspective is sidelined. Our aim in the Australian Marriage Forum has always been to reframe the debate with the child at the centre. We say that a child has the right to look up and see the only two faces on earth that reflect her own: the woman and the man who together gave her existence. A little girl should not have to look up and see two 'married men' posing as her parents. Neither man can be a mother to her; they cannot guide her as a mother would when she is growing from girl to woman, nor model for her the complex relationship of husband and wife. Likewise, any boy needs his father's companionship and example to help him become a man; no matter how competent and caring a lesbian partner may be, she cannot be a dad to a little boy.

Professor Somerville spells out the ethical case for putting the child's needs first:

> Ethical reasons to give priority to children's rights over homosexual adults' claims include that children are the more vulnerable persons and ethics demands that decision making is based on a presumption in favour of the most vulnerable; they cannot give their informed consent to participation in the unprecedented social experiment that same-sex marriage would constitute; and we cannot establish children's "anticipated consent", that is, we cannot reasonably assume they would consent to the mode of their coming-into being or family structure, when their conception is other than between a man and a woman.[39]

Speaking out on behalf of the child

In the next chapter, we have the privilege of hearing from children, now adults, who never gave any sort of consent to be deprived of a biological parent, and who do not think this deprivation should be imposed on other children. They were raised in caring same-sex homes but they still grieve for the missing father or mother. They understand well that their birthright was subjugated to the emotional needs and desires of their same-sex parents, and they plead with us to defend the rights of future children.

In the subsequent chapter we hear from gay men who agree that priority in the marriage debate should be given to the rights of children. They celebrate that they are free to live as they choose and love whom they will, but they say marriage and parenting needs to stay a man-woman thing so that kids can have both their mum and their dad.

And in the final chapter of this section, we learn from decades of social science that children suffer in many ways if the "primal and sacred bond" with their biological parents is broken. Same-sex parenting does exactly that, and it imposes the same disadvantage on kids as any other form of biologically disrupted family structure – such as blended families or single parent families. All fall short of the proven optimal structure of married biological parents. In addition, new research finds harms specific to same-sex parenting. Knowing this, and respecting the best interests of the child, which lawmaker would promote an institution that they know will disadvantage future children?

Society is faced with an inescapable choice. As Somerville observes, the question of same-sex marriage "forces us to choose between giving priority to children's rights or to homosexual adults' claims."[40] That is the choice Australians will face at our national plebiscite on marriage. My hope is that, in the privacy of the voting booth, they choose to stand with the child.

2

CHILDREN OF HOMOSEXUAL HOMES SPEAK OUT

My father's absence created a huge hole in me, and I ached every day for a dad. I loved my mom's partner, but another mom could never have replaced the father I lost.
    Heather Barwick.[41]

'She can't be a father'

If the central offence of 'marriage equality' is that it deprives future children of their mother or father, then the central voice in this debate should be children who can tell us what that deprivation feels like. Such voices have been raised in recent times despite the personal distress of doing so. They have spoken out, as one woman says, because they are sick of reading in the media that genderless marriage and parenting is "all the same" from the child's point of view. "But it's not", wrote Heather Barwick, who was raised by a loving lesbian couple:

> Same-sex marriage and parenting withholds either a mother or father from a child while telling him or her that it doesn't matter. That it's all the same. But it's not. A lot of us, a lot of your kids, are hurting.[42]

Brandi Walton was also raised by a lesbian couple and wrote in April 2015,

> I yearned for the affection that my friends received from their dads. I wanted to know what it was like to be held and cherished

by a man, what it was like to live with one from day to day ... My grandfathers and uncles did the best they could when it came to spending time with me and doing all the daddy-daughter stuff, but it was not the same as having a full-time father, and I knew it. It always felt second-hand. People need to know that some children of gay parents do not agree with gay adoption and marriage, just like some gay people themselves don't agree with it, either! But you will notice that fact is not making headlines.[43]

It did make headlines, briefly, in Australia in August 2015 when Katy Faust, as mentioned earlier, spoke with Tony Jones on *Lateline*:

> **Jones**: Now how is it that the daughter of lesbian mothers has become a leading opponent of gay marriage? How does that work?
>
> **Faust**: Simply because I recognised that while my mother was a fantastic mother and most of what I do well as a mother myself I do because that's how she parented me, she can't be a father. Her partner, an incredible woman — both of these women have my heart — cannot be a father either. Children have a right to be in relationship with their mother and father whenever possible, and as a society, we shouldn't normalise a family structure that requires children to lose one or both parents to be in that household. I got into this discussion primarily because what I heard from the gay lobby was that children don't care who's raising them, right? That children are just fine if it's two men or two women. And the reality is that anybody that's talked to a child who has lost a parent, whether through divorce, abandonment, third-party reproduction or death, kids absolutely care. Family structure matters to children.[44]

Faust explained this further in an open letter to the US Supreme Court prior to its 2015 decision on same-sex 'marriage':

> I am not saying that being same-sex attracted makes one incapable of parenting. My mother was an exceptional parent. This is about the *missing* parent. If you ask a child raised by a lesbian couple if they love their two moms, you'll probably get a resounding "yes!" Ask about their father, and you are in for either painful silence, a confession of gut wrenching longing, or the recognition that they have a father that they wish they could see more often. The one thing that you will not hear is indifference.[45]

These women give voice to the grief of missing out on a father's love in their formative years. They are brave enough to stand up and try to spare future children the same grief, which will increase with the formal institution and promotion of homosexual 'marriage' and parenting.

Other voices have emerged in Australia, not eloquent writers of opinion pieces or guests on *Lateline* but previously unheard of people who ring talkback radio or post a video blog to say they, too, are hurting. A young woman called Amy rang in to speak with me and host Peter Janetzki on Brisbane 96.5FM:

Peter: Amy, hello. What would you like to share with us?

Amy: Hello Peter. I'd like to share my story. Please be patient with me, I get nervous telling you this. I am the adopted daughter of a lesbian relationship. I am 21 years old. Growing through these years was really hard for me because I desperately wanted a daddy. It didn't worry me so much until I got to about 13 and we had sex-ed at school and everybody talking about male and female, and I immediately as a young girl knew that was the way it was meant to be between a man and a woman, and the relationship that my supposed mums had was not normal. When I turned 18 I went searching for my Dad. It was very confronting for him and he was very aggressive at first, but I was persistent. And then he broke down and told me that he was in love with my mother, and that when she found out she was pregnant with me she admitted that she was in a lesbian relationship. She admitted she only used him to have a baby so that she and the woman that she was with, who was my supposed mother, could have the child, so they wouldn't have to go through adoption papers and everything. That's when he snapped and has never been in a relationship ever since. It was hard for me to take that. Obviously I was very angry at my mother – how dare she try and take my life and use it how she wanted it – but I gained a great relationship with my biological father. To this day we have talks – my mother doesn't know ... if she did know I don't know what would happen to me. I just keep it under covers and every single night we chat. His birthday was two weeks ago so we celebrated. It was really lovely; it was at his house. It was a great feeling but it was really different because I'd never known what it was like to be with a daddy. And I said for the first time on his birthday that I loved him, and he broke down and cried because I'm his only daughter. So I just wanted to say, being on that side without having a daddy ... that with this wanting equality and everything: 'marriage' in that sense is not marriage...[46]

Equality? Where is the justice in so-called 'marriage equality' if that means forcing future children like Amy, Heather, Katy or Brandi to miss out on the love of their father? Or Millie. This young Melbourne woman, raised by a lesbian couple, posted an impassioned video-blog in March 2015 in response to our Australian Marriage Forum TV ad about "equality for kids". In a wide-ranging reflection entitled "The real problem with same-sex parenting from a child's point of view", Millie had this to say about "equality": "There's all this talk about equality for women, for gay people, for everybody, but where's the equality for children when it comes to this? ... I am in a position to explain to you the kind of damage it does to a child."[47] At the time of writing, June 2016, I have never met Millie Fontana-Fox, but I admire the courage and conviction that took her from obscurity to addressing MPs in just a few months. At a seminar on children's rights at Parliament House, Canberra, she gave an insight into the pain of fatherlessness:

> The truth is that growing up with two mothers forced me to be confused about who I was and where I fit in the scheme of the world. And it became increasingly obvious as soon as I hit school. You would see every other child embracing who they are on mother's and father's day ... and there I was sitting back wondering what is wrong with me, and why don't I have that connection with my father? Was he such a bad person that that could not be facilitated for me? When I was age 11 I was finally able to meet my father, and it was one of the happiest days of my life. I felt stable and at peace for what was probably the first time in my childhood. I saw my future, I saw my heritage, I saw my other family. And that was something that I am so grateful to have been given at such a critical time in my development. And I cannot believe that LGBT is trying to push an agenda that says that my feelings were not important. Somebody's relationship should always be respected, whether it is homosexual or heterosexual; but when it comes to marriage and how closely intertwined marriage is with child reproduction we cannot say Yes to homosexual marriage without invalidating a child's right to both genders.[48]

We are invalidating and violating primal bonds when we cut a child off from her father, and the wound is real. We dress the wound with a rainbow bandage saying "Love is Love". As Katy Faust writes,

> Now we are normalizing a family structure where a child *will always* be deprived daily of one gender influence and the relationship with at least one natural parent. Our cultural narrative becomes one that, in essence, tells children that they have no right to the natural family structure or their biological parents, but that children simply exist for the satisfaction of adult desires.[49]

'I was confused'

A number of children of homosexual households speak of another obvious problem with single-gender parenting: the social challenge for a child who has no example of the daily interaction of mother and father, man and woman. This affects boys as much as girls. Robert Lopez wrote "Growing Up with Two Moms: The Untold Children's View".[50] He reflects that "I had no male figure at all to follow, and my mother and her partner were both unlike traditional fathers or traditional mothers."

> Quite simply, growing up with gay parents was very difficult, and not because of prejudice from neighbors. People in our community didn't really know what was going on in the house. To most outside observers, I was a well-raised, high-achieving child, finishing high school with straight A's. Inside, however, I was confused. When your home life is so drastically different from everyone around you, in a fundamental way striking at basic physical relations, you grow up weird. My peers learned all the unwritten rules of decorum and body language in their homes; they understood what was appropriate to say in certain settings and what wasn't; they learned both traditionally masculine and traditionally feminine social mechanisms. Even if my peers' parents were divorced, and many of them were, they still grew up seeing male and female social models. In terms of sexuality, gays who grew up in traditional households benefited from at least seeing some kind of functional courtship rituals around them. I had no clue how to make myself attractive to girls. When I stepped outside of my mothers' trailer, I was immediately tagged as an outcast because of my girlish

mannerisms, funny clothes, lisp, and outlandishness.[51]

A Jewish woman and academic, B.N. Klein, testified with pain and some anger to the deprivation of family role models and suppression of her own heterosexuality in her mother's lesbian household:

> When I was growing up only a tiny percentage of the people in the [LGBT] community had children, often the unsightly remnants of their parents' former marriages. Children in the lesbian section of the gay community were seen as the result of male oppression or later as proof that women don't need men and everything is "even Steven". Well, it isn't. I had never seen or could even fathom how families operated. It had all been presented to me as something on a much lower level than what the gay community was striving for. I had no idea what the daily interaction between a husband and wife looked like. I had no idea how two heterosexuals behaved toward their children as mother and father ... I had never had a boyfriend or any male interest because while my mother was preoccupied with my sexuality she was only preoccupied if it matched her values. So in some ways I was not allowed to have sexuality. I was not allowed to express in physical dress anything feminine – this was mocked as tasteless and vulgar and silly (unless it was a butch-femme couple, which was much rarer than butch-butch). I was allowed to knit and sew but this is because their utilitarian value exceeds their female category. I did not know how to flirt or dress.[52]

Dawn Stefanowicz was traumatised by two things: exposure to her father's exuberant homosexuality at home, and the message from the gay male subculture that women were redundant:

> For a little girl to grow up in a gay home and GLBT subcultures damages her sense of femininity and budding womanhood. Women are not the primary recipients of love and kindness; male and female are not considered equal and necessary. I wasn't surrounded by average heterosexual couples. Dad's partners slept and ate in our home, and they took me along to meeting places in the GLBT communities. I was exposed to overt sexual activities like sodomy, nudity, pornography, group sex, sadomasochism and the ilk. There was no guarantee that any of my Dad's partners would be around for long, and yet I often had to obey them. My rights and innocence were violated. I had a twisted view of sexuality, gender, marriage

and did not want to marry or have children. While still a girl, it seemed better if I had been born a boy – Dad even encouraged me to dress manly and wear men's cologne. I felt very stressed and afraid.[53]

The same lesbian judgement that considers men unnecessary as sexual partners also considers men unnecessary as parents. As Heather Barwick observed:

> I grew up surrounded by women who said they didn't need or want a man. Yet, as a little girl, I so desperately wanted a daddy. It is a strange and confusing thing to walk around with this deep-down unquenchable ache for a father, for a man, in a community that says that men are unnecessary.[54]

How does a child cope with this "strange and confusing" clash between her own natural needs and the messages of the adults around her? Typically, by falling in with the values of the homosexual adults until she is old enough and independent enough to assert her own mind. Katy Faust says she had this down to an art form:

> I remember how many times I repeated my speech: "I'm so happy that my parents got divorced so that I could know all of you wonderful women." I quaffed the praise and savored the accolades. The women in my mother's circle swooned at my maturity, my worldliness. I said it over and over, and with every refrain my performance improved. It was what all the adults in my life wanted to hear. I could have been the public service announcement for gay parenting. I cringe when I think of it now, because it was a lie. My parents' divorce has been the most traumatic event in my thirty-eight years of life. While I did love my mother's partner and friends, I would have traded every one of them to have my mom and my dad loving me under the same roof. This should come as no surprise to anyone who is willing to remove the politically correct lens that we all seem to have over our eyes. Kids want their mother and father to love them, and to love each other.[55]

Heather Barwick likewise considered herself a poster-child for lesbian parenting until she was able to think and speak for herself. She described her process of 'coming out' very sensitively in her open letter in *The Federalist*, March 2015, entitled "Dear gay community: your kids are hurting":

> I'm writing to you because I'm letting myself out of the closet: I don't support gay marriage. But it might not be for the reasons that you think. It's not because you're gay. I love you, so much. It's because of the nature of the same-sex relationship itself. Growing up, and even into my 20s, I supported and advocated for gay marriage. It's only with some time and distance from my childhood that I'm able to reflect on my experiences and recognize the long-term consequences that same-sex parenting had on me. And it's only now, as I watch my children loving and being loved by their father each day, that I can see the beauty and wisdom in traditional marriage and parenting.[56]

If all this doesn't break our hearts and make us run from any idea of instituting same-sex 'marriage', nothing will.

'We are either ignored or labeled a hater'

It takes courage for children of homosexual homes to speak out against homosexual 'marriage' and it comes at a personal cost. Not surprisingly, very few speak out. Katy Faust explains that people in her situation often stay silent because they don't want to upset gay family and friends and they don't want the public abuse that comes with opposing homosexual 'marriage':

> Some adult children with gay parents shy away from making their thoughts about marriage public because we do not want to jeopardize our relationships with those to whom our hearts are tethered. The label of bigot or hater has become very powerful and effective tools to silence those of us who choose not to endorse the marriage platform of many gay lobbyists. However, those tactics are no longer strong enough to keep me silent. Advocating for the rights of children, and how they relate to the institution of marriage, is not something that anyone should be timid about. For much of my adult life I was content to keep my opinions on the subject of marriage to myself. I was (and still am) sickened by the accusation that I was bigoted and anti-gay for my belief in natural marriage. For many years those devices kept me quiet. I didn't seek a venue where I could share my views. But I have come

to realize that my silence, and the silence of others, has allowed for the conversation to be dominated by those who claim that only animus, ignorance, or indoctrination could lead one to oppose "marriage equality."[57]

Heather Barwick touched on the same fear of rejection:

> Kids of divorced parents are allowed to say, "Hey, mom and dad, I love you, but the divorce crushed me and has been so hard…" Kids of adoption are allowed to say, "Hey, adoptive parents, I love you. But this is really hard for me. I suffer because my relationship with my first parents was broken…" But children of same-sex parents haven't been given the same voice. It's not just me. There are so many of us. Many of us are too scared to speak up and tell you about our hurt and pain, because for whatever reason it feels like you're not listening. That you don't want to hear. If we say we are hurting because we were raised by same-sex parents, we are either ignored or labeled a hater.[58]

Millie Fontana-Fox also reveals the pressures she felt in speaking out on same-sex parenting:

> Even though I stand here with full conviction in what I'm saying, guilt still hovers over me because I do not want to hurt the people that I love. Not all children will turn out to have these issues, but in truth a lot of us are just too scared to speak up because what is at stake is a family, our lifestyle, our friends. We are considered discriminatory or homophobes more often than not for coming out against the LGBT agenda.[59]

Robert Lopez points out that children still living with homosexual parents are in too dependent a position to express their sadness or anger at missing out on a mother or father. Even adults who do so risk professional repercussions, as he discovered in his capacity as a Professor of English in California.

> I cherish my mother's memory, but I don't mince words when talking about how hard it was to grow up in a gay household. Earlier studies examined children still living with their gay parents, so the kids were not at liberty to speak, governed as all children are by filial piety, guilt, and fear of losing their allowances. For trying to speak honestly, I've been squelched, literally, for decades.[60]

Dawn Stefanowicz agrees that surveys of still-dependent children of gay households are worthless and misleading: "The special interest-groups attempt to tell decision makers and the public that there is no harm to children, often by using *dependent* children, teens and young adults who have not yet left the extraordinary bullying influences of the GLBT environments."[61] She recalls the pressure to stay silent as a child in her essay from April 2015, "My Father Was Gay. Why I Oppose Legalizing Same-Sex Marriage":

> As a dependent child and teen, I was not allowed to say anything that would hurt the feelings of the adults around me. If I did, I could face ostracism or worse. Due to media silencing, political correctness, GLBT lobbying efforts and loss of freedom of speech, it is very hard to tell my story. But I am not alone. Over 50 adult children from alternative households have contacted me. Very few children will share their stories publicly.[62]

What chance is there for the public to reach a fair understanding of the experience of grief and loss for children of homosexual homes? Adults who attempt to speak out are largely ignored or intimidated into silence; other adults and children who tell a positive story of same-sex parenting are given the red carpet treatment. Credulous validity is attached to positive reports by children despite their obvious compromise by being dependent on same-sex parents. And government funding, as always, goes with the 'progressive' point of view: the *Gayby Baby* movie received federal government money[63] and the Victorian Government will fund it along with the compulsory roll-out of "Safe Schools".

The public understanding of the consequences of same-sex parenting would be improved if two guidelines were observed. First, beware of asking children of homosexual homes questions they are not free to answer until they are independent adults. Second, don't demonise adult voices, like these, who testify to the loss and unintended hurt of homosexual parenting.

'This debate, at its core, is about children'

It is inspiring when people speak out with nothing to gain for themselves but ostracism. They speak out about something of incomparable importance: a child's bond to her mother and father. They know from experience that same-sex parenting deliberately breaks this bond and therefore hurts the child. We can learn from their experience and understand why they say, "Don't do it!" Let them sum up:

Millie Fontana-Fox

> This is not equality for children, this is equality for adults, and the very term 'marriage equality' actually offends me, because nobody is thinking about the consequence on the other side of the coin: what comes out of that union. And what comes out of that union is us.[64]

BN Klein

> I believe as long as two people are not hurting anyone they should have the same rights as I have. But same-sex marriage extends past two people. It is a Trojan horse that will damage women and children. It also strays as far as you can get from "not hurting anyone else" and "between two adults." Using one woman to harvest eggs from and another as the long-term gestation uterus goes beyond two people. Next add a third, a child. I count three people. And not hurting? Who says "not hurting"?[65]

Robert Lopez

> I can support same-sex civil unions and some kinds of foster care for gay couples, but I object strenuously to marriage and adoption for gay couples. Both marriage and adoption involve using the force of the state to force unwilling children into emotional relationships with people who are not their parents – and this coercion is permanent, hurtful, and discriminatory, insofar as all children have a mother and father but children placed in same-sex-couple homes are stripped of one of these two figures without their consent. We must honor the universal relationship between children and their father and mother. We must respect the fact that children are 'born that way' with a mother and father, always.[66]

Dawn Stefanowicz

For many of us adult children of gay parents, we have come to the conclusion that same-sex marriage is more about promoting adults' "desires" than about safeguarding children's rights to know and be raised by their biological parents.[67]

Heather Barwick

Gay marriage doesn't just redefine marriage, but also parenting. It promotes and normalizes a family structure that necessarily denies us something precious and foundational. It denies us something we need and long for, while at the same time tells us that we don't need what we naturally crave. That we will be okay. But we're not. We're hurting.[68]

Katy Faust

This debate, at its core, is about one thing. It's about children. There is no difference between the value and worth of heterosexual and homosexual persons. We all deserve equal protection and opportunity in academe, housing, employment, and medical care, because we are all humans created in the image of God. However, when it comes to procreation and child-rearing, same-sex couples and opposite-sex couples are wholly unequal and should be treated differently for the sake of the children. This is not about being *against* anyone. This is about what I am for. I am *for* children! I want all children to have the love of their mother and their father ... We are just the tip of the iceberg of children currently being raised in gay households. When they come of age, many will wonder why the separation from one parent who desperately mattered to them was celebrated as a "triumph of civil rights," and they will turn to this generation for an answer. What should we tell them?[69]

***

This brief survey of some children of homosexual homes who have warned of the harm of homosexual 'marriage' is also an opportunity to thank them for their wisdom and courage. Only they can tell this story, and we need to hear it. If we understand a child's grief at being deprived of her father or mother, how could we contemplate normalising that same grief and loss for future children, through the institution of same-sex 'marriage'?

3

GAY MEN SPEAK OUT

> *A same-sex relationship is different to a marriage, because marriage is at its heart about children, and providing those children with their biological parents. Recognising difference is not discrimination.*
> Paddy Manning[70]

Some gay men go straight to the heart of opposition to gay 'marriage' and make the case bravely and publicly – namely that marriage is not just about adult fulfilment but about giving children a mother and father, and the institution of gay 'marriage' makes that impossible.

The media portrays the gay population as a monolithic voting bloc for 'marriage equality'. Not so. Many thoughtful men and women who are same-sex attracted see that their relationship – fully free and civilly protected as it is – is a different thing to marriage-and-family. Always has been, because only man and woman can undertake the great project of creating a new generation; only man and woman can give the resulting child her own mother and father.

Here are some eloquent examples, among many more, of gay men against gay 'marriage'.

Paddy & Keith

Two gay Irishmen walked into a bar – or more precisely, into a barrage of hostility for their leading role against redefining marriage in the Irish referendum of May 2015. Keith Mills and Paddy Manning copped the predictable abuse of being traitors to the cause and even "homophobes" – see Paddy's comment on that classic line below. Their offence was to point out that gay couples already have the same status and benefits as heterosexual couples (which is the same in Australia) and to warn that unless marriage stays between man and woman, future kids will miss out on their mum or their dad.

Written text cannot capture the charm or convey the sincerity of their presentation – so check out the short video at this endnote link.[71] For the record, this is what Keith and Paddy told their fellow Irish before the referendum.

I'm gay and I'm voting No. Here's why.

> **Keith**: The marriage referendum has been like coming out all over again for me. But it's important to stand up and speak up for what I believe, because there are too many people being bullied into silence. I am a gay man, and I'll be voting No to same-sex marriage because I believe children deserve a mother and a father where possible. For me, marriage is about children and the family, and not a way to measure adult relationships.
>
> **Paddy**: I've been gay for as long as I can remember, and I grew up in an Ireland that was ferociously hostile. I am as far as I know the last person arrested under the *1867 Offences Against the Persons Act*. Young, alone, terrified – that experience nearly killed me. Now I'm being accused of being homophobic because I am against the redefinition of marriage. Yeah, I'm homophobic. I scream when I pass the mirror!
>
> **Keith**: For me this referendum is *not* about equality for two main reasons. We already have civil partnerships in Ireland, and civil partnerships give gay couples protection and recognition. In fact the ceremony is the same as civil marriage, right down to saying 'I do'. If gay couples want constitutional protection, put civil partnerships in the constitution, but don't redefine marriage.
>
> **Paddy**: A same-sex relationship is different to a marriage, because marriage is at its heart about children, and providing those children with their biological parents. Recognising difference is not discrimination.
>
> **Keith**: This referendum is about children because everyone knows marriage is almost always about children, and because the government wants to change the section of the constitution on the

family. To have children, gay men like me need to either adopt or use surrogacy. Surrogacy turns children into commodities, putting adult desires above the rights of children, having babies made to order and wombs for rent. We're seeing in other countries how messy this can get, with surrogacy cases ending up in the court, and where are the child's best interests in that?

Paddy: If this referendum passes, we won't be able to privilege a mother and father model for a child in adoption. That's not fair, and we should vote No to that.

Keith: If you approve the government's amendment, you will be saying that there is no distinction between the union of a man and woman and of two men or two women. There *is* a difference between our relationships and to pretend otherwise is wrong. It's not a matter of better or worse; it's a matter of recognising difference and celebrating diversity. Saying that there is no distinction is ridiculous.

Paddy: There are many people who feel the same way as I do, but they're afraid to speak out because of the extraordinary bullying that's coming from the Yes campaign. We shouldn't bow to that intimidation. We shouldn't be scared of the people who are tearing down the No posters. This is not the way a campaign should be run. Family businesses are being closed, professional careers threatened. We're told Catholic schools must teach the government's vision of marriage. We should not vote for that.

Keith: True equality recognises difference, and it doesn't deliberately take away a child's right to a mother or father. In your heart of hearts, I believe you feel this is true. So get out and vote No

Paddy: You must know that this has been an adult-centred campaign, putting the rights of adults over those of children – a campaign to put surrogacy at the heart of our family law. Once you know this, you need to get out and to vote No.

Keith: If you know that gay people like me already have their love recognised and protected by civil partnerships and that we don't need to redefine marriage, get out and vote No.

Joe the Barrister

I spoke about marriage with Peter Goers on his ABC radio talkback show in Adelaide, March 2015. In the course of a long discussion I made the central point about the injustice of gay 'marriage' forcing future children to miss out on their mum or their dad; Peter preferred the ABC party line about kids just needing two loving 'carers' regardless of gender. Then on came caller Joe to give Peter a roasting:

> I'm a family law barrister so I spent 40 years principally acting for children in the family court protecting them from abuse and so forth. As a gay man in a single-sex relationship for 22 years, I find the concept of bringing children into this relationship selfish and obscene. You bring children into relationships where they have the best possible opportunity of being nurtured in a way that is healthy, that is functional. That is, with a mother and a father. If I want an offspring, as we did – my partner and I – I bought a dog. OK? And I think, Peter, you are completely off whack about all of this. I have to say, I am not a right wing whatever, but David is completely on the money.

Gee thanks, Joe… I think. You can listen to Joe at this endnote link.[72]

The PM's Speechwriter

Another gay man from Adelaide who was happy to have a coffee with this "right-wing whatever" was the late Christopher Pearson, columnist with *The Australian* and former speechwriter for John Howard. Pearson was clear that discrimination against gay people was unjust but that keeping marriage between man and woman, with the inherent connection to creating children, was entirely justifiable. Back in 2010 he wrote, pragmatically:

> Few have argued more consistently over many years than I have done that same-sex partners should get a fair deal on superannuation and other entitlements of that kind. Labor's reforms in the last parliament mean that couples are treated pretty much equally except in the matter of marriage. But the few remaining privileges

reserved for matrimony are there for sound, practical reasons. Men and women tend to have different needs and priorities when they enter a mature sexual relationship. Most men are not naturally disposed to be monogamous, for example. One of the purposes of marriage is to bind them to their spouses and children for the long haul and to give the state's approval to those who enter such a contract and abide by its terms. Another of the purposes of marriage is to affirm that parenthood is a big, and in most cases the primary, contribution a couple can make, both to their own fulfilment and the public good. It follows that societies which want to sustain their population size, let alone increase their fertility level, should positively discriminate in favour of stable, heterosexual relationships and assert the preferability of adolescents making a normal transition to heterosexual adulthood.[73]

Unfashionable: Dolce & Gabbana

When gay European fashion legends Domenico Dolce and Stefano Gabbana made some forthright comments in March 2015 against gay parenting and the artificial reproduction necessary for gay couples to obtain a baby, the all-loving, all-tolerant LGBT community reacted by boycotting their gay brothers.[74]

Dolce and Gabbana told the Italian magazine, *Panorama*, "The only family is the traditional one. No chemical offspring and rented uterus. Life has a natural flow; there are things that cannot be changed."[75] Dolce said, "You are born and you have a mother and a father. At least it should be like this." Gabbana said, "The family is not a fad. In it there is a supernatural sense of belonging." Gabbana had previously told a British paper, "I am opposed to the idea of a child growing up with two gay parents. A child needs a mother and a father. I could not imagine my childhood without my mother. I also believe that it is cruel to take a baby away from its mother."[76]

Elton John (who is 'married' to David Furnish and has taken two babies away from their surrogate mothers) told his fellow artists, "Your archaic thinking is out of step with the times, just like your fashions. I shall never wear Dolce & Gabbana ever again." Elton got tens of thousands of shares for his brave *#BoycottDolceGabbana* tag, and his shrill condemnation was supported by various celebrities, including Courtney Love who said she wanted to burn all her Dolce & Gabbana outfits.[77]

One of the most heartfelt defences of the two designers came from another gay man, Doug Mainwaring. He wrote:

> When a public war of words erupted a few days ago between Sir Elton John and world famous Italian designers Domenico Dolce & Stefano Gabbana, a mostly ignored schism within the gay community was suddenly cast in high relief. Trust me, I know. I'm a gay man opposed to gay marriage. Dolce and Gabbana are bravely standing against a future of state-enforced genderlessness, against a tidal wave of adult selfishness that overwhelms children's rights and their best interests.[78]

That's telling 'em! I think we need to hear more from this Mr Mainwaring...

'Genderless marriage is not marriage at all'

Concern for the right of kids to have both a mum and dad is the heart of Mainwaring's opposition to same-sex 'marriage'. He had come to prominence through an article in 2013 entitled, "I'm Gay and I Oppose Same-Sex Marriage".[79] Like Christopher Pearson, he defended equality of legal status and social benefits for same-sex couples, but said marriage was something completely different.

> I wholeheartedly support civil unions for gay and lesbian couples, but I am opposed to same-sex marriage ... Two men or two women together is, in truth, nothing like a man and a woman creating a life and a family together. Same-sex relationships are certainly very legitimate, rewarding pursuits, leading to happiness for many, but they are wholly different in experience and nature ... Genderless marriage is not marriage at all. It is something else entirely.[80]

He noted the abuse he had received as a gay "traitor" and also commented on the patronizing line that gays who oppose gay marriage only do so for religious reasons:

> I am viewed by many as a self-loathing, traitorous gay. So be it. I prefer to think of myself as a reasoning, intellectually honest

human being. Opposition to same-sex marriage is characterized in the media, at best, as clinging to "old-fashioned" religious beliefs and traditions, and at worst, as homophobia and hatred. I've always been careful to avoid using religion or appeals to tradition as I've approached this topic. And with good reason: Neither religion nor tradition has played a significant role in forming my stance.[81]

In a moving passage he describes his early awareness of same-sex attraction, and then his decision to marry and start a family despite these feelings:

> As a young man, I wasn't strongly inclined toward marriage or fatherhood, because I knew only homosexual desire. I first recognized my strong yearning for men at age eight, when my parents took me to see The Sound of Music. While others marveled at the splendor of the Swiss Alps displayed on the huge Cinerama screen, I marveled at the uniformed, blond-haired Rolfe, who was seventeen going on eighteen. That proclivity, once awakened, never faded ... When all my friends began to marry, I began to seriously consider marriage for the first time. The motive of avoiding social isolation may not have been the best, but it was the catalyst that changed the trajectory of my life. Even though I had to repress certain sexual desires, I found marriage to be extremely rewarding.[82]

After several years of marriage, and some adopted children, Doug Mainwaring and his wife broke up. Only a week before the Dolce & Gabbana controversy erupted, he had written of his remorse for leaving his wife and kids:

> I eventually came to the conclusion that I had committed a grave injustice against my kids by divorcing my wife and attempting to create a family with another man. They deserved to be raised by both their mom and dad under the same roof. Who was I to deny them this most basic of children's rights?[83]

Remarkably, after a decade apart, Doug and his former wife recommitted to giving their children a live-in mum and dad. They re-established their home:

> We have been under one roof for over two years now. Our kids are happier and better off in so many ways. Because of my

predilections, we deny our own sexual impulses. Has this led to depressing, claustrophobic repression? No. We enjoy each other's company immensely. It has actually led to psychological health and a flourishing of our family. Did we do this for the sake of tradition? For the sake of religion? No. We did it because reason led us to resist selfish impulses and to seek the best for our children.[84]

Doug's story concludes with simple observations on what it means for kids to have both a male and female parent in their home:

> Over the last couple of years, I've found our decision to rebuild our family ratified time after time. One day as I turned to climb the stairs I saw my sixteen-year-old son walk past his mom as she sat reading in the living room. As he did, he paused and stooped down to kiss her and give her a hug, and then continued on. With two dads in the house, this little moment of warmth and tenderness would never have occurred. My varsity-track-and-football-playing son and I can give each other a bear hug or a pat on the back, but the kiss thing is never going to happen. To be fully formed, children need to be free to generously receive from and express affection to parents of both genders. Genderless marriages deny this fullness … To give kids two moms or two dads is to withhold from them someone whom they desperately need and deserve in order to be whole and happy. It is to permanently etch "deprivation" on their hearts…[85]

Talk Show Hosts

While we are in Doug Mainwaring's US of A, how could we not tune in to one of their interminable TV talk shows? This episode of the *Ricki Lake Show* was screened in Australia too. You can watch at the link (near the end of the show) as Ricki chats to another talk-show host, Al, about why he (as a gay man) doesn't support gay marriage and parenting.

> **Ricki**: Al is a radio talk show host in Los Angeles who says gay couples don't need to be married to get these rights and he's totally opposed to gay marriage. You're gay, Al?
>
> **Al**: Indeed, last time I checked.
>
> **Ricki**: OK. What do you have to say, very quickly?

Al: I mean, this is primarily being driven by a certain segment of the gay community that wants public acceptance; they want people in this audience to put a stamp of approval on homosexuality. That's not a good reason to change the marriage laws of thousands of years of tradition … Marriage was designed to create a stable home for people to procreate and have children. It was not designed to solve your pension problem, your immigration problem, your need to be accepted by society; that's not why we have marriage.

Ricki: I agree, but if you're going to go there we have to bring up the fact that there are many heterosexual couples that marry and don't intend to have children or procreate

Al: Oh absolutely, but I'm saying Ricki, that the purpose we have marriage as an institution, the reason it's so important, is that the best home for a child, all things being equal, is a mother and a father who are married. That's the best home.[86]

***

Al from LA is just one more example – like Paddy, Keith, Joe, Christopher, Stefano, Domenico and Doug – of a gay man who sees that marriage and parenting is a man-woman thing, because only that way can a child have their chance of a mum and a dad.

Thank you, gentlemen.

4

SOCIAL SCIENCE SPEAKS OUT

> *We should disavow the notion that "mommies can make good daddies," just as we should disavow the popular notion that "daddies can make good mommies."*
> *... The two sexes are different to the core, and each is necessary – culturally and biologically – for the optimal development of a human being.*
> David Popenoe, Rutgers University sociologist.[87]

This is a mountain of a chapter, but it can be climbed in three manageable stages.

We first take the well-trodden path to *Base Camp*, the settled science established over decades of high quality research: that a child does best, on average, when raised by married biological parents. All family structures that fall short of this ideal, that disrupt a child's kinship bonds (including divorced, blended, single-parent, or same-sex parent structures) confer similar levels of disadvantage on the child. We conclude that any policy that deliberately deprives a child of a biological parent (such as same-sex 'marriage') is against the best interests of the child.

The bulk of the climb takes us on a fascinating route to the *No Basis Camp*. Its full name is "There is No Basis for the claim that children of same-sex parents show No Difference in outcomes compared to children of married biological parents". Hence its abbreviated name used by the locals. On the way we pass by the frozen bodies of journalists, academics and activists who, alas, strayed from the path of intellectual integrity and led many simple people off the edge.

At this point of the climb many will have seen enough and be getting footsore; by all means head home because you have covered the most significant terrain. You will be convinced how important it is for a child to have that primal biological link to both mother and father; you will know how to correct any ill-informed person who says, "kids in gay homes do just as well as other kids". The more experienced climbers might like to accompany me to *The Peak*, where conditions are more cloudy and troubled. This final climb is in two stages. First, the partly settled science that finds surprising additional harms to children in same-sex households – especially (note this well) when the same-sex parents are in a legal 'marriage'. Finally, and reluctantly, we must consider the unsettled science on the question of sexual abuse.

I. Base Camp: Settled Science

Imagine for a moment that decades of social science had shown beyond doubt that children do best, on average, with their married biological mother and father. That any form of family where the biological kinship bonds are broken is known to be, on average, worse for a child. Now exercise a little logic: with same-sex parenting, one or both biological bonds are broken; therefore one would expect same-sex parenting to share the disadvantages already known to apply to other biologically disrupted family structures.

Your logic is sound and your expectation is proven correct by multiple studies. But that is not what you will hear in the media; instead you will hear claims that there is "no difference" in outcomes for kids raised by same-sex parents. Might politics and PR be playing some small part in this puzzling claim? Is it not important to get to the truth of the matter, because surely lawmakers would not contemplate establishing a new institution of same-sex 'marriage' if they knew that such an institution would, on average, disadvantage children?

First, let me settle your mind on the settled science. You can read the vast research and be astonished at how much time and money goes into confirming the biologically obvious: mothers matter uniquely; fathers matter uniquely; a child does best with her own married mum and dad. For those who want to read wide and deep and long, the endnote has some links to whet your appetite.[88] For those who don't, let me sum up with the conclusion from Child Trends, a secular research institute in the USA that is rigorous in its reporting of the settled position of decades of social science: "Research clearly demonstrates that family structure matters for children, and the family structure that helps children the most is a family headed by two biological parents in a low-conflict marriage."[89]

That's clear. Any other family structure is not the best structure for kids. We know that many tragic circumstances bring about other family structures – the death or desertion of a parent; divorce and remarriage – but we need to accept that all such structures fall short of the ideal for children. As adults in various domestic arrangements, we must try not to "take offence" at being told that single parenting or step parenting is, on average, "worse for kids". We respect our many family and friends in such circumstances who do the best they can and do it well. But the fact remains that the ideal for a child, statistically speaking, is to be raised by her "two biological parents in a low-conflict marriage."

The same settled science is confirmed, with detailed references, by a group of one hundred scholars of marriage and family in their submission to the US Supreme Court on the same-sex 'marriage' case (*Obergefell*, 2015):

> Compared with children of man-woman couples raised in any other environment, children raised by their two biological parents in a married family are less likely to commit crimes, experience teen pregnancy, have multiple abortions, engage in substance abuse, suffer from mental illness or do poorly in school, and more likely to support themselves and their own children successfully in the future. Accordingly, such children need less state assistance and contribute more to the state's economy and tax base. Indeed, the evidence overwhelmingly establishes that no other parenting arrangement comes close (on average) to that of the child's biological mother and father.[90]

One more summation will suffice to establish this vital truth, this time from Loren Marks, Professor of Child and Family Studies at Louisiana State University:

> Over the past few decades, differences have been observed between outcomes of children in marriage-based intact families and children in cohabiting, divorced, step, and single-parent families in large, representative samples. Based on four nationally representative longitudinal studies with more than 20,000 total participants, McLanahan and Sandefur conclude: "Children who

grow up in a household with only one biological parent are worse off, on average, than children who grow up in a household with both of their biological parents ... regardless of whether the resident parent remarries."[91]

That last point is significant: remarriage to a non-biological parent does not restore advantage to a child. Even a loving stepparent does not confer the advantages of a child's biological parents. The Child Trends review makes the same observation – that it is *biological kinship* that matters, not just having two loving carers:

> Children growing up with stepparents also have lower levels of well-being than children growing up with biological parents. Thus, it is not simply the presence of two parents, as some have assumed, but the presence of two biological parents that seems to support children's development.[92]

Biological bonds are irreplaceable

Count the times you have heard gay activists say that "all kids need is love"; that it doesn't matter if the child is related to the parent or what the gender of parents might be. Next time they say that, tell them they are wrong. One of the largest statistically valid studies of same-sex parenting (Sullins 2015) finds the benefit to children being raised by their biological parents compared to children being raised by same-sex parents is independent of measures of parental "quality" – their socio-economic status and other variables.[93] As Sullins puts it, what appears to matter most to children is having "their own parents", not necessarily having high quality parents: "The primary benefit of marriage for children, therefore, may not be that it tends to present them with improved parents (more stable, financially affluent, etc., although it does do this), but that it presents them with their own parents."

Even a rough and ready pair of biological parents offers something that highly competent same-sex carers cannot: the bonds of blood and belonging. There is something irreplaceably important about having one's own mother and father, one's own biological identity and ancestry. Young people yearn for that; they grieve for it when it is taken from them by tragic circumstance. We know that the ties of kinship and identity matter greatly to indigenous people, but such ties matter to us all.

An institution of same-sex 'marriage' deliberately ruptures those ties of kinship and identity. It imposes similar disadvantage on children as any other biologically broken family structure. The moral difference is that other violations of the child's bond with her mother or father come about through unforeseen family tragedies; this new violation would be brought about by a deliberate, and negligent, Act of Parliament.

Professor John Londregan of Princeton University confirms this comparable level of disadvantage conferred by same-sex parenting: "A picture emerges: in a cross-section of children raised by parents in same-sex relationships, life outcomes tend to resemble those of children raised by single and divorced parents."[94] Let's consider just one "life outcome", the successful completion of high school, which is an established sociological measure of wellbeing. Do both groups of children mentioned by Londregan show a similar disadvantage compared to children of married biological parents? Firstly, here is the evidence for "children raised by single and divorced parents", who are two to three times more likely than children of married biological parents to drop out of high school:

> The cumulative effect of family structure on children's educational performance is most evident in high school graduation rates. Children reared in intact, married households are about twice as likely to graduate from high school, compared to children reared in single-parent or step-families. One study found that 37 percent of children born outside of marriage and 31 percent of children with divorced parents dropped out of high school, compared to 13 percent of children from intact families headed by a married mother and father.[95]

Second, here is the evidence for "children raised by parents in same-sex relationships" compared to children raised by their married mother and father. Douglas Allen's study, "High school graduation rates among children of same-sex households" used a large-sample representative database drawing on a 20% sample of the Canadian Census.[96] Allen found that "Children living with gay and lesbian families in 2006 were about 65% as likely to graduate compared to children living in opposite sex marriage families." So children of same-sex homes are a third less likely to finish high school than children living with their married mother and father. As expected by our "equivalent disadvantage" hypothesis, that is consistent with the dropout rate for children of single parent or divorced homes summarised above. And as expected by the "settled science" of this chapter, both groups are worse off than kids with their own married parents. Allan considered a range of possible explanations for this observed disadvantage for children of same-sex homes compared to children of opposite-sex married parents and concluded with the pointed comment: "In any event, it is time to investigate the difference and reject the conventional wisdom of 'no difference.'"

Surveying all the statistically valid studies in this field, Professor Mark Regnerus sums up: "Population-based surveys of same-sex households with children all tend to reveal *the same thing* regardless of data source … namely, that children who grow up with a married mother and father do best, at face value."[97]

It's time to draw an evidence-based conclusion: that the institution of same-sex marriage, which establishes same-sex parenting as an ideal in our law, would disadvantage children in the same way that other forms of biologically disrupted families disadvantage children. The deliberate creation of such an institution is not consistent with putting the interests of the child first; laws for gay 'marriage' are therefore a deliberate injustice against the child.

Would 'marriage equality' overcome the disadvantage?

One obvious question arises: if we let same-sex couples marry, will the benefits of being 'married' overcome the disadvantage to children that we presently see in unmarried same-sex households? This is the sort of consideration that led the British Prime Minister, David Cameron, to support same-sex 'marriage' – he wanted to share the benefits of marriage more widely, and so benefit the children of such households.

The evidence, regrettably, says no: a legal construct cannot compensate for biological disruption. As we have seen above, an indispensable part of children's wellbeing derives from having "their own parents". Calling a same-sex couple "married" does not restore to the child her missing parent. Calling a same-sex couple "married" does not restore to the child her bonds of biological kinship, and without those bonds the child remains, on average, disadvantaged. As Child Trends noted above, "it is not simply the presence of two parents, as some have assumed, but the presence of two *biological* parents that seems to support children's development." And as Sullins points out, one thing same-sex 'marriage' can never give a child is her two biological parents:

> Whether or not same-sex families attain the legal right, as opposite-sex families now have, to solemnise their relationship in civil marriage, the two family forms will continue to have fundamentally different, even contrasting, effects on the biological component of child well-being, to the relative detriment of children in same-sex families. Functionally, opposite-sex marriage is a social practice that, as much as possible, ensures to children the joint care of both biological parents, with the attendant benefits that brings; same-sex marriage ensures the opposite.[98]

Finally, an extraordinary (if preliminary) finding in a second study by Sullins is that the emotional wellbeing of children is worse in same-sex households where the parents are legally 'married' compared to same-sex households where the parents are not married.[99] Also, the longer the same-sex 'marriage' endures, the worse the emotional detriment to children.

> In the data observed in this study, the greatest harm for children with same-sex parents came from the most stable and most marital family arrangements. This unexpected harm was present despite warm and loving parents who promoted positive school outcomes...[100]

A submission to the US Supreme Court in 2015 co-authored by Sullins, under the auspices of the American College of Paediatricians, elaborates on this effect – bearing in mind the sparse data and therefore the preliminary nature of any such finding:

> [T]he longer the adolescents were with same-sex parents, the worse they fared. Those who resided with married same-sex parents for over ten years, on average, fared much worse than those residing with unmarried, mostly divorced, same-sex parents for only four years, on average. Child harm with same-sex parents may be amplified by a longer time spent with them, or by marriage itself,

or both.[101]

A finding like that requires confirmation by other larger studies, but for now it directly contradicts the well-meaning notion that if we let same-sex couples marry then their children will be better off. We will look more closely at these two Sullins studies in a later section of this chapter, but for now we have some demolition work to do.

II. No Basis for 'No Difference'

All this evidence of disadvantage that comes with disrupted family structures raises the question: how can gay lobbyists continue to claim that "research shows there's no difference" for kids raised by same-sex parents? In an unintended sense they are right; basically there is "no difference" between the *disadvantage* kids experience through homosexual step parenting and the *disadvantage* kids experience through heterosexual step parenting. But do you think that is what the lobbyists are trying to teach you? If so, they would have to rephrase their mantra: "Research shows that kids raised by same-sex parents suffer the same *disadvantage*, on average, as kids raised in other biologically disrupted families. There's no difference". Don't expect that line in a media release any time soon! The political pitch is there to serve the cause of 'marriage equality': that there is *no* disadvantage for kids raised by same-sex couples compared to kids raised by their married mother and father. That is a false claim, as Londregan and Regnerus, Sullins and Marks, McLanahan and Sandefur and many others confirm. Because this false claim is so pervasive and so distorting of the public debate on same-sex 'marriage', we need to take a closer look at it now before returning to some more disturbing findings of harm associated with same-sex parenting.

Politicised science or objective science?

In 2013 the Australian Institute for Family Studies (AIFS) published a review entitled "Same-Sex Parented Families in Australia", a sympathetic treatment of the topic authored by Deborah Dempsey, a founding committee member of the Victorian Gay and Lesbian Rights Lobby.[102] Nevertheless, it contained the important admission that "numerous scholars now agree it is not possible to sustain a claim frequently made in the earlier literature that there are no differences between children raised in same-sex and heterosexual parented families."[103]

Please read that remarkable admission again, slowly... One might have expected the AIFS abandonment of the "no difference" fallacy to filter through to the public debate, but no: advocates for homosexual 'marriage' still repeat "no difference" at every media opportunity. Such a claim neutralises public concern for the wellbeing of children of homosexual households, and as such it is a valuable falsehood.

Among the "numerous scholars" cited in this context by Dempsey is Professor Loren Marks. In 2012 he published a detailed critique of all the small, unrepresentative studies that were the basis of the "no difference" claim for same-sex parenting, and which are being used in the push for same-sex 'marriage'. He opened by considering the political significance of this field of research:

> Social science research with small convenience samples has repeatedly reported no significant differences between children from gay/lesbian households and heterosexual households. These recurring findings of no significant differences have led some researchers and professional organizations to formalize related claims. Perhaps none of these claims has been more influential than the following from the 2005 American Psychological Association (APA) Brief on "Lesbian and Gay Parenting": "Not a single study has found children of lesbian or gay parents to be disadvantaged in any significant respect relative to children of heterosexual parents." Are we witnessing the emergence of a new family form that provides a context for children that is equivalent to the traditional marriage-based family? Many proponents of same-sex marriage contend that the answer is yes. Others are skeptical and wonder – given that other departures from the traditional marriage-based family form have been correlated with more negative long-term child outcomes – do children in same-sex families demonstrably avoid being "disadvantaged in any significant respect relative to children of heterosexual parents" as the APA Brief asserts? This is a question with important implications, particularly since the 2005 APA Brief on "Lesbian and Gay Parenting" has been repeatedly invoked in the current same-sex marriage debate.[104]

It is important to understand that studies which do not meet the

'Gold Standard' of objective research cannot be used to make broader public policy claims. To make such claims, research must demonstrate (1) random, representative sample selection, and (2) sufficient size to achieve statistical significance. That is, they must be large, random and representative. Without this 'Gold Standard', research might be of anecdotal interest but cannot be generalised to the population. Whenever you hear of some new study touted in the media as showing how kids in same-sex homes do "just as well", ask the two questions: is the sample random or biased? Is the sample big enough to be statistically valid?

In his review of the 59 studies which the APA Brief used to justify their claim of "no difference", Marks makes the devastating finding that not a single study achieved this 'Gold Standard'! The hugely influential APA declaration, therefore, was never justified by the small, unrepresentative studies it cites:

> To restate, not one of the 59 studies referenced in the 2005 APA Brief (pp. 23-45; see Table 1) compares a large, random, representative sample of lesbian or gay parents and their children with a large, random, representative sample of married parents and their children. The available data, which are drawn primarily from small convenience samples, are insufficient to support a strong generalizable claim either way. Such a statement would not be grounded in science. To make a generalizable claim, representative, large-sample studies are needed – many of them.

Numerous other scholars, including those arguing for same-sex parenting and marriage, have acknowledged the severe limitations of those earlier studies. Consider a few of the scholars cited in the AIFS review. Wainright (2004) writes: "existing research is still sparse and based on small samples, the representativeness of which is generally difficult to assess."[105] Stacey & Biblarz (2001) write: "There are no studies [of same-sex parenting] based on random, representative samples of such families. Most studies rely on small-scale, snowball and convenience samples drawn primarily from personal or community networks or agencies."[106] Rosenfeld notes in his US Census study (2006): "The universally small sample sizes in the existing literature has left room for several critiques, including the argument that small sample sizes would not have the statistical power to identify the effects of homosexual parents on childhood outcomes even if such effects did exist."

Marks concluded that the state of same-sex parenting research in 2012 could not sustain any generalised conclusions, and that sweeping claims of "no difference" such as that made by the APA in 2005 should not have been made:

> Some opponents of same-sex parenting have made "egregious overstatements" disparaging gay and lesbian parents. Conversely, some same-sex parenting researchers seem to have contended for an "exceptionally clear" verdict of "no difference" between same-sex and heterosexual parents since 1992. However, a closer examination leads to the conclusion that strong, generalized assertions, including those made by the APA Brief, were not empirically warranted. As noted by Shiller (2007) in American Psychologist, "the line between science and advocacy appears blurred".

Take a glance at the "Public Interest" policies of the American Psychological Association and you will find its advocacy hard to distinguish from any Green-left political party.[107] One former president of the APA, Nicholas Cummings, wrote that "the APA has chosen ideology over science" and that "advocacy for scientific and professional concerns has been usurped by agenda-driven ideologues who show little regard for either scientific validation or professional efficacy".[108] Hard words, but the APA is not a unique offender; other professional bodies in different areas of public policy seem to have compromised their scientific objectivity for the greater cause of 'progressive' politics. For policy makers and the public, clinical truth is harder to come by if researchers and peak bodies are compromised by politics. They lose our trust.

The best Australian effort to promote 'no difference'

At this point, let's look at the best-known Australian research: the much-trumpeted "Australian Study of Child Health in Same-Sex Families" (ACHESS) under the auspices of the University of Melbourne.[109] Will it impress us with its 'Gold Standard' rigour? It certainly impressed the Australian Broadcasting Corporation (ABC) when the study was published in July 2014: their headline declared, "Children raised by same-sex couples healthier and happier, research suggests".[110] And the lead researcher for ACHESS, Simon Crouch, certainly knew how to push the ABC's political hot buttons:

> Dr Crouch said the study findings had implications for those who argued against marriage equality for the sake of children. "Quite often, people talk about marriage equality in the context of family and that marriage is necessary to raise children in the right environment, and that you need a mother and a father to be able to do that, and therefore marriage should be restricted to male and female couples," Dr Crouch said. "I think what the study suggests in that context is that actually children can be brought up in many different family contexts, and it shouldn't be a barrier to marriage equality."

Dr Crouch is himself raising children in a homosexual relationship, which might raise questions of conflict of interest in the average reader's mind. Given the lead author's apparent vested interest in this subject, one would expect the study to be scrupulous in avoiding any perception of bias – either selection bias in the recruitment of subjects or reporting bias in the gathering of information. Alas, the study fails on both counts.[111]

On recruitment of subjects, we read in the report: "The convenience sample was recruited using online and traditional recruitment techniques, accessing same-sex attracted parents through news media, community events and community groups." That is a textbook case of selection bias, a self-selecting sample, and gives an immediate 'fail' on the 'Gold Standard' of random subject selection. And for good measure, the sample of parents was unrepresentative of the general population, being better educated and wealthier.

The study fares no better on the matter of reporting bias: "Parents reported information for all children under the age of 18 years." Good for them – that means all the data in this study of "child health in same-sex families" was gathered by asking the same-sex parents themselves what they thought about such things as their child's "self-esteem", "general behaviour", "family cohesion", "emotional problems". Surprise, surprise, the proud parents thought things were pretty rosy. It is interesting, given this intoxicating mix of biases, that the reported emotional advantage for children of same-sex households was only a few percent: "On the Child Health Questionnaire, after adjusting for socio-demographic characteristics, the overall mean score for general behaviour, general health and family cohesion was 3%, 6% and 6% higher respectively for children from the ACHESS compared to population data."

To Crouch's credit he acknowledges the limitations of his study: "The self-selection of our convenience sample has the potential to introduce bias that could distort results. It is clear that the families from the ACHESS are earning more and are better educated than the general population." At that point he could consider pulping the study and desisting from politically charged interviews with the ABC, but he continues: "Whether there are real differences between the ACHESS sample and the normative population or not, it is clear that there are aspects at play in our sample of same-sex families that allow improved outcomes in general behavior, general health, and in particular family cohesion." With respect, what is clear is that well educated and motivated same-sex parents recruited through gay networks in the context of a politically charged debate on gay marriage could be expected to report that they have exceptionally well-behaved healthy kids and a cohesive family. QED.

And most regrettably, Crouch takes the opportunity to promote the "no difference" mantra despite acknowledging the obvious bias risks of his non-random, unrepresentative study:

> The findings suggest that there is no evidence to support a difference in parent reported child health for most measures in these families when compared to children from population samples, which was also found with the previous smaller studies and those of lesbian families.

If this sort of research is touted (modestly, by Crouch) as "a significant contribution to the literature", is there any way we can have confidence in the rest of the research literature on same-sex parenting? Are there any studies sufficiently free of bias and with sufficient statistical power that we can use them to inform public policy? Yes there are, but very few. Professor Marks notes that, "To make a generalizable claim, representative, large-sample studies are needed." So if we are to have any scientific basis for informing public policy on same-sex parenting, and therefore same-sex 'marriage', we have to look for the "representative, large-sample studies" of the effects of same-sex parenting on children. And you will be glad to know that, as best I can ascertain as of March 2016, there are only nine such studies.

What do the nine valid studies show?

The Australian Institute for Family Studies (AIFS) review tallied up the statistically valid studies that were published by 2013:

> There have now been several randomly sampled comparative studies published on educational outcomes for children from same-sex and heterosexual families (Potter, 2012; Rosenfeld, 2010), and also social outcomes (Regnerus, 2012; Wainright, Russell, & Patterson, 2004).[112]

Potter and Rosenfeld will get passing mention below. Regnerus we have touched on, and will revisit. Jennifer Wainright and her colleagues (including Charlotte Patterson, a principal researcher for the APA "no difference" position on same-sex parenting[113]) in fact published three separate studies using the same database (and therein lies a tale – stay tuned).[114] Add to those six the three more recent studies we have already mentioned: Douglas Allen's on high school completion rates and Paul Sullins' two studies of emotional problems in children of same-sex households, which we will return to in the next part of the chapter. Then add one more study published by Sullins in 2015 which found increased rates of ADHD in children of same-sex parents compared to opposite-sex parents.[115] That gives a total of six "representative, large-sample studies" published by 2013 and four published after, giving a total of ten for our consideration.

But didn't I say there were only nine? Yes, because in my view the Rosenfeld study needs to be scratched from the field.[116] It used US Census data that had previously been shown by researchers at the California Centre for Population Research (CCPR) to be corrupted by miscoding.[117] His study found that "children of same-sex couples are as likely to make normal progress through school as the children of most other family structures" but his modest "no difference" conclusion is discredited by the fact that his data was, to put it mildly, compromised. Up to forty per cent of the "same-sex couples" he claimed for his study were actually opposite-sex couples. Awkward, that! Until Rosenfeld's study is reanalysed using the correct coding, his study, in my view, remains in the sin-bin.

That reduces the total to just nine "representative, large-sample studies" which address the question of whether same-sex parenting has adverse effects compared to opposite-sex parenting. That's all the studies there are! All the small shabby studies that give big happy headlines in newspapers about how "kids of gay parents do best" must be dismissed as of anecdotal value only. These nine are the only ones, to my best knowledge, that are sufficiently powerful to allow generalisation to the population and therefore deserve consideration by policy makers. For a tallying up of these nine studies and what they say about the harm or lack of harm to children in same-sex households, skip to the next section, "Partly settled science". For now, for completeness, a quick comment on the last two studies on our list.

Potter does the math; Regnerus is roasted

Daniel Potter published "Same-Sex Parent Families and Children's Academic Achievement" in 2012.[118] He analysed the database of 19,000 children in the USA Early Childhood Longitudinal Study – Kindergarten Cohort which included 72 same-sex parent families. Importantly, his number crunching included the one comparison that really matters: children of same-sex homes with children of *married* biological parents. He found that "Children in same-sex parent families appeared to have lower baseline math scores, on average, than their peers in married, two-biological parent families, and this association was robust to select sociodemographic factors". This decrease in a key measure of school performance is what we would expect under the "broken biological bonds" hypothesis of this chapter. Also, as we expected, it is not specific to same-sex parenting. In this study, children of all disrupted family structures (single parents, divorced and blended families) suffered disadvantage similar to the same-sex parented children when compared to children of married biological parents. Potter chooses to attribute the adverse finding to the trauma of past family breakups, shared by all groups except "married, two-biological parent families" saying "the difference was nonsignificant net of family transitions". Attentive readers will note that he is merely confirming the "settled science" outlined at the start of this chapter. His results show that same-sex step parenting carries the same disadvantages as other forms of biologically disrupted family; in all such cases, children have necessarily undergone "family transitions", or family deconstruction, and lack the presence of their two biological parents. Are you starting to see a pattern?

One study remains, Mark Regnerus' 2012 analysis of data from the New Family Structures Study, "How different are the adult children of parents who have same-sex relationships?"[119] It caused a political furore for daring to find a wide range of harms to children who had a parent in a same-sex relationship at some point in their childhood. One of the best defences of the Regnerus paper is found in the Amicus Curiae brief to the US Supreme Court in 2015 under the auspices of the American College of Pediatricians (with professors Sullins, Regnerus and Marks as co-authors).[120] They outline the study and its limitations:

> Regnerus published the findings of a retrospective study based on representative national sample of 2,988 adults, including 248 whose mother or father had been in a same-sex relationship at some point during their upbringing ... Regnerus found that well-being for the adults who reported a parent having been in a same-sex relationship (during the respondent's childhood) was significantly lower than in the general population, particularly when compared to persons who had grown up with parents who are still married or were married until one of them died. The differences were striking ... The Regnerus study was limited in that few of the reported same-sex parents had been in a same-sex relationship for very long. Critics pointed out, correctly, that factors other than parental sexual orientation may account for the differences observed. Nevertheless, the study demonstrated that, even with an attenuated sample, large statistically significant differences were present where the "consensus finding" body of research had long claimed there were none. And the burden to show that other factors (rather than exposure to or residence with a same-sex parent) explains the differences rests with the critics, not Regnerus. So far, none have done so.

Important findings of the Regnerus research stand firm, as do the

Sullins findings – which suffered a similarly ferocious ideological attack. Valid data cannot be erased by vitriol. These authors were attacked, in my view, because they challenged the rainbow party line that "science shows there is 'no difference' for children of same-sex households and therefore politicians should support gay 'marriage'." Sullins hinted at the politicisation of this field of social science in the conclusion of his second study:

> As noted in the introduction, a steady drumbeat of dozens of studies based on small, non-random samples has been celebrated by the American social science establishment as definitive proof that having same-sex parents is innocuous for child wellbeing. In the face of mounting evidence to the contrary, the American Psychological Association continues to claim: "Not a single study has found children of lesbian or gay parents to be disadvantaged in any significant respect relative to children of heterosexual parents." The present study definitively demonstrates that statement to be false. To those convinced that the no differences thesis is true, the evidence presented in this study is unexpected and possibly inconvenient. Whether future evidence upholds, modifies or rebuts these findings, they suggest that much of the received social science wisdom about such relationships is mistaken, and we have just begun to try to understand the effect on children of having two parents of the same sex.[121]

III. To the Peak

The first part of this chapter confirmed the settled science that the family headed by married biological parents is best, on average, for children. The second part showed the mischief of the "no difference" campaign and demonstrated that same-sex parenting carries the same disadvantage for children as other forms of biologically disrupted family structures. This final part goes further. It considers the evidence for additional harms from same-sex parenting above and beyond the expected disadvantages of step parenting generally. If those additional harms exist, it would be negligent beyond belief for legislators to establish same-sex 'marriage' and parenting as a norm.

(i) Partly settled science: additional harms

Those additional disadvantages are found, on present evidence, in the field of emotional and psychological harm to children. We know there is a baseline level of emotional disadvantage common to all biologically disrupted family structures compared to the optimum context of married biological parents. By way of summary:

> Children from stable, married families are significantly less likely to suffer from depression, anxiety, alcohol and drug abuse and thoughts of suicide compared to children from divorced homes.[122] One recent study of the entire population of Swedish children found that Swedish boys and girls in two-parent homes were about 50 percent less likely to suffer from suicide attempts, alcohol and drug abuse, and serious psychiatric illnesses compared to children reared in single-parent homes.[123] A survey of the American literature on child well-being found that family structure was more consequential than poverty in predicting children's psychological and behavioral outcomes.[124]

The question is: what evidence do we have of additional emotional harm above and beyond this baseline when children are raised in same-sex households? We will ask sociology professor Paul Sullins to be our guide.

A closer look at the first Sullins study of emotional harm

Sullins' study "Emotional problems among children with same-sex parents" (2015) is one of the largest random-sample representative studies yet conducted in this field.[125] His findings are statistically robust and were published in a journal that has one of the highest rankings possible for rigour of the peer-review process.[126] Drawing on the US National Health Interview Survey database of 207,000 children, including 512 from same-sex households, Sullins concluded that "emotional problems were over twice as prevalent for children with same-sex parents than for children with opposite-sex parents". Specifically, serious emotional problems were found in 17.4% of children with same-sex parents versus 7.4% of children from opposite-sex parents. That rose to almost four times the risk (3.6) when compared to the optimum subgroup of children with married biological parents.

Sullins was careful to address the inevitable criticism that the worse psychological outcome for a child of same-sex parents was due to something other than their experience of same-sex parenting, namely the experience of family instability (e.g. going through divorce). The fortunate group of children with their own married biological parents had been spared this trauma. Sullins eliminated this possible confounding factor of "instability" in the obvious way: he compared the children from same-sex stepparent families with the children from opposite-sex stepparent families. All these children had been through transitions, so this compared instability with instability, apples with apples. And the findings? The increased risk for children in same-sex stepparent families remained higher than children in opposite-sex stepparent families, at 2.2 times the risk.

That, ladies and gentlemen, is among the most robust evidence we have that there is additional harm to children from same-sex parenting above and beyond the disadvantage expected of all step parenting.

What did the "no difference" crowd make of these ruggedly objective findings, where most of the differences are statistically significant at 0.001? The American Psychological Association (APA) and the American Sociological Association (ASA) tried three main lines of attack on the Sullins study, each of them more intellectually embarrassing than the one before. Far from praising Sullins for his efforts to address the question of family instability by making the apples-with-apples comparison of homosexual stepparent families with heterosexual stepparent families, the APA said that "creating more differentiated categories of children of opposite-sex couples (children residing with married versus single or divorced parents)" was a "methodological flaw". Some people are just hard to please. Be sure that, if Sullins had not differentiated the categories, the APA would have criticised him for not controlling for the role of family instability in his findings! To read more of the ASA's and APA's attempts to discredit this research, including misguided criticism of coding classifications and unwarranted sneering at the publishing journal, see the endnote.[127]

Sullins was also careful to test for any role of stigmatisation and bullying in the adverse emotional outcome for children of same-sex homes, and his findings were a surprise: "Contrary to the assumption underlying this hypothesis, children with opposite-sex parents are picked on and bullied more than those with same-sex parents." Did you catch that? In one of the largest random, representative samples of same-sex households ever studied, children of gay parents were bullied *less* than other kids, not more. Therefore stigma and bullying could not plausibly be the explanation for the worse emotional state of children from same-sex homes.

Sullins' high quality study finds a significant increase in serious emotional problems for children raised by same-sex parents compared to children raised by opposite-sex parents, especially when compared to the subgroup of children raised by their married biological parents. While that research stands – and it does, despite the contortions of its detractors – no policy maker should support the deliberate institution of same-sex 'marriage' and therefore same-sex parenting as an ideal in our law. We cannot knowingly consign children to a family structure that carries double or quadruple the risk of emotional harm.

The second Sullins study and more 'unexpected harm'

In a second study in 2015, Sullins confirmed the earlier finding of greater emotional distress for children of same-sex parents, but with a new twist. Sullins called his study "The unexpected harm of same-sex marriage: a critical appraisal and re-analysis of Wainright..." and the reasons he calls it "unexpected" will become clear.[128]

Sullins reanalysed a 2004 study by Jennifer Wainright and her colleagues, "Psychosocial adjustment, school outcomes, and romantic relationships of adolescents with same-sex parents", which drew on an in-depth database of over 20,000 young people between age 10 and 17, the US National Longitudinal Study of Adolescent to Adult Health (AddHealth).[129] Her study revealed a significant advantage for children of lesbian households in the criterion of "school connectedness", whatever that term means. But this is where it gets interesting. Sullins identified serious database errors in the Wainright study. Of the 44 cases of children of "lesbian parents" identified by Wainright from the AddHealth database, most of them were not in fact children raised by lesbian parents. The questionnaire actually reported that 27 of those children had both their father and mother living with them. What sort of lesbian household has the child's father living with the child? Even if the mother was having a lesbian affair on the side, an essentially mother-father household does not meet any definition of "same-sex parenting".

Sullins reanalysed the data using only the genuine lesbian and gay couple households and two important negative findings emerged: first, that children of same-sex households suffered a statistically significant increase in anxiety compared to their peers from mother-father households. Second, that the adverse emotional effect was worse for children of "married" same-sex couples than for children of "unmarried" same-sex couples, and it got more severe the longer the couples were "married". That latter unexpected finding, as mentioned earlier, challenges the hopeful guess that children will benefit from 'marriage equality' for their same-sex parents. That guess is a key plank of the conservative platform for same-sex 'marriage', but if this data is correct, that plank is not safe to stand on.

On the positive side of the equation, the corrected Wainright data in Sullins' study still finds better "school connectedness" for children of lesbian homes, and indeed a new finding of higher average GPA score at school in the children of lesbian households. This is plausible: children who are anxious about their home situation might find security in "connectedness" with their peer community, and parents know that the more anxious child is often the more diligent with homework. So yes, there appears to be marginal higher achievement in school for children of homosexual households, but in my view – surely any parent's view – that advantage is outweighed by the adverse finding of elevated emotional distress in such children.

Summing up the science

So where does all this "large-sample representative research" – Sullins, Allen, Potter, Regnerus and the reanalysed Wainright study – leave the complacent APA claim from 2005 that "Not a single study has found children of lesbian or gay parents to be disadvantaged in any significant respect relative to children of heterosexual parents"?

To return to the tally room, as promised: of the total of nine 'Gold

Standard' studies, six found various adverse educational and emotional outcomes for children raised by same-sex parents. One of the remaining three studies by Wainright shows a mixed picture of benefit and unexpected harm once the coding is corrected, where the benefit in terms of higher GPA and "school connectedness" is weighed against higher levels of anxiety. The other two Wainright studies (as I understand) have not yet been reanalysed using the uncorrupted database, and their findings cannot be relied on until that is done.

The 'marriage equality' PR team wants us to believe that children raised by same-sex parents do just as well as children raised by their married biological parents, but where are the large-scale representative studies to support their case? Apart from the "school connectedness" and GPA rise of Wainright, they have nothing to show. The findings so far are overwhelmingly one-way: children raised by same-sex parents suffer disadvantage on many different measures. As a general baseline, they suffer similar disadvantage to children raised in other biologically disrupted family structures. On the specific question of emotional harm, evidence so far suggests they suffer at about twice the rate of children in other biologically disrupted family structures. When compared to children raised by their married biological parents, evidence suggests children of same-sex households suffer nearly four times the rate of emotional harm.

If that is the case, what sort of society would enshrine this new way of disadvantaging children, this new structure of biologically disrupted family, as an ideal in our law?

Stop Press! Does a new study prove 'no difference' at last?

It's April 2016 and it is proving difficult to finish this chapter. I have to mention a new paper which has joined the exclusive ranks of "large representative studies". Ten now, not nine. And this one has really sent the "no difference" lobby into ecstasy: *Slate* magazine declares that, with this study, "The scientific debate over same-sex parenting is over."[130] The Centre for American Progress announces, "The conservative argument against same-sex parenting just fell apart."[131] Typical lazy journalism. Science is not a process with a sudden ending, a dramatic dropping of the curtain. Any scientific debate continues to amass evidence for and against a thesis, and the extra evidence in this latest study is of very little mass indeed, which makes it all the easier to spin.

The study is entitled "Same-Sex and Different-Sex Parent Households and Child Health Outcomes: Findings from the National Survey of Children's Health".[132] It compares stable lesbian households with stable opposite-sex households. The study makes only one significant finding: that lesbian couples are more irritable and angry with their children. It reveals worrying associations between this raised "parental stress" and a corresponding rise in childhood emotional difficulties and decline in coping behaviour and learning behaviour, but these associations did not reach the level of statistical significance. Achieving statistical significance is always a problem when studying stable same-sex households since there are so few of them: from ninety-five thousand phone surveys, only ninety-five continuously-coupled same-sex households with children made the study. It is hard to find statistical significance with those numbers – but, cheekily enough, that very inability to get a big enough sample to show statistical difference is trumpeted as evidence for finding "no difference"! Bear this in mind as you read the spin in the concluding lines of the study with its take-home message to policy-makers:

> Our analyses reveal that although female same-sex parents acknowledge more parenting stress, their children demonstrate no differences in general health, emotional difficulties, coping behavior, and learning behavior from children reared in different-sex parent households. These findings are relevant to clinicians, public policy analysts, litigators, and legislators who are consulted on matters pertaining to same-sex parent families.

With respect, no finding is relevant to legislators unless it is statistically significant, and the only finding that is statistically significant is that lesbian couples get more cranky with their kids. Why this apparent spin? Should it matter that the main driving force behind this study, according to the left-wing group Centre for American Progress, was the Williams Institute, "an LGBT think tank at the UCLA School of Law"?[133] Apparently this Institute was trying to "call Regnerus' bluff" with this study; in response, Professor Regnerus was both gracious and stubbornly objective. He said:

> In the pecking order of good study qualities, it has several things going for it, and I am happy to give credit generously where it is due. First, it focuses on "continuously coupled" households, which were profoundly rare in my 2012 study ... Second, it originates with a nationally representative sample — another big plus. However, when you start with tens of thousands of eligible cases but whittle down to comparing 95 female same-sex households with 95 opposite-sex ones, you quickly arrive at territory where statistical significance is going to be hard to locate.[134]

He then points to the one and only "significant finding":

> Here's what the new study claims: "No differences were observed between household types on family relationships or any child outcomes." Here's what the study actually signals (and it didn't take a PhD to see it): female same-sex parents report more anger, irritation, and comparative frustration with their (apparently misbehaving) children than do opposite-sex parents.

So much for the knockout study to end all further debate! It only confirms, once again, a form of disadvantage to children raised in same-sex households — unless it is now considered desirable for a household to have more stressed, irritable parents?

As a reward for so patiently reading the chapter so far, let me share one more joke about this study. The third paragraph looks back for support to a few large representative studies we are now familiar with: Wainright, Rosenfeld and Potter. But this new study blithely quotes Wainright's and Rosenfeld's "no difference" finding without mentioning the corruption of their databases! It claims Potter in support of the "no difference" thesis without admitting that Potter found a significant educational disadvantage for children of same-sex homes compared to married biological homes! So much for this all-conquering new study: it has no significant finding except that lesbian parents get angrier with their kids, and it claims support for its "no difference" thesis from studies which, on proper analysis, give no such support.

(ii) Unsettled science: the question of abuse

Regrettably, this final question cannot be ignored. In the Amicus Curiae brief to the US Supreme Court mentioned above, the most disturbing question raised was the apparent higher rate of sexual abuse of children in same-sex households.[135] Let me state at the outset that I am not convinced that the size and quality of the databases – even though they are among the largest and best we have – gives sufficient confidence about these troubling findings. What I am convinced about is that further research is imperative to confirm or dismiss any statistical association between same-sex households and increased rates of child sexual abuse.

The Amicus brief refers to worrying data in two key studies of same-sex parenting by Sullins and Regnerus.[136] On the Regnerus study it states:

> Some of the largest, and most sensitive, differences were in reported childhood sexual abuse: the children of lesbian mothers were, as children, ten times more likely to have been sexually touched by a parent or other adult and four times more likely to have been forced to have sex against their will. (Regnerus at 761, Table 2)[137]

In the other study, the AddHealth database used by Sullins was noteworthy for being one of the few large-scale questionnaires to ask adolescents about possible sexual abuse and to ask it in a way that allowed for a frank and confidential response. Sullins comments on the methodology and findings:

> To increase accuracy, adolescents entered their answers to these sensitive questions anonymously into a laptop computer in response to recorded questions they heard using earphones. Adolescents who had ever had sexual intercourse were given a series of follow-up questions that included being asked about forced sex ... 10% to 12% (SE .73-.92) of those with opposite-sex parents reported having been forced (or forcing someone) to have sexual intercourse. This proportion doubles with same-sex unmarried parents (24% SE 23), and almost triples again with same-sex married parents. Over two-thirds (71% SE 30) of the children with same-sex married parents who had ever had sexual intercourse reported that they had been forced to have sex against

their will at some point. All the "yes" responses for this group are from female adolescents, meaning that these are all reports of being forced, not forcing someone else, to have sex relations. In fact, strikingly, every sexually active female adolescent living with married same-sex parents (which are all lesbian parent couples) responded "yes" to having experienced forced sex.[138]

What are we to make of this disturbing, yet statistically fragile finding? I cannot be confident in findings based on so small a number of individuals, and yet given the fact that, of all couple households with children, only one in a thousand are same-sex households,[139] it requires very large studies to get sufficient numbers to achieve greater confidence. If the AddHealth study surveyed some twenty thousand young people to get just a couple of dozen subjects raised in same-sex homes, it would take a study of five or ten times that size to achieve the certainty we need on questions such as child sexual abuse. I cannot see that happening any time soon.

We are left in a disturbing predicament: if we take these preliminary and tentative findings seriously, we will be accused of casting generalised aspersions on the character of homosexual couples. If we sweep these hints of hidden tragedy under the carpet and they do indeed reflect an aspect of a hypersexualised, radical gay and lesbian subculture that puts children at risk, then we are abandoning children.

We should not dismiss this dilemma lightly. We can already hear the voice of abuse and abandonment in testimony like this from B.N. Klein in her submission to the US Court of Appeal, fifth circuit, in 2014:

> I grew up with a parent and her partner in an atmosphere in which gay ideology was used as a tool of repression, retribution and abuse. I lived with gay abuse for years ... By the time I was 11, I also found that the gay community had an obsessive unhealthy invasive preoccupation with their children's sexuality. They in fact encouraged sexual activity – because "they were open..." I do not believe that children abused in the gay community have the ability to safely come forward or be received and protected and believed. In the current climate, people are too afraid of being called homophobic and a bigot ... Within the gay community, abusers have complete impunity and complete protection from a code of honor that puts gay adults first. Then there is a network

of social and legal services that do not and will never consider the best interest of a child. If you imagine that children are not aware of this you are mistaken. I certainly knew that no one would help me ever no matter what.[140]

That is her story. No responsible person can read an account like that (and others) of growing up in a homosexual subculture, then read the Sullins and Regnerus data on sexual abuse in homosexual households, and then just turn a blind eye. Nor can any reasonable person make generalised conclusions that are not substantiated by the present preliminary data.

The one thing necessary is for our government to commission research to settle this distressing question. If the statisticians say we need a few hundred young people raised in same-sex homes to achieve certainty on the question of sexual abuse, we would need to survey a few hundred thousand adolescents – with the same comprehensiveness and provision of privacy as the AddHealth survey. We are capable of that as a sophisticated nation, and we have a duty to seek the truth on this matter – for the sake of future children like B.N. Klein.

Conclusion

This survey of the science has confirmed one finding as 'settled': that children do best, on average, when raised by their married biological parents. As Rutgers sociologist David Popenoe put it: "Few propositions have more empirical support in the social sciences than this one: compared to all other family forms, families headed by married, biological parents are best for children." The related fact is that same-sex parenting confers on a child the disadvantage that all biologically disrupted family structures confer. Therefore any policy that enshrines and encourages same-sex 'marriage' and parenting deliberately disadvantages future children. That is a legislative step we should never take.

On top of the settled science there is evidence of additional harm to children raised in same-sex homes, above and beyond the expected harm of any biologically disrupted family structure. This tough truth is politically incorrect in the present climate, but as Sullins, Regnerus, Marks et al conclude:

The longer social scientists study the question, the more evidence of harm is found, and the fact that children with same-sex parents suffer significant harm in that condition, compared to children with opposite-sex parents, particularly among same-sex parents who identify as married, has been established beyond reasonable doubt. Despite intense political bias to suppress the findings set forth herein, evidence from large, nationally-representative studies has demonstrated that children raised by same-sex parents, particularly those who identify as married, do not fare as well as those with opposite-sex parents, and many experience substantial harm.[141]

The evidence shows that the institution of homosexual 'marriage' would bring various forms of harm to the children of such unions. Which of our politicians is so negligent, so captive to fashion, so indifferent to the best interests of the child, as to sign such an institution into law?

Part II

Stealing Childhood

5

LGBTQ Sex-Education at Your 'Safe School'

Parents don't have the power to shut this down. There's an insignificant minority that might have an issue with it.
    Joel Radcliffe, Safe Schools Coalition Project Officer.[142]

Gay 'marriage' means gay sex-education, and parents will have no say.

At present, parents can object to radical LGBT sex-education programmes like "Safe Schools", and we can repel those who would impose indecent and disturbing material on our children. But once homosexual 'marriage' is the law of the land, parents will have no grounds to push back. The logic is simple: if the law says homosexual/bisexual/transsexual 'marriage' is normal and right, schools will be obliged, by anti-discrimination law, to teach that homosexual/bisexual/transsexual behaviour is normal and right. Vote for genderless 'marriage' and you get Safe Schools on Steroids.

After New York State passed its same-sex 'marriage' law in 2011, gay journalist Daniel Villarreal wrote,

> I and a lot of other people want to indoctrinate, recruit, teach, and expose children to queer sexuality AND THERE'S NOTHING WRONG WITH THAT ... I for one certainly want tons of school children to learn that it's OK to be gay, that people of the same sex should be allowed to legally marry each other, and that anyone

can kiss a person of the same sex without feeling like a freak. And I would very much like for many of these young boys to grow up and start f-----g men.[143]

Then, with an intelligent question that brings us back to the Safe Schools juggernaut rolling through our schools, Villarreal writes, "Why would we push anti-bullying programs or social studies classes that teach kids about the historical contributions of famous queers unless we wanted to deliberately educate children to accept queer sexuality as normal?"

Safe Schools Coalition Australia (SSCA) is a misleadingly named and government-funded programme that has been smuggled in under the pretext of reducing bullying, but in effect is a means of sexually radicalising your child's mind without you knowing about it. This is the programme, launched nationally by the Labor government in 2013, that has taught eleven-year-olds to "imagine you are sixteen" and going out with a person of the same sex that you are "really into"; that directed students to a site advertising sadomasochistic bondage workshops for young people and towards adult LGBT sites that are clearly pornographic; that advises students on how to hide their internet browsing history from their parents; whose associated resources instruct young people in the arts of "chest binding" and "penis tucking" to disguise their unwanted sexual characteristics; that frowns on the terms "boy" or "girl" as being too heteronormative and binary; instead, gender is taught to kids as "fluid", to be freely explored along the rainbow spectrum from mostly boy to mostly girl and all combinations in between.[144]

Because of parental outrage, the Coalition government pruned the existing SSCA programme in March 2016. Pruned, not uprooted, just awaiting more favourable conditions for regrowth. The federal Labor leader Bill Shorten declared himself "absolutely supportive" of the Safe Schools Coalition material and in Victoria the Labor Government of Premier Daniel Andrews decreed that the uncensored version shall be compulsory at all state schools by 2018. By contrast, former Prime Minister John Howard told Sky News in June 2016: "Something like that Safe Schools programme, I'd throw that in the dustbin – lock, stock and barrel."

Safe Schools is not a harmless frolic by fringe ideologues. It confuses and sexualises our children at a very suggestive age. Already I know of children deeply distressed after Safe Schools classes – one a distraught boy with a learning disability who thought from the role-play lesson that he must be gay; it took a week for him to get over the upset. Another boy from a religious family who was told to go home and find a picture on the internet of a male that he found "sexually attractive"; another girl who told me she was humiliated in class for not agreeing with the Safe Schools position on gender fluidity. Her teacher at a high school in Adelaide told her, "Well, I hope we have changed your views by the end of the class."

The people shaping your child's mind

If parents are not shocked into action by the indoctrination of their children through Safe Schools, which is a foretaste of the enforcement of gender ideology across society under laws for 'genderless marriage', then nothing will activate us. For those parents who are not yet shocked because they are not yet acquainted with the Safe Schools Coalition Australia, let me make the introductions.

Ms Ward and cultural Marxism

Meet two key players. The main architect of the SSCA curriculum, Roz Ward, is an out and proud Marxist. Catechising children into queer sexuality is consistent with the quest of cultural Marxism to undermine traditional marriage and family (see Chapter 9, Children of the State). Ms Ward keeps the red flag flying, as *The Australian* newspaper reported in February 2016:

> Addressing the Marxism 2015 conference in Melbourne, Ward railed against the "push to fit people into gender constructs that promote heterosexuality". "Programs like the Safe Schools Coalition are making some difference but we're still a long way from liberation," she said. "Marxism offers the hope and the strategy needed to create a world where human sexuality, gender and how we relate to our bodies can blossom in extraordinarily new and amazing ways that we can only try to imagine today.[145]

Ms Ward's passion for liberation and the socialist red flag was nearly her undoing. In May, she was briefly suspended by La Trobe University for "engaging in misconduct" after she posted a rainbow flag to her Facebook page along with the words, "Now we just need to get rid of the racist Australian flag on top of state parliament and get a red one up there and my work is done."[146] The suspension was brief, as the National Tertiary Education Union (NTEU) rallied to her defence with threats of lawsuits against the university. NTEU Victorian Secretary, Dr Colin Long, condemned La Trobe's bad behaviour: "It is this kind of moral and intellectual cowardice and bullying that underlies the bullying and victimisation of young people of diverse genders and sexualities, against which Roz Ward has dedicated her professional life." Clearly Ms Ward needed a Safe Universities programme to protect her from bullying. Dr Long then gave us this gem: "We are very concerned that La Trobe University management seem to think that political views should be a criterion for employment, as was the case in the Soviet Union." There would be little concern, surely, for Ms Ward's employment prospects back in the USSR? In any case, the University backed down within days and Ms Ward was welcomed back to work, marching in her red jacket through an NTEU guard of honour with clenched fist raised in salute.[147] Off to prepare more gender lessons for your kids.

Ward's commendable frankness has put the lie to the PR line, repeated in every news bulletin on the subject, that the Safe Schools programme is designed "to prevent bullying" of LGBT students. She cuts through the spin in a leaked video filmed at the Safe Schools Coalition National Symposium in Melbourne on 13 June, 2014. Ward makes it clear to the audience that stopping bullying is not the purpose of the programme:

> Safe Schools Coalition is about supporting gender and sexual diversity. Not about stopping bullying. About gender and sexual diversity. About same-sex attraction. About being transgender. About being lesbian, gay, bisexual – say the words – transgender, intersex. Not just 'Be nice to everyone. Everyone's great'.[148]

This programme is promoted as an anti-bullying programme because nice people can't say no to that. Ward's department at Latrobe University which undertook the research and advocacy that underpins Safe Schools was admirably honest about the deliberate framing of this programme in the respectable terms of "safety". It is also frank about its taxpayer-funded activism (they use a more sophisticated term than activism: "creating and supporting processes of social change"):

> The marketing of this research was consciously directed towards creating and supporting processes of social change. A focus on safety was thought to be a socially responsible way to disseminate the research. Safety for all young people was a basic human right, particularly in school, to which everyone could respond, irrespective of their personal moral stance. The safety paradigm endowed the cause with respectability; anyone could get behind such a banner without fear of suspicion and criticism. In short it removed seemingly insurmountable blockages to action and cleared the way for social change.[149]

Yes, all decent people would get behind such a banner of "safety", even if it was a banner used as a cloak. Even if it was an unnecessary banner, since we already have several school programmes that do the important job of minimising bullying of any student for any reason. As one example, the PEACE Pack was developed a decade ago at Flinders University by Professor Phillip Slee and is now being exported to other countries to deal with the whole gamut of bullying at school.[150] As we shall see in the next chapter, claims of a plague of gay-based bullying are overblown, but framing LGBT advocacy in terms of "safety" helped endow the cause with respectability and taxpayer money. The actual objective of SSCA, as Ms Ward confirms, lacks such easy respectability, promoting marginal and disturbing sexual ideas to our children.

Of course there is value in the right sort of sex education, but it needs to be free of gender ideology and soft porn titillation. Give kids in class a cold serve of the relevant biology and some stern ethics and then get back to maths and spelling. Rare children with gender confusion are best helped privately by specialist teachers and doctors, remembering always that most of the students who think they are gay or transgender will no longer think of themselves as gay or transgender within a matter of months to years – so relax a little![151] Don't hassle kids in a transient stage of sexual confusion to "come out" prematurely and be celebrated; hassle them, rather, to attend to their basic competencies – which are going backwards in Australia in direct proportion to the number of activist issues cluttering the curriculum. If young people of any orientation want to flaunt their sexuality in their own private time, so be it, but not at school. An approach like that makes sense to this parent, at least.

Ms Fink and transgender activism

The other person parents need to meet is Margot Fink, Director of the Safe Schools *All of Us* programme presently being rolled out to hundreds of Australian schools. She is the chief author of several joint ventures between the Safe Schools Coalition and Minus18 ("Australia's national organisation for LGBT youth"). In one of those jointly produced resources, *OMG I'm Trans*, Fink gives a biographical insight into her passion for the subject: "For me personally I identify as a bisexual girl, but was assigned male at birth. What that means is I strongly identify as female, and can be attracted to other people of multiple genders the same or different from my own."[152]

Fink and Roz Ward are the "Proof and Edit" team for *OMG I'm Trans*, and their booklet includes instructions (p.30) for gender-confused youth in the above-mentioned "chest binding" and "penis tucking" as ways to fabricate the desired gendered appearance. Fink's essay on "medical transition" (p.11) for youth who want surgery and hormones to change their gender appearance is, in my view, gravely irresponsible. Amidst the enthusing about "a lot of great options" and descriptions of genital and chest surgery and puberty blockers there is no mention of two vital facts. First, that most young people with gender confusion – up to 97% in some studies – will get over their confusion around the time of puberty.[153,154,155] Fink does not even mention this statistic to the young readers! Only at puberty do new hormonal forces and physical changes come into play that affirm the young person's actual sex. A medical journal review drew the conclusion:

> As children with GID [gender identity disorder] only rarely go on to have permanent transsexualism, irreversible physical interventions are clearly not indicated until after the individual's psychosexual development is complete. The identity-creating experiences of this phase of development should not be restricted by the use of LHRH analogues that prevent puberty.[156]

Which policy maker in their right mind would recommend medical interference for a gender-confused child when there is every expectation the young person's confusion will resolve around puberty? So why let this notion be peddled to kids using taxpayer money? Fink's second omission: there is no mention of the dire long-term psychological outcomes for those who submit to these "great options" of medical and surgical intervention. The best study we have reveals short-term relief lasting a few years followed by a long-term suicide rate twenty times higher than the matched non-trans population.[157] Could it be that we are treating the wrong thing: perhaps we should be mending a wounded mind, not mutilating a healthy body?

Kids are impressionable. Is it any coincidence, as these troubling ideas are promulgated in schools, that there is a sudden epidemic of confused children seeking medical help to change their gender? In July 2015, journalist Kate Legge wrote a review, "Transgender children: what's behind the spike in numbers" and noted,

> Requests to help transgender students have skyrocketed since mid-last year when the federal Education Department funded a national initiative called the Safe Schools Coalition aimed at creating "inclusive" learning environments… "The numbers are enormous," says Dr Michelle Telfer, the leading specialist at Melbourne's Royal Children's Hospital… From one patient in 2003, the hospital expects to see 200 children and adolescents this year.[158]

Correlation is not causation, but any reasonable person can see that, if grown-ups give children glossy presentations about the normality of homosexual, bisexual and transsexual behaviour and use their authority to teach children to get over their binary ideas of "male" and "female"[159] and that if a boy wears a girl's school uniform he "is a girl",[160] this is the result we would expect. Perhaps such growth in gender-confused children is as a pleasing result for the architects of Safe Schools, but I do not think this is the result parents want when they entrust their child to the local state school.

I will defer further discussion on transgender matters to Chapter 8 (The Abolition of Male and Female), but I hope this brief introduction to two of the main players gives parents a flavour of the mindset and values behind this programme – and that parents will join the pushback.

Parent power

There have been two successful pushbacks by parents against the Safe Schools Coalition. In the video mentioned above, Roz Ward specified how she expected school principals to deal with parents who object to the programme: "The school leadership can very calmly and graciously say, 'You know what, we're doing it anyway. Tough luck'." Credit for bravado, even if that is not very becoming in an academic, but for now the tide of luck has turned against Ms Ward.

2014 – 'Two virginities'

The first small victory for worried parents was back in 2014, when the attention of politicians was drawn to the Minus18/SSCA booklet *OMG I'm Queer* which was featured as a resource on the (uncensored) SSCA website. On page 10, entitled "Doing It", schoolchildren are given the following advice by contributor Alice Chesworth:

> It may come as a surprise, but there is no strict definition for virginity, especially if you're queer. Penis-in-vagina sex is not the only sex, and certainly not the *ultimate* sex ... I'm bisexual, so I ended up thinking of myself as having two virginities, my first time with a chick and my first time with a dude. How you think about it is really up to you![161]

Your taxes at work. Amidst the demands of business and home life, upset parents took time to contact MPs and Senators, and there was robust discussion in the corridors of power as to why this stuff was still being funded under a Coalition government. The authors of the booklet quietly removed page 10, "Doing it", and a smaller-target online version appeared in 2015. Having said that, the 2014 version is still available in hard copy at schools, and even on certain school websites. For example, one parent let me know that Golden Grove High School in South Australia, "part of the Safe Schools Coalition Australia", still makes the original version available at its "Wellbeing Hub".[162] The 2014 version is also preserved at a number of sites online because it would be a pity if that publicly-funded advice on "Doing it" became unavailable for taxpayer and parental scrutiny.

2016 – 'He doesn't need to deal with this'

Then there was the major pushback against Safe Schools in early 2016. Two main factors led to this triumph. First, a mother in Victoria, Cella White, went public with her decision to withdraw her children from a school that was using the SSCA programme. The Melbourne *Herald Sun* reported on February 8th,

> A mother has withdrawn her children from Frankston High School after the introduction of a new program to promote transgender awareness. Cella White says her 14-year-old son was told he could wear a dress to school and that male-born students who identified as female could use the girls' change rooms and toilets. The government-funded program by the Safe Schools Coalition is designed to promote inclusiveness for 'same sex attracted, intersex and gender diverse' students, but critics say it is indoctrinating children in sexual identity politics under the pretence of a bullying program.[163]

Ms White had two children with medical conditions that, she felt, would make them especially vulnerable to the confusing ideas contained in the programme:

> "It was announced in science class that boys could wear school dresses next year," Ms White said. "They're telling my children to call transgender children by their requested pronoun. What is the benefit to my son? He's got a learning disability, he's struggling with his times tables, he doesn't need to deal with this." The mother of four was particularly concerned about any changes in bathroom policy that could see her daughter sharing a bathroom with a gender diverse student. "It could be a year 12 student of the opposite-born sex in the bathroom with my year 7 daughter who is blind," Ms White said. "This isn't about safe schools, it's transgenderism and gay activism bought into the classroom. I know other parents who are not happy."

In a powerful short video that attracted half a million views on Facebook in five days, Ms White explained why she had to withdraw her children, and why she was motivated to speak out publicly:

> Most people think that you have to be religious to have any concerns about the Safe School Coalition. It's not so. I'm not of

any religious affiliation. I just feel so violated, so violated, because I handed in a non-permission to the school and they overrode it. Now I really wanted an opt-out, much the same as you would with religious education... I just figure, if as a parent you deem it harmful, why would you send them to school to learn it?[164]

Other parents also withdrew their children and went public with their concerns. A father from the same part of Victoria describes his dismay when he looked into the programme in early 2016:

And so I went onto their website and was immediately shocked with what was being presented to me and the other things that were being linked off to; all the little banners that were on the website and what was being promoted... I thought, is this something that I want my kids to be learning about... People say, teaching about penis tucking and breast binding: I saw the links. I saw the material there. People talk about teaching kids to hide their internet history: I saw that, that was there.[165]

There was no political agenda for parents like Cella White any more than there was a religious agenda. It was more primal than that; it was the instinct of a mother to defend her child from harm:

At the end of the day I just want the best for my children, like any other parent. This is why we had to leave the school, to escape the Safe Schools programme. I think there's many other ways you can teach kids to be kind, respectful, tolerant, diverse, inclusive. It can be done in the home and it can be done at school, and it can be done with a true anti-bullying programme – without the sexualisation of children. Without LGBT activism, I would call it, within the school.

There will be no escape from Safe Schools and its progeny, dear parents, once homosexual/bisexual/transsexual 'marriage' is enshrined in law as the new normal.

Indecent exposure

The second factor in the 2016 taming of Safe Schools was bold action by federal Coalition backbenchers. Speeches in the Parliament and a petition to the Prime Minister signed by the majority of Liberal and National MPs in February led to a review of the SSCA programme. Among the backbenchers, George Christensen MP gave the most forensic analysis in Parliament, and his documentation of Safe Schools' links to adult sites deserves close attention:

> I rise as a voice for the thousands of parents who have been shocked when they discovered how the ironically named Safe Schools program is indoctrinating their children. When those parents consider just how unsafe this program is, they will wonder why the federal government is allowing it to be implemented in schools, much less spending $8 million of taxpayer money to fund it. The things that the Safe Schools Coalition Australia are recommending to school students include pornographic web content, sex shops, adult online communities and sex clubs. The Safe Schools 'All of Us' teaching resource directs students to the LGBT organisation Twenty10. On 19 January this year, Twenty10 hosted a hands-on workshop for youth on sex toys and sadomasochistic practices. All of Us also directs students to the website of the LGBT youth organisation Minus18, which produced most of the Safe Schools resources. Minus18 advised the students on chest binding, penis tucking, sex toys and sex advice such as 'penis-in-vagina sex is not the only sex and certainly not the ultimate sex'. Minus18 links to The Tool Shed - an online pornographic sex shop offering a range of sex toys, sadomasochistic items and pornography. Minus18 recommends Scarleteen – a teen sex advice site that promotes group sex, sex toys and sadomasochism. Minus18 is an event partner with Melbourne gay bar the GH Hotel, which features erotic homosexual entertainment. Safe Schools recommends the transgender organisation Seahorse Club Victoria, which in turn recommends the Abode fetish club. Abode is located at the same address as The Parlour Lounge sex club, which provides sadomasochistic entertainment and rooms for sex. Safe Schools is funded via the Foundation for Young Australians, whose partner agencies implement the Safe Schools program. Tasmanian partner Working It Out recommends YouTube channels featuring such things as 'Gay guy sees first transgender vagina' and 'Anal for FTMs'. These links to sexually explicit web content and external organisations of an adult or erotic nature raise serious concerns about child safety. Further, Safe Schools provides instructions to children on how to hide their internet browsing history. It advises

them to ask for restricted websites that are blocked at school – and would be blocked at home – to be unblocked by their teachers without parental knowledge. If parents knew their children were being exposed to this type of material, they would probably not let them go to school. If someone proposed exposing a child to this material, the parents would probably call the police because it sounds a lot like the grooming work that a sexual predator might undertake. Child and Adolescent Sexual Assault Counselling Incorporated is a New South Wales peak body for child sexual assault counselling. This is how that body describes the process of grooming:

- Sexualisation of the relationship through conversation and exposure of the child to sexual material such as images;
- taking undue interest in the child's sexual development;
- assuring the child of the rightness of what they are doing;
- telling the child the acts will not hurt them;
- alienating the child from their parents and family so that they do not feel close to them;
- and shaping the child's sexual preferences and manipulating what the child finds exciting.

That all sounds very familiar. The Safe Schools program focuses heavily on child and teenage sexual activity and sexual attractions; justifies almost any sexual activity; diminishes possible risks and harms; encourages young people to hide their activities from their parents; and provides links to adult sex clubs, adult online communities and sex shops. What is more, the program portrays all of this as normal and wraps it up in a taxpayer-funded package and calls it an anti-bullying campaign. The Safe Schools program is in fact an unsafe schools program and it leaves students open to being groomed on websites advertising adult sex venues. I commend the government for undertaking a review of this program and I call on schools using this program to immediately suspend it pending the outcome of that review. I urge all members of this House, particularly those with young children, to take a close look at what Safe Schools is delivering.[166]

Mr Christensen made serious claims of gravely improper links from

Safe Schools material to adult sites, and I could find no error in his claims. On the night of his speech, the links he mentioned to sites like The Tool Shed were mysteriously removed. Concerned readers will be glad to know that the uncensored axis of Safe Schools / Minus18 / adult sites as at February 2016 has been preserved for posterity. A closely documented submission to the NSW Parliamentary Inquiry into Sexualisation of Children and Young People maps out all the links in graphic form and confirms the claims made by Mr Christensen.[167] The question remains: has anyone at Minus18 and Safe Schools been held responsible for setting up or promoting these indecent links to Australian children? Is that a matter for the police, or just the educational authorities?

All of Us - What's all the fuss?

And the question for parents now is, "What is left after the pruning process of March 2016, and is it acceptable that there be anything left of such a subversive and corrupting programme?" The *All of Us* programme, flagship of Safe Schools and Minus18, sailed on unchanged for months after the March review. This joint venture of Margot Fink and Roz Ward's team describes itself thus:

> *All Of Us* is an innovative new teaching and learning resource jointly developed by Safe Schools Coalition Australia and The Minus18 Foundation that aims to increase students' understanding and awareness of gender diversity, sexual diversity and intersex topics. It is approved by the Australian Government.[168]

It's nice to be approved by the Government, but the blurb does not mention the Government's disapproval of the links provided by *All of Us* to LGBT sites like Twenty10 (with its bondage and sex toy classes for young people) and of the programme's intensely sexualised and politicised content. To get a feel for that original content – which remained online long after the Birmingham review was announced and is still found in schools in hard copy form – just look at lesson two.[169] I would ask teachers to consider whether or not this is a form of pedagogical abuse.

Intimidating children

Your year 7 class is about to watch a video of Jaimee, who identifies as lesbian. You are first to undertake a class activity with the apparent objective of bringing maximal peer pressure and personal embarrassment to bear on any student who has inhibitions about same-sex relationships. To start with, separate students from their usual friendship groups. Then instruct these eleven and twelve year old students to imagine themselves as sixteen year olds going out with a person they are "really into". Half are to be in heterosexual relationships and half homosexual. The students then answer ten questions about how easy it is for them to live out their sexual relationship, gay or straight. Questions include "When you go out with a group of friends to the movies, would you feel comfortable giving your partner a kiss or hug?" or "Would you be able to talk to your friends about what you did on the weekend with your partner without worrying about their reaction?" and "If you were in a sports team, would you confidently tell your teammates about your sexuality?" One wonders what normal year 7 student would want to engage her teammates in a conversation about her sexuality, but this is the world of Ward and Fink.

Then the children all stand up – separated, you remember, from their "usual friendship groups". Those who are most comfortable in their sexual role-play and answered yes to all the questions sit down first, leaving standing those students who found it all very uncomfortable. Finally there is one child standing, in the homosexual role-play group no doubt, who was able to say yes to only one or two of these weird questions. Maybe the child is on the verge of tears. Maybe the child is from a Christian home or just doesn't understand all this strange sexual talk. Lesson learnt, kid: there is something wrong with your attitude.

By the time the student has endured a few more emotionally disorienting *All of Us* lessons on the normality of bisexual relationships and transgender identity, the poor kid will probably be desperate to show that she is a nice person just like the others in her class by signing her name to the highly politicised pledge to be an LGBT "ally" who "stands against homophobia and transphobia."[170] She can then join wholeheartedly in the recommended activities like celebrating the International Day Against Homophobia and Transphobia (IDAHO). In my view, this is pedagogical abuse for ideological ends. In the words of one parent, "It has been a cause of stress, anxiety and tears for my child who strongly agrees with the anti-bullying message but does not support all values endorsed by and associated with the LGBTIQ movement. Students who take issue with some aspects of the Safe Schools program are themselves feeling bullied and are being told they are ignorant and homophobic."

"Tough luck", to quote Roz Ward. What matters is that another young mind has been successfully formed in gender fluid and sexually permissive attitudes, freed from the homophobic prejudices of their parents' generation.

Rats in the torchlight

Yes, the review by Education Minister Simon Birmingham in March 2016 was a major setback for the Safe Schools programme, but the Government did not do what Mr Howard advised and throw it in the dustbin – lock, stock and barrel. If I check on our half-dozen hens at night, my torch will disturb some sleek young rats. They will scurry from the light, but they will be back as soon as I turn away. That, I regret to say, is what will happen with Safe Schools. The light of public scrutiny has sent it scurrying for a while, but this plague on our schools will be back worse than ever under a regime of genderless 'marriage'.

We know that Labor and the Greens want it back in its full ideological rigour; we know that Daniel Andrews' Labor government in Victoria has defied Minister Birmingham and will continue the full-blooded rollout to all government schools.[171] And even the Birmingham review leaves far too much standing.[172] The Minister required, among other things, that the material now be limited to high schools and be shorn of its external links; that the *All of Us* content be made more "appropriate" and that future materials be subject to departmental approval. Also, that schools should first consult parents before introducing the programme, but good luck with that when parents in Queensland and now NSW are blocked from even knowing which schools use the programme – the Queensland Labor government rejected a petition of 11,000 residents and a formal FOI request for the information! Yes, it is progress (starting from a very low base) that *All of Us* no longer directs students to sadomasochistic get-togethers; that eleven-year-olds no longer role-play being sixteen and in a same-sex relationship; that the "ally" pledge has been deleted. Yet the censored version of May 2016 remains saturated in gender theory and sexualised to the hilt. Lesson 4 of the post-pruning *All of Us* programme is pure dogma on the social construction of male and female:

> Up until this point, many students may believe that gender can only be either male or female, and that they have specifically related behaviours and characteristics. By completing this exercise, students will be able to explore the concept that gender exists outside this binary and that societal expectations of gender are shaped by the world in which they live.[173]

The current version still has Nevo, a young woman who identifies as male, telling students via video "about growing up with the knowledge that the female sex assigned to him at birth did not match who he knew he truly was"; likewise Margot still confides to students "what it's like to grow up being told you're a boy when you know you're a girl". The dogma of *All of Us* does not permit the alternative view that Nevo and Margot's transgender identity might be a problem with the mind, not the body. Sexual identity is still described in casual terms to twelve-year-old students as being "who you love, like and hookup with" (p.24) and the children are told, "There are lots of different components that make up your sexuality. You can be attracted to a whole spectrum of masculinity, femininity, both or even none." Children who are still struggling with their times-tables are instructed in the subtleties of gender fluidity; uncontested assertions are made that "it's up to the individual to decide what gender identity fits them best", and that kids can choose from such categories as genderqueer, trans guy, sister girl, or agender (p.34). And lesson 6 still alerts the child to the evils of "heteronormativity"; it is clearly bigoted to believe that the division of mammalian life into male and female is somehow 'natural' or that man-woman sexual attraction is somehow 'normal'. To start expunging such unacceptable thoughts from young minds the teacher helps the students "think of everyday examples where this worldview is reinforced":

> Some suggestions include: asking new parents whether their baby is a boy or a girl; always asking boys if they have a girlfriend rather

than a girlfriend or a boyfriend; telling a girl not to express herself in masculine ways because it is not 'lady-like'.[174]

Why in the world does the government continue to use our money to subject our children to this mind-messing gender theory? We must laugh if we are not to cry, so let me note with grim delight that the only element of *All of Us* that has been entirely erased, "thrown in the dustbin – lock, stock and barrel", is Ms Ward herself. From being listed as author and featured prominently on the front cover of the first version of *All of Us*, she has been "disappeared" down the revised version's memory hole, to use an apt Orwellian phrase. That face-saving swiftie by Safe Schools seems to me to epitomise the disdain this programme shows for parents: that Ms Ward will be falsely de-authored, hidden from sight, to keep parents in the dark about its Marxist writer-in-residence.

This two-year tale of parent power is heartening, but the gender ideologues are only biding their time; they shall return. They know that the battle will be won for them once genderless 'marriage' becomes law. As we have seen overseas, parents will be told that the state now has an obligation to treat LGBT and heterosexual relationships as identical and there is no longer any basis for complaint about what is taught in school. Just consider one real-life testimony from parents overseas who live under a law for 'marriage equality'.

Overseas case study: 'We had no right to object'

Robb and Robin Wirthlin were parents of a primary school child in Massachusetts when the courts imposed same-sex 'marriage' in 2003. Their son's grade two teacher read his class the story *King & King* in which a handsome prince spurns the traditional princess and lives happily ever after with the princess's brother.[175] The Wirthlins heard about this lesson from their son and they objected to the school. The teacher told them that the theme of that day had been weddings and that since "gay marriage is legal," she "wanted to present all points of view."[176] The school principal told the parents that no, they could not remove their son from such lessons, nor would they be given notice of such lessons.

The Wirthlins were not going to give up without a fight and they joined with another couple from the same school, David and Tonia

Parker, in a court case asserting their "rights to direct the moral upbringing of their own children".[177] This of course reflects Article 26 of the Universal Declaration of Human Rights: "Parents have a prior right to choose the kind of education that shall be given to their children." The parents' legal team made the case that the school was guilty "of intentionally indoctrinating very young children to affirm the notion that homosexuality is right and moral, in direct denigration of the plaintiffs' deeply-held faith".

They fought all the way to the Appeals Court, but they lost: "The courts said we had no right to object or pull them out of class," said Mrs Wirthlin.[178] The opinion of Judge Sandra Lynch, one of President Bill Clinton's appointees, shows us that the fundamental right of parents to direct the moral upbringing of their children must give way to the fundamental intention of 'progressives' to trash traditional morals.[179] "We do not suggest that the school's choice of books for young students has not deeply offended the plaintiffs' sincerely held religious beliefs," says Her Honor, but "the reading of King and King was not instruction in religion or religious beliefs". Do you follow Her Honor's reasoning here? Teaching a child to accept a view of marriage and sexual relationships that is in direct contradiction to the core moral and religious beliefs of the child's family is not "instruction in religion or religious beliefs". It's destruction, not instruction, so that's cool. Judge Lynch fully acknowledges that this was an exercise in "influencing" the child's beliefs, but what the conservative parents call anti-religious indoctrination the 'progressive' judge (who has all the power) prefers to call "influence towards tolerance":

> King and King ... affirmatively endorses homosexuality and gay marriage. It is a fair inference that the reading of King and King was precisely intended to influence the listening children toward tolerance of gay marriage. That was the point of why that book was chosen and used. Even assuming there is a continuum along which an intent to influence could become an attempt to indoctrinate, however, this case is firmly on the influence-toward-tolerance end.

Such is the supercilious logic of the elite: indoctrination of your children is just "influence-toward-tolerance", and quite good for them.

So schools in Massachusetts can continue to "affirmatively endorse homosexuality and gay marriage" without parental consent. Schools in Australia will do the same and treat parental authority with the same disdain once we have a law for homosexual 'marriage'.

Win the battle but lose the war?

Australia's pushback against the cultural Marxists and sexual radicals of the Safe Schools Coalition is a significant victory for the right of parents to determine what is taught to their children. But there are two problems. First, there are several other programmes being rolled out in our schools that derive from the same disturbing "gender theory" as Safe Schools (see Chapter 8 for details) and the pressure by certain academics will be unrelenting. Second, parents will lose all power to push back against these programmes once there is a law that enshrines homosexual and bisexual and transsexual relationships as the equivalent of natural marriage.

So, parents of Australia, vote for 'marriage equality' and you are voting to relinquish control of your child's moral education to sexual radicals. Vote for 'marriage equality' and, based on President Obama's executive order in May 2016 to all 96,000 public schools in the US, you are voting for your daughter to have to share change-rooms with disturbed young men who claim they are women – all on the basis of genderless 'equality'. Vote Yes in the same-sex 'marriage' plebiscite and you will get Safe Schools on Steroids, and your children and grandchildren will live with the consequences.

6

BULLYING, BLACKMAIL, AND 'BORN THAT WAY'

Without any intervention whatsoever, three out of four boys who think they're gay at age 16 aren't by 25.
    Dr Jeffrey Satinover, psychiatrist

The three main arguments used to justify programs like Safe Schools are the same three arguments used to justify same-sex 'marriage'. We will hear these arguments unendingly over the course of the national debate: first, that we must normalise homosexual 'marriage' and homosexual behaviour in order to combat bullying of LGBT people; second, that society must agree to this or be culpable for gay depression and suicide; third, that we must grant gay 'marriage' as a matter of natural justice, since gay people are 'born that way'. None of these claims withstand scrutiny.

I. To combat bullying

To the first argument: that there is a crisis of gay-based bullying in our schools, and the best way to reduce that bullying is to celebrate homosexuality in the curriculum and affirm same-sex 'marriage' in our laws.

The factual basis of that proposition is doubtful. Rates of bullying are rarely compared between homosexual and heterosexual populations, but one large study published in the *British Journal of Psychiatry* in 2003 compared a thousand homosexual and heterosexual adults.[180] The researchers found no increase whatsoever in bullying of gay men compared to heterosexual men, whether at school or subsequently, whether verbally or physically. The researchers noted, "Reports that gay and lesbian people are vulnerable to such experiences because of their sexuality are often taken at face value." A study in 2015 drawing on the US National Health Interview Survey database of 207,000 children examined the assumption that kids of same-sex households are more likely to be bullied. It found that, "Contrary to the assumption underlying this hypothesis, children with opposite-sex parents are picked on and bullied more than those with same-sex parents."[181]

There are many reasons to be bullied at school – for being too smart, too dumb; too fat, too weak; too shy, too odd-looking; or for being "gay" even when you are not gay. That is something many of us go through and the claim that homosexual people or kids in homosexual homes suffer disproportionate bullying appears to be "taken at face value". But the claim has immense political value. We saw in the last chapter how the publicly funded Latrobe University research that underpins the Safe Schools programme chose "safety" as the theme that would be most likely to make government sit up and pay up: "The safety paradigm endowed the cause with respectability; anyone could get behind such a banner without fear of suspicion and criticism. In short it removed seemingly insurmountable blockages to action and cleared the way for social change."[182] There is a clear benefit for advocates of "social change" to stand behind the banner of bullying-prevention, despite the principal author of the Safe Schools material, Roz Ward, admitting that the programme is "not about stopping bullying".[183] And this narrative of gay-child-as-victim comes straight from the 1990 textbook of homosexual activism, *After the Ball* by Kirk and Madsen, which understood that the way to win over "straight society" would be to play on their protective instincts. Note their famous quote, perhaps the single most influential insight of the last quarter century of gay activism: "Gays must be portrayed as victims in need of protection so that straights will be inclined by reflex to adopt the role of protector."[184]

Suppressing our reflex for a moment, and bearing in mind the political overtones to this alleged crisis of gay-based bullying, let us consider that the claims might be overblown. That they are poorly supported by the data we have. That dubious studies are being used as a bludgeon to shame people into supporting homosexual 'marriage' and LGBT sex-education. Scholars should be challenging this politically charged proposition that gay-based bullying is disproportionately worse than general bullying. But they probably won't, so I will.

Are LGBT kids really bullied more?

Hard data on homophobic bullying is hard to come by; there is a strange shyness about gathering it and reporting it. For example, in NSW, which has had its own "Proud Schools" programme countering homophobia and heterosexism, the Education Department does not even keep a tally of episodes of gay-based bullying. In May 2015 the NSW Minister for Education and Communities, Adrian Piccoli, was asked the following Question on Notice regarding bullying in public schools:

> With respect to formally reported incidents of bullying in 2014, including cyber bullying, in the following New South Wales High Schools, what was the (a) most frequent reason given by complainants for the bullying reports; (b) second most frequent reason given by complainants for the bullying reports; and (c) third most frequent reason given by complainants for the bullying reports?[185]

The question then helpfully listed every high school from Airds to Young making it nine pages long. The answer was much shorter. The Minister said, "The NSW Department of Education and Communities does not collect data at a systemic level on incidents of alleged bullying in schools." Puzzling response, since there is indeed a system of "safety and security incident reports" in NSW public schools. Sydney's *Daily Telegraph* had its education reporter, Bruce McDougall, monitor the NSW Department of Education incident reports of violence and other problems at schools for seven years. He did not find a single report relating to homophobia.[186]

We can at least establish a valid figure for the general rate of bullying across all school students. The Australian Covert Bullying Prevalence Study (ACBPS, 2009) was commissioned by the Federal Government and conducted by Edith Cowan University. This massive tome takes us back to that nasty *Lord of the Flies* phase of life:

> Students reported that girls are more likely to engage in behaviours such as spreading rumours; talking behind another's back; name calling; passing notes; saying mean things about others; exclusion; gossip; teasing; telling secrets; mean looks; writing letters; and physical actions such as pulling hair, biting, slapping, pushing and preventing access to the toilets, whereas boys were reported as more likely to engage in behaviours that are physical such as punching, kicking, pushing, or hitting; name calling or teasing; threatening; sending notes; saying nasty things; spreading rumours; hand gestures; swearing; gossiping; and staring.[187]

Chapter 4.3 details "Rates of bullying" across different year groups:

> Year 4 students were more likely to report they were bullied for most of the listed forms of bullying (covert and overt), with approximately two-thirds of these students reporting that they were teased (71%) and excluded from groups (66%). Year 8 students reported the next highest levels of bullying behaviour, with 57% reporting they were teased and 47% reporting they had hurtful lies told about them.[188]

Those numbers are high and worth keeping in mind when we consider the claims for gay-based bullying. The ACBPS study does not specify reasons for bullying, only noting established research that "both covert and overt bullying are selectively directed at certain children who tend to be anxious, cautious, sensitive, with low self-esteem, or who are considered by the group to have 'unattractive' physical, behavioural or social-cultural features, such as obesity, physical disability, arrogance, or who belong to a different ethnic group."[189] No mention of sexuality. Which reminds us that there are a hundred and one reasons to be bullied, and over-emphasising the small proportion of bullying attributed to homophobia is unjust to the majority of victims bullied for other reasons.

Accordingly, the ACBPS does not seek to impose radical gender theory on students or prohibit the use of "boy" and "girl", but proposes something saner and more general to deal with the mainstream of bullying:

> Effective school policies to prevent and deal with covert bullying

will require the development of programs aimed at: enhancing a positive school climate and ethos which promotes pro-social behaviours; providing pre-service and in-service training of all school staff to assist them to recognise and respond appropriately to signs of covert bullying; creating physical environments that limit the invisibility of covert bullying..."[190]

Compare and contrast this broad approach with the Safe Schools *All of Us* advocacy programme focussed narrowly on homophobic bullying (except it isn't really, as author Ms Ward just told us). Here is their core factual claim: "We know that 75% of same sex attracted young people experience some form of homophobic abuse or bullying ... A staggering 80% of this abuse and bullying occurs while young people are at school."[191] Staggering? It depends on how much is substance and how much is spin. It's time for a reality check on their 75% claim.

Fixing the figures

The *All of Us* figure of 75% is based entirely on one study, *Writing Themselves In Three: The 3rd national study on the sexual health and wellbeing of same sex attracted and gender questioning young people*.[192] This research was conducted by La Trobe University's Australian Research Centre in Sex, Health and Society, which is the home of Safe Schools and co-creator of *All of Us*. A little incestuous, perhaps?

When *All of Us* uses the strong phrase "homophobic abuse or bullying" experienced by the 75%, we learn from *Writing Themselves In Three (WTI3)* that the phrase covers everything from the 69% who report feeling "socially excluded by peers" or have rumours spread about them through to the 61% who experience direct teasing and the 18% who are physically bullied.[193] Note how comparable these figures are to the ACBPS figures, above, for all Year 4 students feeling socially excluded (66%) and teased (71%). Yes, other year levels in the ACBPS did not have such high figures – but wait a little longer, since I have not finished with the incredible shrinking *All of Us* figure for homophobic bullying. For a start, we need to knock a fifth off that figure, because only four-fifths of it occurred at school[194] (recall the "staggering" finding that "80% of this abuse and bullying occurs while young people are at school" – therefore

20% did not) whereas the ACBPS data was 100% at school. Let's correct the 75% *All of Us* figure to 60% for actual school-based bullying. That is now well below the ACBPS data across all kids in Year 4 (71%) and comparable to Year 8 (57%). But wait, there's more… Fewer than half of the young people contributing to the *All of Us* figure were actually at school (41%) while others were at university (40%) or out working![195] How is that meant to give us a valid figure for school-based bullying? I will leave it to statisticians to decide how much more needs to be knocked off the number.

Then despair of the validity of even that reduced number, for four solid reasons: first, the study suffered from overt *selection bias* (a self-selecting convenience sample of LGBT youth mainly recruited on the internet and via sexual diversity youth workers); second, the sample was unrepresentative of the Australian population by sex or ethnicity; third, there was no control group of non-LGBT students to compare rates of bullying with. Fail, fail, fail! But the really big, fourth and final nail in the coffin of the *All of Us* figure for rates of homophobic bullying is its *reporting bias*, and it was hammered in, astonishingly enough, by one of the authors of *WTI3*. In April 2016 we read in *The Australian*,

> University of New England academic Tiffany Jones appears to have broken ranks from many colleagues in the field by highlighting the deficiencies of some advocacy-driven research studies, particularly those presenting gay, lesbian, bisexual, transgender, intersex and queer (GLBTIQ) youth as victims of homophobic bullying. It is an extraordinary admission given Professor Jones's role as a collaborator on a high-profile research project, the 2010 *Writing Themselves In 3* study, which has propagated this view and formed the basis for education policy across the country, including the Safe Schools gender and sexual diversity program.[196]

I don't think Jones has broken ranks. She has just done the professional thing as an academic and identified the weaknesses in *WTI3*, particularly the way it is structured to elicit the desired "victim" narrative from students. Discussing *WTI3* and similar studies she writes,

> The studies were often linked to GLBTIQ education networks interested in humanising the GLBTIQ student as a 'victim' of schools. Research tools frequently asked whether participants had

experienced verbal and physical homophobic bullying, depression, suicidal intentions and self-harm in a way that created a kind of 'expected narrative' for the GLBTIQ student.[197]

Jones writes that such a methodology: "privileged the bullied, depressed and suicidal position by repeatedly enquiring, and ultimately reporting on, this aspect of GLBTIQ life." As an example of the practical ways this 'expected narrative' might be gleaned from students, Jones reproduced a thirteen-point questionnaire from *WTI3* (p.116). She wrote,

> [The] survey's list of impacts for a question on how homophobia impacted GLBTIQ students' schooling did offer participants the opportunity to say it had no impact, or had inspired activism, but 10 of 13 impacts offered were educational deficits:
>
> In what ways, if at all, has homophobia impacted on your schooling? (Please tick all boxes that apply).
>
> 1. I couldn't concentrate in class.
>
> 2. My marks dropped.
>
> 3. I moved schools.
>
> 4. I left school altogether.
>
> 5. I missed classes.
>
> 6. I missed days.
>
> 7. I hid at recess/lunch.
>
> 8. I couldn't go to the toilet.
>
> 9. I couldn't use the change-rooms.
>
> 10. I dropped out of a sport/extra-curricular activity.
>
> 11. I became involved in activism.
>
> 12. It hasn't affected me at all.
>
> 13. Other (please specify)[198]

End quote. It would be an admirably stubborn kid who could get through the first ten suggestions without ticking at least one box that the researcher invites him to tick. Research and ye shall find. And ye shall be funded, as Jones notes:

> They often offered clear policy implications for government, political and educational leadership. Their dramatic findings garnered media coverage with their detailed descriptions of violence and easy to understand statistics, and some reports from Western countries showed how the accumulation and dissemination of data on student well-being had over time assisted activists to obtain funding for GLBTIQ-specific educational interventions...[199]

The last line in *The Australian's* report on Jones' study noted that "her analysis has attracted the support of University of Sydney health sciences academic James Athanasou." I corresponded with Professor Athanasou, and he holds a low view of the validity of the *WTI3* research that has justified the Safe Schools programme:

> This is a study of self-reports from a sample of convenience that is not representative. The findings may not be accurate. There is no control group(s) built into the study. It disenfranchises the majority of school students who experience other forms of bullying and abuse.[200]

I rest my case. When subjected to scrutiny, the *All of Us* claim that 75% of LGBTQ youth suffer abuse and bullying shrinks further and further to nothing different to that suffered by school children generally. So why accede to activist demands to impose specific anti-homophobic bullying programmes, especially if they are a cloak for imposing radical sexualisation and gender theory on our kids?

Bullying and activism: stop them both

We already have general anti-bullying programmes that have proven effective.[201] If children are being given a hard time because of sexual identity issues, that is disgraceful and must be stopped just like bullying of any child for any cause. If LGBTQ activists and their academic supporters are being slippery with the data to create an impact for political purposes, that is also disgraceful and must be stopped. When that spawner of Safe Schools, La Trobe University, shows us properly conducted studies with a non-biased, statistically valid, representative sample and a methodology that does not elicit the answers that the researcher seeks, then we will show due respect. Meantime, unsubstantiated claims of disproportionate levels of gay-based bullying should not be used to impose LGBTQ sex-education on our children nor bludgeon the public into granting gay 'marriage'.

II. To combat depression

The second main argument is that if we do not normalise homosexuality in schools and celebrate same-sex 'marriage' in our culture, we are culpable for depression and even suicide in young same-sex attracted people. That is an increasingly influential argument – and it is outrageous.

Emotional blackmail

On 12 August 2015, *Sky News* presenter Peter van Onselen suggested to the Hon. Bruce Billson, Federal Minister for Small Business, that the Coalition would have blood on its hands because of its decision not to hold an immediate parliamentary vote on same-sex 'marriage' but to defer the decision to a national plebiscite in a year or two. He said, "Can you first just explain to me why it is an acceptable thing, the number of young Australians who are homosexual that will commit suicide between now and when the government finally gets its act together to have a plebiscite on this issue?"[202] On the same day in the *Sydney Morning Herald*, Justin Koonin, convenor of the NSW Gay and Lesbian Rights Lobby, specified my full-page newspaper ad[203] for the Australian Marriage Forum as "toxic" and an example of the "bigoted opinions that we know cause harm to same-sex attracted and gender diverse young people".[204] In an earlier report about the Australian Marriage Forum television ad aired during Mardi Gras in March 2015,[205] the director of Australian Marriage Equality, Rodney Croome, said our ad was "actually harming the many Australian children being raised by same-sex couples".[206]

Do you see how this game works? If anyone makes the case for keeping marriage between man and woman, the mere act of raising such an argument is "actually harming" children. There is only one solution: shut up and agree with Mr Croome and Mr Koonin. Breathing a word makes us culpable for depression and suicide in young people! Can the gay lobby not see their argument for the emotional blackmail it is, and the most uncivil insult to their fellow citizens who are merely upholding the law of the land?

What causes LGBTQ depression?

Nobody denies that same-sex attracted people suffer disproportionately from depression and emotional distress, but never once, in my experience as a GP, has a patient's depression or distress been due to the "bigoted opinions" of straight society. It has always been due to something private and personal: perhaps the trauma of domestic violence from a lesbian partner, or self-disgust at their own compulsive sexual behaviour, or unresolved anger at childhood sexual abuse, or the spiritual grief of holding values that conflict with their unwanted sexual impulses – not to mention the trauma of a diagnosis of HIV or other STD so heavily focused on the male homosexual population.[207] This is what drives their depression and distress, in my experience, not whether or not there are laws out there for gay 'marriage'.

Psychiatrist Dr Jeffrey Satinover brings a sense of proportion to this multi-factorial suffering:

> Some of this is in fact, as activists claim, because all-too-often he experiences from others a cold lack of sympathy or even open hostility ... But it is not true, as activists claim, that these are the only or even the major stresses. Much distress is caused simply by his way of life – for example, the medical consequences, AIDS being just one of many (if also the worst). He also lives with the guilt and shame that he inevitably feels over his compulsive, promiscuous behavior; and too, over the knowledge that he cannot relate effectively to the opposite sex and is less likely to have a family.[208]

And on the question of depression, we know that those living the gay lifestyle have close to double the rate of substance abuse, both alcohol and drugs, compared to the heterosexual population and that this is associated with increased depression and suicide. For example, the Australian Institute of Health and Welfare in 2010 found the prevalence of illicit drug use by homosexuals to be more than double that of heterosexuals (34% to 14%) while the rate of excessive alcohol intake was 25% to 16%.[209] The previously mentioned study in the *British Journal of Psychiatry* cautioned:

> It may be that prejudice in society against gay men and lesbians leads to greater psychological distress ... Conversely, gay men and lesbians may have lifestyles that make them vulnerable to psychological disorder. Such lifestyles may include increased use of drugs and alcohol.[210]

Law reform as 'therapy'

If we change the *Marriage Act* to make gay people 'feel normal', is that going to change the depression-causing elements of the gay lifestyle? In Canada, four years after same-sex 'marriage' was introduced, it didn't seem any sunnier. A formal Human Rights Complaint by homosexual lobbyists still said that "GLB people are significantly impacted by homophobia and heterosexism", and still cited that subculture's use of illicit drugs (up to 19 times higher), rate of alcoholism (up to seven times higher) and depression (up to three times higher) as a reason for Health Canada to provide extra funding.[211] Does changing the *Marriage Act* improve the mental health of the LGBT youth that we are apparently driving to substance abuse and depression by our laws? There is no convincing link. Associate Professor Rob Cover from the University of Western Australia, himself a gay man, finds "the relationship between the legalisation of marriage and GLBTIQ youth health and wellbeing is more complex and it is important not to assume that legislative amendment leads directly by itself to a reduction in youth suicidality."[212] He observes that the rate of GLBTIQ suicide "has not dropped significantly despite a whole host of other legislative changes and protections, from de-criminalisation of homosexuality, to anti-vilification laws, to institutional anti-discrimination policies in schools and youth recreational organisations." Why then, one might ask, would 'marriage equality' be the magic legislative wand that makes LGBT depression disappear? After all, as noted in the opening chapter, gay couples in Australia have already achieved the same legal status and social benefits as married couples. And if most gay couples don't want to get married – as we see in Holland – just how is this reform going to improve their health? Gay people are ambivalent about marriage; researchers are ambivalent about any link between 'marriage equality' and LGBT youth mental health. Speaking for himself, Cover says, "My own partner of seven years and I find the idea of marriage a tad distasteful, and of all our coupled friends and colleagues none have stated they would marry given the opportunity. Ultimately, the right to marry is a positive, but whether or not this very 'adult' issue is a priority in light of queer youth issues such as suicide needs more understanding." That would include acknowledging our lack of understanding as to whether, in fact, same-sex attracted people in Australia do have a higher suicide rate. Certainly they have a higher rate of suicide attempts but that does not necessarily mean a higher rate of completed suicide; women, after all, have a higher rate of suicide attempts than men, but a lower rate of completed suicide. As Rob Cover acknowledged: "the actual rate of GLBTIQ youth suicide and self-harm is not fully known."

Alas, educated ambivalence about the speculative link between marriage rights and youth depression rates is not what we will hear during the plebiscite debate. The message from 'progressive' types among the medical fraternity will be that LGBT people must be given 'marriage equality' to improve their mental health - and anyhow it won't do any harm to heterosexual marriage. That position was summarised well in an article in *Australasian Psychiatry*, "Marriage equality is a mental health issue", co-authored by Lisa Pryor and Dr Warren Kealy-Bateman.[213] Pryor is a former journalist turned medical student, wife of *The Chaser's* Julian Morrow. Kealy-Bateman is a psychiatrist living in a long-term gay relationship.[214] They make several bludgeoning claims about the source of LGBTI ill-health, the sure-fire benefits of marriage rights, how all their 'progressive' mates agree with them, and how there's no way redefining marriage would cause any harm:

> Lesbian, Gay, Bisexual, Transgender and Intersex (LGBTI) people disproportionately face negative health stressors and negative health events compared with the general population and this is related to the stress of being a stigmatised minority group. The evidence strongly supports the proposition that marriage equality is related to improved health outcomes. A diverse range of professional health groups advocate for the legislative progression

to marriage equality. The authors found no evidence that marriage equality harms opposite-sex marriage.

Harming marriage

I'm sure they didn't. Others, however, have. One hundred scholars in the field of marriage and family studies submitted evidence to the United States Supreme Court in 2015 on the structural harm to the institution of "opposite sex marriage" that comes when its meaning is changed.[215] They identified a roughly 5% decline in opposite-sex marriage in jurisdictions where 'marriage equality' has been introduced. This decline was in addition to any existing downward trend – and it makes good sense. Homosexual 'marriage' takes natural marriage off its pedestal as the irreplaceable vocation of a male and female of the species who are uniquely empowered to extend the human family into a new generation. It degrades marriage to the self-fulfilling romantic "bestie" relationship of any two adults (or three, or four, in due course) without reference to nature, to children, to the archetypal life-giving collaboration of man and woman. Who gives a damn, really? Why be surprised if young people don't bother marrying, when it is nothing different in the eyes of law and culture to the two blokes and their cocker spaniel in the unit upstairs?

The scholars analysed the data for individual US states that had introduced state-based 'marriage equality' and concluded, "in every U.S. jurisdiction for which such data are available, after the adoption of same-sex marriage the opposite-sex marriage rate declined by at least five percent – in comparison to a national marriage rate that, in the past few years, has been fairly stable."[216] They found a similar decline in man-woman marriage rates in other nations that have introduced same-sex 'marriage', for instance Belgium (7.4%) and Canada (4.3%).[217] Spain saw a 36% drop in opposite-sex marriage in the nine year period after bringing in same-sex 'marriage', but it introduced more permissive divorce laws at the same time so the exact contribution of 'marriage equality' will never be known; it can be assumed to be substantial, since no nation has seen such a decline in marriage after liberalising divorce laws. In Holland, the overall decline in the marriage rate for women aged 18-22 that followed its pioneering 'marriage equality' law in 2001 was 5% after adjusting for a pre-existing trend of 2.8%. Interestingly, the scholars reported marked differences between the more secular and more religious sectors of Dutch society (a similar finding was made in Massachusetts between more and less religious counties). In Holland, the decline in marriage rates among young women in the four largest, more secular, urban areas was an astonishing 31.8%, while there was a slight rise in the more religious, rural areas. The decline among native Dutch women, as opposed to the immigrant population, was 13.4%. Perhaps this indicates that religious and ethnic subcultures will sustain natural marriage while it crumbles in secular circles. In any case, gay 'marriage' is probably the last demographic rite for ageing secular Europe.

As a matter of social justice, a decline in man-woman marriage is going to have its most damaging impact on the least resilient people. The scholars note,

> Making marriage genderless may have little impact on those who are already married or who are well educated, well-to-do, religious and/ or otherwise committed to the marital norm of sexual intercourse only between husband and wife. But *marginal* marriage candidates – including the poor, relatively uneducated, irreligious or others who are highly influenced by cultural messages promoting casual and uncommitted sex – likely will be affected.[218]

The scholars further assessed the consequences of such a degradation of marriage culture in terms of harm to children. As we saw in Chapter 4 (Social science speaks out) children do best, all things being equal, with their married biological parents, so a further 5% decline in married parents is *ipso facto* harmful to a lot of future children whose parents won't be married. The scholars also estimate the statistical consequences for future children in the womb, whose prospects of reaching birth are known to be diminished where the parents are not married. They note:

> If a forced redefinition of marriage caused only a five percent permanent decline in U.S. opposite-sex marriage rates, under reasonable assumptions and over the next fertility cycle (30 years), that decline would result in nearly 1.3 million fewer women marrying. That would lead to an additional nearly 600,000 children born into nonmarital parenting situations, and nearly 900,000 more children aborted.

I would not be confident in quantifying the numbers affected, but the direction of the effect is clear. All of this is predictable harm – unless you consider a culture of abortion to be a good thing and a weakening of marriage culture among poorer people desirable and the gender-neutering of man and woman an ideological boon and the demographic death spiral of the west entirely welcome. Add that to the broader harms contained in the "package deal" of same-sex 'marriage', namely the emotional injury from violating a child's kinship bond with mother or father; the moral damage from imposing radical LGBTQ sex-education on all children; the civic distress from using law to intimidate conscientious objectors… but perhaps I have already mentioned that.

And all of these diverse harms, known and yet to be known, are to be justified by some dubious claim of "improved mental health" for same-sex attracted youth? Surely that proposition lacks proportion.

The dangers of casting LGBTQ youth as victims

There is a real risk in continually telling young LGBTQ people they are victims of society's homophobia and expecting them to be depressed and suicidal until we give them 'marriage equality'. I think Tiffany Jones was sincerely motivated by such a concern in the paper discussed earlier, when she noted:

> [The] Gay & Lesbian Alliance Against Defamation (GLAAD 2011) warned staff against perpetuating 'suicide contagion' among GLBTIQ youth … Harwood and Rasmussen (2004) argued that the focus on GLBTIQ youth discrimination and suicide encouraged students to express GLBTIQ identity using a conflated woundedness…[219]

One valuable voice expressing the same concern is Melinda Selmys, who formerly lived as a lesbian:

> I am exceedingly wary of attempts to put the onus for gay suicide on "heterosexist" culture … It is not in the interest of any teenager – gay, straight, transsexual, or non-sexually identifying – to be told that suicide is a natural reaction to their reality. I have struggled with depression and suicidal temptations since youth; the removal of moral culpability has never been a help and a comfort when I

am working through feelings of inadequacy and self-hatred. On the contrary, more than once, the only thing that kept me from taking my own life was a feeling that I was profoundly culpable, that I was responsible to the people who would suffer for my decisions. To be able to say, "It's not my fault, I had no choice, too much was expected of me, society made me do it" has only ever helped make it easier to entertain thoughts of self-annihilation.[220]

Even the spokeswoman for Parents and Friends of Lesbians and Gays (PFLAG), Shelley Argent, plays with the same fire when she uses youth suicide as an argument not to have a plebiscite debate, saying "it's better to wait than to be walking over bodies as you walk down the aisle".[221] Yes, that is a sound bite with emotive force, but parents and friends should beware of suggesting to an impulsive adolescent mind "that suicide is a natural reaction to their reality", and beware the demoralising effect on an individual of being continually told they are weak.

Regardless of how affirming or hostile the surrounding society might be, the emotional and moral dissonance of same-sex attraction can cause deep inner distress. But there are as many causes of inner distress as there are individuals. It infantilises same-sex attracted individuals if we treat them as victims who cannot cope, just as it trivialises their suffering if we blame it primarily on the external environment. The associated claim that we must change the external environment by legalising same-sex marriage or we are culpable for gay suicide is political blackmail, and should be treated with all due respect.

III. To do justice to people who are 'born that way'

The final argument for affirming homosexuality in the curriculum and in our marriage laws is a powerful claim of justice: that gay people are simply 'born that way', so natural justice demands they should have equal marriage rights. This moral argument has great influence on public thinking, but it is embarrassingly false and needs to be put to rest.

"If God made them that way", asked a female Anglican priest of my acquaintance, "how can we deny them their fulfilment as sexual beings?" Or as Lady Gaga put it in her same-sex anthem, *Born This Way*: "It doesn't matter if you love him or capital H-I-M...'cause God makes no mistakes." On the contrary, all our lives are marred with mistakes of both nature and nurture, and we have to adapt. For some people who suffer unwanted homosexual impulses, their capacity to adapt is helped by understanding that they are not in fact 'born that way'.

The 'inborn' myth

No science supports the 'born that way' theory. The American Psychiatric Association says: "the causes of sexual orientation (whether homosexual or heterosexual) are not known at this time and likely are multifactorial including biological and behavioral roots which may vary between different individuals and may even vary over time.."[222] Even the avowedly pro-gay American Psychological Association states, "No findings have emerged that permit scientists to conclude that sexual orientation is determined by any particular factor or factors."[223] The director of the Human Genome Project, Francis Collins, notes, "sexual orientation is genetically influenced but not hardwired by DNA, and whatever genes are involved represent predispositions, not predeterminations."[224] Finally, as studies of identical twins conclusively demonstrate, there is no simplistic gay gene.[225] One of the biggest and best studies used the Australian twin database (Bailey, 2000) and examined how often a homosexual person's identical twin was also homosexual.[226] If there is such a thing as a 'gay gene' then the concordance should be high, even 100%, since the two individuals have the same genes. However, the concordance was weak; indeed so weak (just 20%) that the study "did not provide statistically significant support for the importance of genetic factors for that trait." The concordance was closely linked to a shared family environment, which is consistent with a complex nature-nurture cause of same-sex attraction, not a simplistic 'born that way' claim.

Two years later, a study of twins by Bearman and Bruckner drawing on the high quality US National Longitudinal Study of Adolescent Health found "no evidence of genetic influence on same-sex preference".[227] The concordance between identical twins was only 6.7%, similar to non-identical twins (7.2%) and ordinary siblings (5.5%) and the researchers observed, "Clearly, the observed concordance rates do not correspond to degrees of genetic similarity ... If same-sex romantic attraction has a genetic component, it is massively overwhelmed by other factors."

In the same way, psychological mechanisms are not sufficient to explain every case and for many individuals the causative factors of same-sex attraction remain obscure. All one can conclude is that the phenomenon is multi-factorial in origin, with predisposing and precipitating factors; a deeply ingrained but potentially modifiable condition, not an innate identity.[228] Much more detail on the 'born that way' myth is available at a major review in *The New Atlantis*, August 2016.[229]

The 'immutable' myth

If gay and lesbian people are not 'born that way', it is not surprising that some don't 'stay that way'. Senators at the May 2012 inquiry into the Marriage Equality Amendment Bill 2010 heard from a man who had been actively homosexual for most of his adult life but was now married with three children.[230] A little earlier, the high-profile founder of Young Gay America, Michael Glatze, left the gay world. Both of these men changed without seeking professional help, as I understand; they just came to a point in their lives where they wanted out. That, I suspect, is the case with the majority of people who consider themselves gay at one stage of their life but then leave that phase behind.

The story of Glatze 'going straight', this pin-up boy for gay culture, was the subject of a remarkable feature article in the *New York Times*, "My Ex-gay Friend," as well as the subject of much vitriol.[231] Glatze gave an interview in 2014 not long after he married his girlfriend, Rebekah:

> **Q**: So you were in a gay relationship ... did you live with a man for a while?
>
> **Glatze**: Oh yeah, I did, for almost 10 years.
>
> **Q**: With the same man?
>
> **Glatze**: Yes. And sex with a man is - as I have told Rebekah – a fantasy-world: like a couple of guys playing games with each other. That's all they are ... fantasies, playing around like those guys on Pleasure Island, in Pinocchio. They're in the perpetual Peter-Pan Syndrome and living that way, they never grow up ... But when you leave homosexuality,

there's a sense of growing up. There is a sense of leaving adolescence behind, of becoming whole. I can't explain it any further than that...

Q: So when your heterosexual self looked at your homosexual behaviors, interests, thoughts, etc, how did the heterosexual self explain the homosexual desires?

Glatze: A lot of it goes back to the sadness that lies behind it. Let's just say if I were to encounter a homosexual desire, if it was ten years ago, I would just assume that that meant I was a gay person because I have these desires. Then I would try to make myself feel good about those desires in every possible way. I would try to assume that since I'm a loving, kind person, then this must just be another form of love. It must be a homosexual form of love. That would be the process that I went through, and I think most other people I knew would also say "I'm not lusting, I'm not dirty, I'm loving."

Q: "That this is just my own particular way of expressing love..."

Glatze: Right. But when we recognize the truth, we see things differently. And so now I say, "I am a whole heterosexual man; so how do I deal with these desires?" When I look a little deeper, I see behind it a longing pain in there. I see the fact that there is a craving for something that's missing within me.

Q: So when you looked in the light of truth, what was behind it – was it a pain, or was it sadness?

Glatze: It was pain ... and I recognize the futility of the longing that comes from the pain. The longing is nothing more than an attempt to grab hold of something that I don't actually need because I have it somewhere in myself, and I can rebuild that masculine sense of self that is somewhere inside me. But of course, anyone reading this who is in the gay mindset would say, "I don't feel pain... I'm emotionally attracted, I feel love..."

Q: You've had sex with men and now, you're with a woman... what's the difference for you?

Glatze: I want to be respectful, obviously, and not distasteful in my answer. So I'll just describe the personal awareness of "awesome" that I feel right now ... Coming out of homosexuality has been the most liberating thing I have ever felt. I said before, seven years ago, that it was like coming out of a cave and breathing fresh air. Today I can say, being married, that it's entirely an inversion of homosexuality. It as though you have a rudder pointed in one direction and then you take the rudder and turn it 180 degrees; now it's been turned around in the correct direction. It doesn't feel as though I've lost any of my sexuality, it just is working in the right alignment. There's no part of me that's wavering from my true nature. I feel aligned with my mind, my body, my spirit, my sexuality, with creation... they are all aligned, and that alignment is evidenced through the fact that my relationship with my wife is so real, so natural...[232]

If the founder of Young Gay America can leave homosexuality behind and marry his girlfriend, obviously happy and fulfilled like never before, where does that leave the theory of being 'born that way'? Men like Glatze should not exist under that theory. And yet a remarkable number of individuals will consider themselves gay at one stage of their life and no longer gay at a later stage. Let me show you just four independent lines of evidence demonstrating this spontaneous change in sexual orientation (with more in-depth recent clinical analysis available at *The New Atlantis*).[233]

First, a large, representative study in 2007 by Savin-Williams, using the AddHealth database, looked at adolescents who described themselves as same-sex attracted around age 16 and found that about two thirds of them changed to describe themselves as opposite-sex attracted by their early twenties.[234] There was negligible percentage drift in the other direction. Second, a study of some 14,000 adolescents by Ott and Corliss in 2010 found that two thirds of those who initially thought they might be homosexual eventually became exclusively heterosexual.[235] Third, the US National Health and Social Life Survey in the 1990s found that around 8% of students age 16 identified as homosexual, but that halved to around 4% by age 18, and dropped again to 2.8% by age 25.[236] That is more than a two-thirds drift away from a homosexual identity from age 16 to adulthood. This finding was referred to in the testimony of psychiatrist Dr Jeffrey Satinover to the Massachusetts Senate in 2003 during its enquiry into a State Bill for same-sex 'marriage'. He said, in part:

> The most comprehensive, most recent and most accurate study of sexuality, the National Health and Social Life Survey (NHSLS), was completed in 1994 by a large research team from the University of Chicago and funded by almost every large government agency and NGO with an interest in the AIDS epidemic. They studied every aspect of sexuality, but among their findings is the following, which I'm going to quote for you directly: "7.1 [to as much as 9.1] percent of the men [we studied, more than 1,500] had at least one same-gender partner since puberty. ... [But] almost 4 percent of the men [we studied] had sex with another male before turning eighteen but not after. These men...constitute 42 percent of the total number of men who report ever having a same gender experience." Let me put this in context: Roughly ten out of every 100 men have had sex with another man at some time - the origin of the 10% gay myth. Most of these will have identified themselves as gay before turning eighteen and will have acted on it. But by age 18, a full half of them no longer identify themselves as gay and will never again have a male sexual partner. And this is not a population of people selected because they went into therapy; it's just the general population. Furthermore, by age twenty-five, the percentage of gay identified men drops to 2.8%. This means that without any intervention whatsoever, three out of four boys who think they're gay at age 16 aren't by 25.[237]

As the fourth line of evidence of spontaneous change, let's return home and compare two studies from Latrobe University, one establishing the percentage of homosexual identification among Australian adults and one among Australian students. The adult study, "Sex in Australia: Sexual identity, sexual attraction and sexual experience among a representative sample of adults", was published in the *Australian and New Zealand Journal* of *Public Health* in 2003.[238] It found that 97.5% of Australians identify as heterosexual. The number who identify as homosexual is 1.2% (being 1.6% men, 0.8% women). Bisexuality adds another 1.2%, giving a total same-or-both-sex identification of 2.4% among Australian adults. The prevalence of same-sex attraction among Australian students is claimed to be 10%, according to the Safe Schools Coalition Australia document, *All of Us*. That is based on the Latrobe research, *Writing Themselves In Three* and yes, it is certainly an exaggeration given the selection bias of the study, but let's accept it for sake of argument.[239] That 10% figure includes bisexual attraction, so we should compare it with the 2.4% combined homosexual/bisexual figure for Australian adults. That still confirms at least a two-thirds drift away from a homosexual/bisexual identity between the school years and adulthood. Spontaneously, without any intervention.

What these four lines of evidence show is that most sexual confusion in adolescence clears away if left to itself. Please let the significance of that sink in. These young people did not have to seek professional help; they did not need to be persuaded; they just changed the way they felt. LGBT people are sure not 'born that way' if two-thirds of them don't stay that way between school and adulthood!

The '10%' myth

This might be the right time to dispel the influential folk myth about the percentage of people who identify as homosexual. The 10% figure haunts the popular imagination. This is partly because, as Satinover mentioned, close to 10% of teenage males have had some passing homosexual experience - but most of them leave that behind and do not consider themselves 'gay'. The other source of the 10% figure is the discredited work of zoologist Alfred Kinsey and his child-abusing 'researchers' in the 1940s.[240] With an activist's contempt for scientific process Kinsey deliberately oversampled prison populations of sex offenders to achieve his finding that a full 10% of American adults were homosexual. As the leading American statistician, John Tukey, said after his exasperated dealings with Kinsey, "A random selection of three people would have been better than a group of 300 chosen by

Mr Kinsey."[241] Kinsey's 10% myth has been perpetuated because it is so useful for LGBT politics; as Larry Kramer, cofounder of the pro-gay group ACT UP famously said in the early nineties, "The 10% figure became part of our vocabulary ... Democracy is all about proving you have the numbers. The more numbers you can prove you have, the more likely you'll get your due". Kramer had the ear of President Bill Clinton at the time. An article in *Time* magazine, "The shrinking ten percent", noted the consternation of Kramer and friends when a national survey found only 1% of American men were homosexual, not the 10% figure Clinton and others had been led to believe: "Here they were, about to sit down face to face with the President in the Oval Office, when a major national survey abruptly shrank their population to a tenth of what it was once touted to be".[242]

Wildly inflated numbers are still used by the gay lobby to make businesses think they need to chase the pink dollar and make politicians think they need to placate the pink vote. Take the example of the British Treasury which decreed in 2011 that 6% of UK citizens were gay or lesbian - don't ask how; they just knew. And we read in *The Guardian* how business scrambled to factor Treasury's figure into their strategy:

> Publication of the figure comes as big name companies such as Barclays bank, Hilton hotels and cosmetics giant L'Oreal join the growing rush to cash in on a gay economy which is worth tens of billions of pounds ... Barclays spokesman Michael O'Toole admitted the bank is very keen to woo Britain's gays and lesbians by portraying itself as sympathetic to gays' desire for equality.

But nothing can match the gullibility of the American public: in 2011 a Gallup poll found that most Americans put the figure for gay and lesbian people at an incredible, credulous 25%, and only a third thought it was less than 15%.[243] Don't the activists for same-sex 'marriage' just love that illusion of numbers, winning over pollies and companies alike! Here in Australia, haven't we been told what a boost for the economy all those gay weddings will be? The boost goes a little limp faced with a 1.2% figure for the gay population, just 1% of couples being same-sex, and only about a fifth of those couples even wanting to marry - hence the need to "talk ten per cent".

So file this in the "I'm not a mug" folder: just as the "Sex in Australia" study found 1.2% of adults identifying as gay or lesbian, the official figure for the US is 1.6% and for the UK is 1.1%. The US National Health Interview Survey for 2013 reports, "96.6% of adults identified as straight, 1.6% identified as gay or lesbian, and 0.7% identified as bisexual."[244] The UK Office for National Statistics found a slightly lower number in 2014, with 1.1% of adults identifying as gay or lesbian; bisexual adults took the total figure to 1.6%.[245] And may I note in passing that the phenomenon of a "two thirds drift" away from an initial homosexual identity is again confirmed by the UK data: "The likelihood of an adult identifying as lesbian, gay or bisexual decreased with age. Around 2.6% of adults aged 16 to 24 years identified themselves as lesbian, gay or bisexual. This decreased to 0.6% of adults aged 65 and over." That's more than a three-quarters spontaneous change away from homosexuality; count that as a bonus fifth line of evidence.

Gay people who acknowledge changeability

Some gay and lesbian people are quite relaxed about the changeability of same-sex attraction in some people and how this makes a mockery of the 'born that way' dogma. Prominent UK gay rights activist Peter Tatchell writes:

> There is a major problem with gay gene theory, and with all theories that posit the biological programming of sexual orientation. If heterosexuality and homosexuality are, indeed, genetically predetermined (and therefore mutually exclusive and unchangeable), how do we explain bisexuality or people who, suddenly in mid-life, switch from heterosexuality to homosexuality (or vice versa)? We can't.[246]

Lesbian writer E.J. Graff reflects on these mid-life switches in "What's Wrong With Choosing to Be Gay?"

> ... I know many women who say that they were once so identified with one direction of desire that it never occurred to them it would ever vary - and yet fifteen or thirty years later, are stunned to find that their attractions take a U-turn. Some women who spend their younger adulthood identifying as lesbians shift in midlife and get involved with men. Some straight women have serious, meaningful relationships with men – and are stunned when they fall hard for a woman, not with a mild crush, but with full-on love and desire. These women often don't call themselves "bisexual." They say: at one point I was straight and then became gay (or vice versa). And that involves choice.[247]

Most changes in sexual attraction seem to happen spontaneously without any professional guidance, but the redoubtable lesbian warrior Camille Paglia sees no problem with getting a bit of expert help to reach your goals. She writes in her book *Vamps and Tramps*:

> If a gay man wants to marry and sire children, why should he be harassed by gay activists accusing him of 'self-hatred'? He is more mature than they are, for he knows that woman's power cannot be ignored. If counseling can allow a gay man to respond sexually to women, it should be encouraged and applauded, not strafed by gay artillery fire of reverse moralism.[248]

The implications of spontaneous change

Several lines of evidence confirm that the majority, perhaps two thirds, of young people who think they are gay spontaneously change and live a heterosexual life.[249] In addition, some adults experience varying degrees of change in later life. The relevance for educators is that the Safe Schools approach of affirming adolescents in their 'gay identity' is premature, since most will get over their confusion, avoiding the grave physical and emotional harms of a homosexual lifestyle. Even using the simplest, most objective measure of harm – the burden of venereal disease (and in Australia it remains the case now, as for the last 30 years, that around three quarters of new transmissions of HIV are in "men who have sex with men"[250]) – it is obviously harmful to lock young men into a lifestyle that they might have avoided. Just let them be, give them time, and don't set their transient confusion in activist concrete by urging them to "come out" and declare their gayness.

The relevance for legislators is that there is not the same obligation to grant gay people 'marriage equality' as there was to grant black people civic equality. We know people are born black; we have no evidence they are born gay, and there is no legislative duty to institutionalise an irregular, sometimes changeable, homosexual disposition. Our legislative duty is to protect the one institution that gives a child her mother and her father. Every baby, every mammal, is born that way.

Part III

Repealing Nature

7

MUTATIONS OF MARRIAGE

Marriage means the union of a man and a woman to the exclusion of all others, voluntarily entered into for life. Certain unions are not marriages.
  Australian Marriage Act (1961)

Lying about marriage

We need to reject Senator Penny Wong's disingenuous words to the National Press Club in Canberra, July 2015, that nothing will really change with same-sex 'marriage': "the sun will still rise, and children will still eat more ice cream than is good for them."[251] That is not what her fellow lesbian activist Masha Gessen told the Sydney Writer's Festival in 2012:

> Fighting for gay marriage generally involves lying about what we are going to do with marriage when we get there. Because we lie that the institution of marriage is not going to change. And that is a lie. The institution of marriage is going to change and it should change, and again I don't think it should exist.[252]

We have heard US activist Michelangelo Signorile urge gays "to fight for same-sex marriage and its benefits and then, once granted, redefine the institution of marriage completely, because the most subversive action lesbians and gay men can undertake … is to transform the notion of 'family' entirely."[253] We have read lawyer Paula Ettelbrick's declaration that "Being queer means pushing the parameters of sex, sexuality and family … and of radically reordering society's view of reality." Feminists who despise the idea of marriage as patriarchal and religious welcome this latest radical takedown of the institution; for instance, Ellen Willis writes,

> Feminism and gay liberation have already seriously weakened marriage as a transmission belt of patriarchal, religious values; conferring the legitimacy of marriage on homosexual relations will introduce an implicit revolt against the institution into its very heart...[254]

Lying about marriage, redefining it completely, introducing an implicit revolt… and remember lesbian writer E.J. Graff saying that "same-sex marriage is a breathtakingly subversive idea".[255] These are not the words of easy-going citizens who just want to fit in with the established norms of marriage and family. These are the words of culture warriors intent on taking the despised heteronormative institution and "radically reordering" it in their own image. Yes, the sun will still rise, but on an unrecognisable human scene.

'Monogamish'

In this gay new world, "pushing the parameters of sex, sexuality and family", faithful monogamy is the essential repressive element that has to go. On the same Sydney Writer's Festival panel as Masha Gessen, academic Dennis Altman told us:

> Now I am going to speak now as a gay man: one of the things about gay male culture is that it is not a monogamous culture. All the evidence we have suggests that monogamy is a myth. There are many longstanding gay relationships. There are virtually no longstanding monogamous gay relationships. I happen to think that this is a good thing.[256]

The US gay activist Dan Savage agrees, saying gay marriage can at best be "monogamish", not monogamous; a primary emotional commitment but not 'to the exclusion of all others'. Being gay means being open, adventurous, exuberant; best leave monogamy to the "breeders", as they call us. Melinda Selmys confirms this from her own experience of the LGBT community:

> Most homosexuals, and particularly homosexual men, are quite frank about this. They admit that their relationships are open; that although they consider themselves "married to" or "in love with" a single person, there are usually other people on the side. They state, simply, that they see no reason why heterosexual notions of monogamy and fidelity should be grafted unnaturally onto homosexual relationships. Some have thought quite deeply about this and are able to recognize a tension within themselves between the deep desire to have a relationship that is a foundation for identity…and the reality of homosexual life.[257]

And she references a celebrated study by David McWhirter and Andrew Mattison of 156 stable homosexual couples: of the 100 couples who remained together after five years, not a single couple remained sexually faithful.[258]

> "My parents were faithful to each other, and I expected us to be the same," said one man, expressing the non-infrequent ideal. But such hopes, the authors document, are simply contrary to homosexual yearnings.[259]

McWhirter and Mattison, themselves a gay couple, rationalised the non-monogamous nature of gay relationships by redefining "fidelity" in terms of "emotional dependability" rather than sexual exclusivity. On page 285 of their book they write, "We found that gay men expect mutual emotional dependability with their partners, and that relationship fidelity transcends concerns about sexuality and exclusivity". A relationship of "emotional dependability" while the partners explore outside sexual adventures is light years from the humble ideal of faithful monogamous marriage. The sexually open cohabitation of homosexual couples is a different undertaking to "the union of a man and a woman, to the exclusion of all others, voluntarily entered into for life".

It is quite reasonable for homosexual partners to eschew the demands of monogamy and permanence since their relationship is a private matter. By contrast, natural marriage needs to be monogamous and permanent, built around the needs of vulnerable offspring who require long nurture and permanent connection to their mother and father. These are two quite different projects, and same-sex couples should find a different word. Instead, activists want to use the same word and give it a different, false meaning.

'Love Makes a Family'

What else might the future hold for marriage? First, as a matter of legal logic, gay 'marriage' must surely lead to group 'marriage'. Lord Daniel Brennan, former Chair of the Bar Association in the UK, wrote in March 2012: "After all, if you can abolish the most important pre-condition of marriage – namely that it requires a person of each sex – why should you be able to retain other pre-conditions, such as limiting it to only two people?"[260] And in June 2015, the Chief Justice of the Supreme Court of the USA, John Roberts, made the same point in his dissenting statement about same-sex 'marriage':

> Although the majority randomly inserts the adjective 'two' in various places, it offers no reason at all why the two-person element of the core definition of marriage may be preserved while the man-woman element may not ... It is striking how much of the majority's reasoning would apply with equal force to the claim of a fundamental right to plural marriage.[261]

These two top legal minds understand that, once marriage is separated from family formation and reduced to a mere emotional commitment between consenting adults, there is no clear reason to restrict the celebration of that commitment to just two people. And 'progressive' political minds will discern a new form of discrimination to be stamped out. The same week as Justice Roberts made his comments in the US, the Green Party leader in the UK, Natalie Bennett, was staking out a tentative position on group 'marriage', saying "We have led the way on many issues related to the liberalisation of legal status in adult consenting relationships". As *The Telegraph* reported,

> The Green Party is "open" to the idea of three-person marriages, Natalie Bennett has said. Ms Bennett said she was "open to further conversation and consultation" about the prospect of the state recognising polyamorous relationships. She made the comments in conversation with PinkNews, the LGBT website.[262]

The polyamorous (meaning "multiple loves") push for 'marriage equality' is slowly breaking through into public consciousness. Ellen Willis asked in 2004, "If homosexual marriage is OK, why not group marriage – which after all makes a lot of sense at a time when the economic and social fragility of family life is causing major problems?"²⁶³ A decade later, in 2014, the *New York Post* featured three women in wedding dresses under the heading, "Married lesbian threesome expecting first child".²⁶⁴ In February 2015 the same paper introduced us to "the world's first gay married throuple" in Thailand.²⁶⁵ On October 15, 2015, we read in the *Daily Mail* of the gay Canadian threesome who "plan to have children with their sisters as surrogates". One of the threesome, Adam, uses the one-liners we know so well: "We just want to say that love is love … we are all equal in our relationship and in marriage." Here in Australia, polyamorist Rachelle White told Radio 6PR in Perth, "I do think we need to address same-sex marriage before we do move forward and look at polyamorous marriage."²⁶⁶

And on August 24, 2016, the ABC TV show "You Can't Ask That: Polyamorous" did everything possible to normalise such relationships, complete with giggly good humour and the childlike innocence of the backing music. Speaking for the male threesome, Will Fennell from Sydney tells the ABC, "We are a family, the three of us." His charming French partner, Mathieu, acknowledges that the group sex "gets exhausting"; Will laughingly agrees, "There's so many legs, with six legs, do you know? It can get a bit porn-movie". Anne Hunter speaks for another threesome in asserting that if two is good, three is better for raising a family: "Kids raised by multiple loving adults do better. More role models to choose from. More people to bring home the bacon." So why is it taking so long for society to recognise throuples as normal married families with kids? Bec and Albey and "the other partner who lives with us, who we both share" realise that it will take a little longer for society to respect their group relationship. Bec tells the ABC, "I'd love to be able to say, 'Oh, my other partner', but I don't think society's quite ready for that yet. Fingers crossed, one day."

Perhaps one day sooner than you think, for the logic of gay 'marriage' will work its inexorable way towards group 'marriage'. If we redefine marriage as nothing more than the love and commitment between consenting adults, on what rational ground can we deny 'marriage equality' to three or four loving adults who are deeply committed to each other and want society to honour their relationship? "Love is love" and "love makes a family". Their love is as good as your love, you bigot!

'Love knows no boundaries'

In this brave new boundary-free world, even incestuous couples make a case for marriage equality. In April 2016, we learnt about "Kim West – the 51-year-old who entered a romantic relationship with her child 30 years after giving him up for adoption ... Now they want to get married and start a family."[267] Four years earlier, in April 2012, an incestuous relationship came to the European Court of Human Rights.[268] Patrick Stuebing from Leipzig argued that he and his sister had the right to a "family life". The case had inspired calls in Europe to legalise familial sexual relations, but the ECHR refused, saying it was necessary for "the protection of marriage and the family" to punish incestuous relationships. That's nice, but for how long will courts uphold this quaint notion of "the protection of marriage and the family" once homosexual 'marriage' has breached the levee of sexual taboo that alone protects the natural order of marriage and family life?

An Australian couple, Jenny and John Deaves, have overcome the taboo against incest. Jenny is John's daughter. In April 2008 Jenny told *60 Minutes* about their "normal, sexual loving couple relationship" and how they and their three children were "a happy normal family".[269]

The question to supporters of homosexual marriage is this. Your banners say that "love is love", and your T-shirts say, "love makes a family". How, then, can you deny marriage equality to Kim West and her son without implying that their love is not as good as your love? How can you deny Jenny and John Deaves their "loving couple relationship" and their "happy, normal family" without making them feel like second-class citizens - and without making their children feel like there's something wrong with their family? Just think of the emotional harm you are causing those kids of an incestuous family by denying them the security and stability of married parents. You might even be driving them to depression and suicide by your incestophobic attitudes, don't you think?

For a while, society will irrationally accept one form of false marriage but not the other, but eventually the sequence of ideas that led to the acceptance of 'homosexual marriage equality' will lead to the acceptance of 'incestuous marriage equality'. First, popular science will tell us that incestuous love is a genetic condition (implying 'born that way'); that couples can't help it and shouldn't be asked to suppress their sexuality.

Journalist Charlotte Gill takes a step in this direction:

> Genetic Sexual Attraction (GSA) describes a powerful sexual attraction that occurs when biological relatives – parent and offspring, siblings or half siblings or first and second cousins – meet for the first time as adults ... When people criticise (Kim) West, they overestimate her degree of control in the situation. Often GSA sufferers feel powerless - as if their feelings are impossible to change.[270]

Second, the academic journals will question the rational basis for this longstanding assumption of sexual deviancy and challenge the need for legal sanctions. One scholar, Vera Bergelson, has set about this task, putting incest taboo down to irrational prejudice:

> It appears that the true reason behind the long history of the incest laws is the feeling of repulsion and disgust this tabooed practice tends to evoke in the majority of the population. However, in the absence of wrongdoing, neither a historic taboo nor the sense of repulsion and disgust legitimizes criminalization of an act.[271]

The academics will also downplay concerns about genetic harm to children of incestuous inbreeding. Jenny and John's first baby died of congenital heart defects but, undeterred, they produced three other inbred offspring. There's no real problem with this, says the academic Bergelson:

> ...it is far from clear that inbreeding presents a threat to society. The number of serious genetic disorders associated with inbreeding is quite limited. Moreover, some scientists believe that, in the long run, populations may suffer from the prevention of consanguineous marriages...[272]

Hey, it's probably good for society! Next, with a safe space cleared by pseudo-science and permissive legal opinion, we will witness the proud and sentimental "coming out" by the incestuous couple:

> West, who works as an interior designer, told Alley Einstein of *New Day*: "This is not incest, it is GSA. We are like peas in a pod and are meant to be together. I know people will say we're disgusting, that we should be able to control our feelings, but when you're hit by a love so consuming you are willing to give up everything for it, you have to fight for it."[273]

Finally, progressive poseurs will urge an attitude of welcome and inclusion for this new "love that dares not speak its name". As with homosexuality, the real problem is society's attitudes: the task is to help such couples overcome their 'internalised incestophobia' and to stand proud against society's bigotry. Journalist Gill does not go that far, but she hints at the need for openness towards a closeted minority:

> It is only (Kim West's) pride in her relationship that has perplexed others, as many GSA couples feel deeply upset about what's happened to them. There are even communities online for them to anonymously discuss their relationships. In the future, I hope they won't have to hide away.[274]

Just ponder the situation of Kim and Ben, Jenny and John, and the needs of their children. Compare and contrast with homosexual couples who say they are just a normal family and we must not make their kids feel second-class. On what clear legal and logical principle will you draw a line between these two scenarios and deny 'marriage equality' and 'family normality' to our incestuous fellow citizens? LGBT activists say that 'marriage equality' will let gay couples and their families "come in from the cold". I put it to them: on what grounds will you keep incestuous couples and their families out in the cold? After all, love is love; love knows no boundaries; love makes a family.

Such is the surreal but plausible future when the rugged structure of marriage as a truth of nature and a core task of culture is pulped into the mush of mere "love".

Where will it end?

When marriage and family gets so radically reordered that the "natural and fundamental group unit of society" is unrecognisable, then all that remains to order society is the State. Repeal the natural and fundamental relationship of man and woman and you repeal the natural and fundamental relationship of parent and child along with broader kinship bonds. Words like husband and wife, mother and father stand for the deepest human relationships and their subversion is momentous. Brendan O'Neill wrote, "Those who say "They're only words, who cares?" clearly don't know their Orwell. The policing of language is very often a policing of attitudes, a reengineering of societal values so that they better accord with the elite's view."[275]

We need to revisit our Orwell. We need to see, in the next chapter, how the corrosive notion of "gender theory" with its roots in cultural Marxism is dissolving the idea of the natural family in the minds of our children. We need to understand, in the subsequent chapter, how collectivist ideologies have sought for over a century to subject the family to the power of the state — and how that elusive goal is finally within reach with the deconstruction of man-woman marriage.

Stepping back, we can see that these chapters in Part III are like three Russian dolls, obviously from the Soviet era, fitting one within the other. The smallest and central Babushka doll is 'marriage equality', which mutates the fundamental group unit of society — father, mother and child. That Babushka becomes the core of the larger doll of 'gender theory', which subverts the truth of male and female, the bonds of biological kinship and the boundaries of sexual right and wrong. With that dissolution of sex, marriage, morality and kinship complete, the largest doll — the 'total state' — can engulf and consume its only rival structure of authority: the natural family.

If all this sounds strange it's because we don't know our Orwell, or the century-long assault by the empire of ideas that Orwell so detested and which we review in Chapter 9 (Children of the State). 'Marriage equality' and the resulting deconstruction of family is a major capitulation to the collective by a once-free and sane society. Yet we, useful idiots that we are, believe Senator Wong that nothing is going to change if we institute homosexual 'marriage'. The sun will still rise.

8

THE ABOLITION OF MALE AND FEMALE

Only you know whether you are a boy or a girl. No one can tell you.
The Gender Fairy, a story for Australian four year olds by Jo Hirst, with teacher notes by Roz Ward.[276]

Policy makers and the media are doing no favors either to the public or the transgendered by treating their confusions as a right in need of defending rather than as a mental disorder that deserves understanding, treatment and prevention.
Professor Paul McHugh, former director of psychiatry, Johns Hopkins University.[277]

People I have known

He was just nine back then and must be thirty now, but I will never forget the exquisitely feminine gestures and bearing. This little boy had been emotionally and physically abused by his father and, so it seemed, rejected the idea of being like that man in any way. He clung to his mother, who was also a victim, holding out against this frightening man, taking on the mannerisms and outlook of the female world.

Another wounded patient from another city had a similarly troubled past. Sexually abused as a child, sunken to the point of homosexual prostitution, he now presented as a caricature of a woman: the fake nails, the hair and makeup, the flamboyant dresses and more flamboyant name.

Somehow a sex-change operation was going to make everything OK, and he was saving up; meantime the oestrogen softened his skin and reduced his beard but only added to his weight, and his sexual partners still beat him up.

Memories like these make me ask one question when I read the tinselly news stories of a little boy who is so happy now that he "is a girl", or a man who poses for the cameras with a contrived female body: what has wounded this person? Why would doctors even consider messing with hormones or amputating genitals when the problem is a wounded mind?

These troubled souls are useful for ideologues who want to portray rare abnormal circumstances as normal and so muddy the whole notion of biological sex. The gender campaign seeks to make us believe that the elemental polarity of male and female - the biological fact on which most of our cultural customs, art and literature, and sense of self and community is built – is an illusion; that gender is fluid for everyone; that it is natural for boys to want to wear girls' uniform and use the girls' bathroom; that it is quite reasonable for girls to bind their breasts and take masculinising hormones; that anyone who thinks something has gone deeply wrong here is guilty of that newly invented attitudinal disorder called "transphobia".

I think of another patient, a big bloke working as a labourer, who has Klinefelter's syndrome. That means he has an extra X chromosome, making him XXY instead of the usual male pattern of XY. That imbalance interferes with his testosterone levels, his secondary sexual characteristics and his fertility, but with testosterone supplements he is hard to tell from a typical male. And yet some people – including the authors of the Safe Schools Coalition - claim such a man for the "intersex" category of individuals who are neither male nor female! They then use such cases to suggest that none of us are really men or women but fluid players on a continuous gender spectrum. Try telling my patient that he isn't a man and he would likely flatten you. Try telling schoolchildren that people who think they are male or female are just victims of narrow social prejudice and should be free to explore a rainbow of gender possibilities, and you will get government funding.

Similarly, I think of a young woman with Turner's syndrome, where she has only one X chromosome. That deficiency left her with the typical shorter stature and infertility, but breast growth could be stimulated to some extent with oestrogen supplement. She was obviously a very intelligent woman, albeit with this impairment, and yet she too is claimed by the gender spinners as "intersex". Her affliction is exploited to strengthen the strange proposition that gender is a continuum from cis male to trans guy to genderqueer to androgynous to agender to sister girl to cis female and all stops in between.

These two categories, transgender and intersex, are the T and the I at the end of the LGBQTI rainbow, and we need to understand them better so we can see how these complex clinical conditions have been misrepresented to serve political ends. But first we need to understand the worldview that underlies this push for the abolition of male and female. We need to be fully aware of how our children are being targeted and disturbed by these ideas and we need to be astonished at how governments are feebly falling into line with this latest aspect of the LGBQTI agenda. Armed with all this knowledge, we can stand against this most subversive assault on the natural relationships underlying marriage and family.

The flow of this chapter will therefore be:
I. Gender theory: a dangerous idea
II. Targeting the minds of children
III. Government collaborators & enforcers
IV. Transgender conditions: "A mental disorder"
V. Intersex conditions: no basis for abolishing male and female
VI. Clinging to reality

I. Gender theory: a dangerous idea

"Gender theory" is a mind-messing ideology coming soon to a public toilet and preschool near you.

That notoriously good-natured gentleman, Pope Francis, called it "demonic" and a form of "ideological colonisation" like we saw with "the dictators of the last century".[278] His scholarly predecessor, Benedict, warned of "the anthropological revolution contained within it":

> According to this philosophy, sex is no longer a given element of nature that man has to accept and personally make sense of: it is a social role that we choose for ourselves, while in the past it was chosen for us by society ... People dispute the idea that they have a nature, given by their bodily identity, that serves as a defining element of the human being.[279]

A less illustrious philosopher, former federal Labor leader Mark Latham, agrees that gender theory's insidious colonisation of our schools is a threat to our children and even to our civilisation:

> The craziest trend in Australian politics is to teach Neo-Marxist genderless programs in our schools through the Orwellian-named Safe Schools and Building Respectful Relationships (BRR) curriculum ... Safe Schools seeks to eradicate the use of terms like "his and her" and "boys and girls". It believes genderless language will produce a genderless generation of young Australians, self-selecting their sexuality as a fluid identity ... As parents we need to make our views known to election candidates and school leaders alike. Anyone who has researched this issue will know we are fighting for the future of our civilisation.[280]

The gender theory creed runs like this: binary is bad; male and female are social inventions not biological realities; gender is a sliding scale from mostly masculine to mostly feminine; whatever gender you feel yourself to be is what you are and nobody has the right to question your judgement. The implications are that we must stop using binary terms like boy and girl; we should affirm children in moving freely between the masculine and feminine poles of gender; we must ensure people are free to use the toilets and change rooms of their preferred gender identity and use the power of the state to punish citizens who don't get with the programme.

The pressing objective of the gender strategists is to achieve genderless 'marriage', which will cement this genderless madness into our law and from there into the wider culture. The logic of this approach is irresistible: if we agree there is no objective gendered meaning to husband and wife then we must agree there is no objective gendered meaning to mother and father – and ultimately, no meaning to male and female. Benedict notes what such an abolition of natural structures will mean for the child:

> If there is no pre-ordained duality of man and woman in creation, then neither is the family any longer a reality established by creation. Likewise, the child has lost the place he had occupied hitherto and the dignity pertaining to him ... perforce, from being a subject of rights, the child has become an object to which people have a right and which they have a right to obtain.

It is to be expected that leaders of the Christian church would take up arms against this old enemy, for gender theory is a modern manifestation of gnosticism. This ancient philosophical warp of the human mind blossomed in the second Christian century as a series of heresies; it views the material world as less than real and defines reality by a secret inner knowledge, or "gnosis". Today's slogan taught to our kids, that gender "is not what's between your legs, but what's between your ears" is a cartoonish modern statement of the gnostic flight from the objective to the subjective.

Sherif Girgis, a Rhodes scholar and graduate of Yale Law School, reflected recently on the gnostic quality of the US Supreme Court's decision last year to change marriage from an objective biological gendered bond to a subjective emotional genderless bond. He shows how the Court's high-minded doctrine, now untethered from the natural world, will be used to enforce increasingly strange assertions about gender:

> Beyond marriage, this doctrine entails that [biological] sex doesn't matter, or that it matters only as an inner reality. Since I am not my body, I might have been born in the wrong one. Because the real me is internal, my sexual identity is just what I sense it to be ... The Court didn't simply free people to live by the New Gnosticism. It required us, "the People," to endorse this dogma.[281]

Genderless 'marriage' is the capstone for the overarching structure of genderless dogma. If we vote for 'marriage equality', the whole oppressive gnostic edifice will be near-impossible to bring down.

The origins of gender theory

Who started building this edifice, anyway? The word "gender" as opposed to "sex" was first used by the New Zealand psychologist, John Money, in a 1955 article published in the *Bulletin of the Johns Hopkins Hospital*, where he worked for many years.[282] Money made the distinction between a person's sex and the "gender role" they might choose to take on. That seems harmless enough; what was not harmless was when Money tried to apply his new theory of the "social construction of gender" to a baby boy who had been through a botched circumcision and lost most of his penis. That was in 1967; the baby was Bruce Reimer (later Brenda, later David - it's complicated) and Money advised the parents to simply tidy up the wound with a cosmetic vaginal fold and raise the child as a girl, since a child's gender (on his new theory) is whatever society teaches a child to be.

Disaster ensued. Decades later, Money was exposed for misrepresenting this tragic case as a success in a series of published papers. He reported that Reimer had changed happily to the feminine gender, when in fact the child (now called Brenda) never identified as a girl and found the psychological and medical 'treatment' deeply traumatic. When Reimer was finally told, age 14, about his actual sex as a boy he took on the new name of David and tried to undo the hormonal feminisation by a double mastectomy, testosterone injections and penile reconstruction.

Historically, this misrepresented case study was used as the justification for surgically reassigning the sex of hundreds of babies. Only in 1997 did David Reimer go public with his story to John Colapinto of *The Rolling Stone*, and the grim truth was exposed:

> For Dr John Money, the medical psychologist who was the architect of the experiment, this case was to be the most publicly celebrated triumph of a 40-year career that recently earned him the accolade "one of the greatest sex researchers of the century." But as the mere existence of this young man in front of me would suggest, the experiment was a failure, a fact revealed in a March 1997 article in the *Archives of Adolescent and Pediatric Medicine*. Authors Milton Diamond, a biologist at the University of Hawaii, and Keith Sigmundson, a psychiatrist from Victoria, British Columbia, documented how the twin had struggled against his

imposed girlhood from the start. The paper set off shock waves in medical circles around the world, generating furious debate about the ongoing practice of sex reassignment.[283]

Distressing details were reported of the methods Money allegedly used to feminise the young Brenda. *The Guardian's* article in 2004, "Being Brenda", referred to the "regular therapy sessions with Money in Baltimore" which Reimer's twin brother, Brian, also attended:

> According to Colapinto's [book-length[284]] account, they soon degenerated into horrifying encounters that deeply traumatised the two children. Showing the children "explicit sexual pictures" was seemingly central to Money's theories of gender reassignment. David Reimer later recalled, as Brenda, "getting yelled at by Money ... he told me to take my clothes off, and I just did not do it. I just stood there. And he screamed 'No!' I thought he was going to give me a whupping. So I took my clothes off and stood there, shaking."[285]

David Reimer married in 1990 and was father to three stepchildren, but fourteen years later his wife said she wanted to separate. This young man of 38 who had suffered so much through infancy, youth and manhood, gave up and took his life.

Behold the first experiment in applied gender theory. A theory that first arose in the mind of John Money; a sexually unusual mind according to *The Guardian's* research:

> Raised in a conservative religious family in New Zealand, he had rebelled and become a self-described "missionary of sex", revelling in shocked responses to his tireless advocacy of open marriages and – a particular favourite - bisexual group sex. At their most extreme, Money's public statements had appeared to endorse, or at least not to condemn, incest and paedophilia.

Money's false reports of success in raising Reimer as a girl were grist to the mill of the sexual revolution: "This dramatic case," *Time* magazine reported at the time, "provides strong support for a major contention of women's liberationists: that conventional patterns on masculine and feminine behaviour can be altered."[286] Late in his career, Money looked back with pride: "It is impossible to write about the political history of the second half of the twentieth century without reference to the concept of gender. This is particularly true with respect to the women's movement in politics."[287] And in the first half of the twenty first century, his concept remains particularly influential in the hands of gender theorists messing with our children's minds.

II. Targeting the minds of children

Some philosophies are so bizarre, only an academic could believe them. The problem is that some academics do believe the philosophy of "gender theory" and they are teaching our children to believe it too. Consider the 'gender' headlines in Australia from the first few months of 2016. In February, *The Australian* newspaper revealed,

> Eleven-year-old children are being taught about sexual orientation and transgender issues at school in a taxpayer-funded program written by gay activists. The Safe Schools Coalition teaching manual says that asking parents if their baby is a boy or a girl reinforces a "heteronormative world view".[288]

Regrettably, as Mark Latham alluded to above, Safe Schools is not the only assault on our kids' common sense. In March, the *Herald Sun* reported:

> Toddlers will be taught about sex, sexuality and cross-dressing in a controversial national program being rolled out at childcare centres and kindergartens next month ... Early Childhood Australia spokeswoman Clare McHugh said the program would reduce domestic violence because "rigid views on gender" were associated with violence and domestic violence. "Children are sexual beings and it's a strong part of their identity, and it is linked to their values and respect," she said. It comes after the federal government ordered a review of a Safe Schools program for secondary students including lessons on how to bind breasts and tuck in male genitalia.[289]

And in April, *The Australian* reported on yet more ideological gold for kiddies at the end of the genderless rainbow:

> Preschoolers should be introduced to the concept of same-sex marriage, according to a leading early education academic who is advocating against the notion of "compulsory heterosexuality"

in the classroom. Melbourne University research fellow Kylie Smith, a contributor to the education curriculum in Victoria, has published a paper about the importance of political activism in the early childhood sector, focusing on the marriage equality debate and ideas around gender. Echoing proponents of the controversial Safe Schools program, Dr Smith, who works in the university's Youth Research Centre, laments the degree to which early education resources represent gender and sexuality as "fixed" rather than "fluid and changing". She refers to her experience teaching "Lydia", who had said she wanted to grow up to be a boy. She had told the young girl that "it might not be easy but she can and people like doctors can help". The paper [was] titled "And the princesses married and lived happily ever after: challenging compulsory heterosexuality in the early childhood classroom".[290]

Just pause there and ask what experiences might have made little Lydia so unhappy being a girl; also ask by what authority a university academic encourages a little girl in her quest to become a boy. And by what authority do other academics, like the transgender Margot Fink, impose their gnostic notions on our children in an entirely unchallenged, uncritical way? For that is what Fink does, as director of the Safe Schools *All of Us* programme with its glossy promulgation of gender theory and transgenderism. She is also the main editor of *OMG I'm Trans* (with Roz Ward on the team) and her column on page 6 is pure gender dogma:

> For a lot of people gender might not be strictly male or female. It could be somewhere in between, or something else entirely! I have friends who experience gender more fluidly, it can shift and change over time. An important thing to understand is gender isn't about the physical stuff. It's much more about how you identify and feel most comfortable, not your body, not the sex you were assigned at birth, and definitely not what anyone else thinks![291]

"Spoiler alert" says this document. "It's a total lie that all guys have dicks, that all girls have vaginas."[292] This is the document noted above that teaches confused students how to conceal their unwanted gender's sexual features by "chest binding" or "penis tucking", not to mention the more constructive "penis padding".[293] As mentioned in Chapter 5, Fink reports uncritically on "a lot of great options" for students to transition gender, including hormone treatments and genital surgery, as if such an approach was harmless and uncontroversial. Worse than that, one Safe Schools document which escaped the March 2016 government review subverts the role of parents in the care of their gender-confused child. In the *Guide to supporting a student to affirm or transition gender identity at school* we read this advice:

> If a student does not have family or carer support for the process, a decision to proceed should be made based on the school's duty of care for the student's wellbeing and their level of maturity to make decisions about their needs. It may be possible to consider a student a mature minor and able to make decisions without parental consent.[294]

Oh, the urgency of gender activism at school! Press on, teachers, even if the parents don't want you to do it! Press on, because you might be caught out by the awkward fact that the vast majority of gender-confused students will get over their confusion around puberty and live as their natural sex. [295,296,297] No time to lose!

And so new programmes keep rolling off the press. In August 2016 we learn of a trial of transgender teaching to five year olds in South Australia:

> Children as young as five have been used for story time sessions featuring books with transgender characters, introducing concepts ranging from cross-dressing to gender reassignment surgery, as part of a university study being used to advocate for the expansion of the Safe Schools program into primary schools … One of the books, *My New Daddy*, written by transgender author and LGBTI rights advocate Lilly Mossiano, follows the tale of a young boy who is told by his mother that "nature made a mistake" and "she should've been born a boy like him". "Mommy begins transitioning, and Charles calls her daddy," says the blurb for the book. "Daddy goes to see a doctor and has an operation. Charles now has a new daddy who loves him and he loves his daddy."[298]

This is the world we are allowing radicals to create for our kids, where Mossiano's character tells our five year olds, "Now I am a lucky little boy because my mommy is my new daddy. He will always love me and I will always love him." Just what we want our kids to be taught in their first year at school.

A warning from Canada

So where will this path lead our children? In Canada, which has had same-sex 'marriage' for a decade, the full genderless agenda is being implemented in schools. Unlike Australian parents, who have partially repelled some of these obnoxious programmes, Canadian parents no longer have any grounds to push back. By normalising homosexual 'marriage', Canada normalised homosexual behaviour (and all the ideological baggage that goes with it including full-blown gender theory) with the force of law. The Education Department in the province of Alberta specifies what the rainbow package deal means for their schools.[299]

- A child's gender in Alberta is whatever he or she says it is, according to the directives from the Department: "An individual's self-identification is the sole measure of their sexual orientation, gender identity or gender expression."

- We must invent new pronouns to suit these self-identified students: "Some individuals may not feel included in the use of the pronouns 'he' or 'she' and may prefer alternate pronouns, such as 'ze,' 'zir,' 'hir,' 'they' or 'them,' or might wish to express themselves or self-identify in other ways."

- School uniforms must avoid being "gender-exclusive, such as implying that a certain type of clothing, such as skirts, will be worn by one gender only." The tradition of uniforms that grace a girl or make your son look more of a man – this must go.

- All distinctively boy or girl activities must be downplayed - "Reduce gender-segregated activities to the greatest extent possible" – in deference to a tiny number of children going through a typically transient stage of gender confusion.

- But if you do want team sports for girls, be ready to let the gender-questioning boys play in their team, and when they need a shower afterwards, ensure the boys on the girls' team "are able to access washrooms that are congruent with their gender identity".

How deep does the rot go?

Perhaps we assume that our young people will just laugh off such loopiness. Alas, the slow marination of young minds in today's greens-left curriculum, the atrophy of their common sense under the tyranny of "tolerance", is far advanced. Just look with wonder on the finished products of an expensive western education (the short video is well worth a view).[300] Here are the responses of university students interviewed on an American campus in 2016 on the subject of male and female:

"Is there a difference in your mind between men and women?" the interviewer asks. "Possibly", says one young woman. "In general, yes", says another, "but I don't know why I think that", looking a little worried at holding an incorrect view. "Currently, yes", says an eloquent male student, "but there is no need for that difference to exist scientifically or logically". Says another, "There's not much difference besides what society forces on people". The interviewer moves on: *"And how do you know the difference between men and women?"* Says a female student, "I don't think there's any one way to really distinguish between a man or a woman, and I don't think it's necessary". Getting right down to it, the interviewer asks, *"What would you say I am?"* The worried student says, "A male… based on how I look at you". When challenged, *"Do you think that's a problem"* she is contrite, "Yeah, probably". But the full penetration of gender theory into the student mindset is only evident with the final question, *"Then is there a reason to have those labels, male and female?"* Says the first female student, "I don't think so. I think that it's a social construct of this binary that we're given at birth."

Behold the brain-addled future. If we care about our children and grandchildren we will not rest until the last vestige of gender theory has been uprooted from the school curriculum – thrown in the dustbin, lock, stock and barrel. Let the Marxist Ms Ward direct her ideological fervour towards adults, by all means, but not towards children. Let the transgender Ms Fink debate with clinicians like Professor McHugh who considers the condition "a mental disorder that deserves understanding, treatment and prevention",[301] but not declare it as gospel to our children.

III. Government collaborators & enforcers

If only this mass confusion were limited to student campuses! It is not, and our governments increasingly validate it. In Australia, the tipping point for the gender agenda might be dated to Australia Day, 2016. The former Chief of Army and then Chairman of the Diversity Council of Australia, Lieutenant General David Morrison, was appointed "Australian of the Year". The Diversity Council noted, "During his tenure as the Chief of Army, David took a strong public stand on matters of military culture, especially those related to increasing gender diversity and LGBTI-inclusion in the Army."[302]

Morrison pipped a past subordinate of his, Lieutenant Catherine McGregor, for the prestigious award, and the defeat was not taken graciously. McGregor, after all, was an embodiment of diversity itself, having been Malcolm McGregor for most of his career in the army before transitioning to "Catherine". Lieutenant McGregor told the LGBT magazine *Star Observer*, somewhat churlishly, that giving Morrison the award was "a weak and conventional choice ... I think I'll die without seeing a trans Australian of the Year and I think that's terribly sad."[303] There was also personal offence taken at Morrison's use of McGregor's "former male name" in media interviews following his win; in addition, *Star Observer* notes, Morrison "used the wrong pronouns."

At present, Australians are not fined a quarter of a million dollars for using the wrong pronouns for a man who wants to be addressed as a woman, but in New York City such fines are now an option for repeat offenders.[304] Fair enough if it amounts to harassment, but no citizen should be punished for simply refusing to speak falsehoods. Transgender adults are free to cross-dress or cross-live to relieve whatever psychological need they have, but they should not presume on the courtesy of strangers in always playing along with their fetish or confusion or delusion. Most of us will be courteous in our use of words in the presence of such people, but that is a concession to their vulnerability, not a concession to truth.

The Australian feminist controversialist Germaine Greer prefers truth to courtesy and she poured scorn on the idea of a feminised man demanding admission to the sisterhood. In an interview in late 2015, in the context of former Olympic athlete Bruce Jenner declaring himself to be Caitlyn, she described such men as a "ghastly parody" and said, "Just because you lop off your dick and then wear a dress doesn't make you a f***ing woman. I've asked my doctor to give me long ears and liver spots and I'm going to wear a brown coat but that doesn't turn me into a f***ing cocker spaniel."[305] Point made, loudly. Another Australian provocateur and professional cross-dresser, Barry Humphries (aka Dame Edna Everage) concurred: "I agree with Germaine. You're a mutilated man, that's all. Self-mutilation, what's all this carry-on?"[306]

Because some people don't want all that surgery, the most gnostic of the gender enforcers are now proposing to let a man change his sex to female, officially on his birth certificate, while still keeping 'her' original male gear! We read in *The Australian* in August 2016,

> [Tasmanian Anti-Discrimination] Commissioner Robin Banks has recommended to the state government that it change the Births, Deaths and Marriages Registration Act to remove the requirement people must have a sex change operation before they can legally change their sex. The reforms, being considered by Attorney-General Vanessa Goodwin, would make changing sex as easy as changing names for anyone older than 16, and allow people to change sex as frequently as once a year.[307]

As with Germaine Greer, it was the Tasmanian feminists who sounded the alarm, with Women's Liberation Front (WOLF) spokeswoman, Tessa Anne, saying this would "legally erase the existence of female people". Real ones, that is. She told *The Australian,* "By allowing any person to self-identify their sex, it effectively redefines what 'sex' means under law ... It stops being a reflection of a physical biological reality and becomes a social construct and a reflection of how a person subjectively feels about themselves."[308]

Exactly – but that is what the *All of Us* booklet is teaching our children right now! These bizarre ideas taught to children have real-world consequences. The Women's Liberation Front gave examples:

> On a practical level, the group believed Ms Banks's amendments would undermine protections under the Sex Discrimination Act that allow for women-only services such as domestic violence shelters and support groups, gyms, sports, events and clubs. It feared the changes would allow men who self-identify as women

to legally demand access to such services, as well as roles currently reserved for women. This could mean organisations employing carers to provide intimate care for aged or disabled women, such as help with toileting and showering, being forced to employ men in such roles.[309]

If this sounds insane, remember that the Commissioner's proposal makes complete gnostic sense. It is part of the same theory that 'effectively redefines what marriage means under law'; where marriage itself "stops being a reflection of a physical biological reality and becomes a social construct". Behold the seamless garment of the genderless agenda. That is why we will meet Commissioner Banks again in Chapter 10 in her role as Inquisitor into a Catholic Bishop who dared teach the "biological reality" of marriage.

We live in surreal times. Returning to Germaine Greer, importantly she took the trouble to distinguish her "ghastly parodies" from the grievous afflictions some babies suffer (see later in the chapter) when rare genetic and hormonal disorders malform the genitalia and disturb sexual development: "I do understand that some people are born intersex and they deserve support in coming to terms with their gender but it's not the same thing. A man who gets his dick chopped off is actually inflicting an extraordinary act of violence on himself."

Extraordinary acts of governance doing violence to common sense have followed. In the US in April 2016, the *Washington Times* reported on an uncivil war brewing between states who stand with the transgender programme and those who think, "What's all this carry-on?"

> The governments of New York, Connecticut, Minnesota, Vermont and the District of Columbia have barred official travel to Mississippi and North Carolina, which have enacted laws protecting common sense and the privacy of boys and girls alike by requiring transgender students to use restrooms that match their biological sex. Such laws may not last long. The 4th U.S. Circuit Court of Appeals ruled last week that a Virginia public school cannot bar a high school girl who thinks she's a boy from using what used to be the boys' restroom. A dissenting judge wrote that the decision "completely tramples on all universally accepted protections of privacy and safety that are based on the anatomical differences between the sexes."[310]

The 'gay marriage President' extends his campaign

But what chance has biology and anatomy got against gender ideology! The combined forces of progressive contempt were brought to bear on North Carolina: the Obama administration called its law "mean spirited" and threatened withdrawal of federal funds; 100 CEOs from companies like Apple and Bank of America called for its repeal with PayPal scrapping plans for a major development in the state capital (a campaign of boycott had caused two other states, Georgia and Indiana, to back down from similar laws); sporting associations threatened to pull major events and celebs like Obama-barracker Bruce Springsteen cancelled concerts.[311] All in the noble cause of letting troubled men use women's change-rooms. It would have been simple enough to agree on Unisex toilets in public facilities which would have satisfied all and troubled none but that would not have taught stubborn states the necessary gnostic lesson: that transgender men *"are* women" and therefore have a right to use *women's* toilets.

Note two things about the transgender crusade in America. First, the President and his entourage didn't miss a beat moving from their victory in normalising genderless 'marriage' to their campaign to normalise genderless bathrooms, showing again that gay 'marriage' is just the battering ram for the broader rainbow agenda. Second, that the self-righteous rhetoric of progressivism was the same in both campaigns, with proponents of both causes claiming the high ground of "equality" and opponents of both causes being branded as no better than racists. Explicitly, Obama's Attorney-General Loretta Lynch "cast the bathroom bill issue as the latest civil rights struggle of the era." CNN reports her barbed comments: "It was not so very long ago that states, including North Carolina, had other signs above restrooms, water fountains, and on public accommodations, keeping people out based on a distinction without a difference. We've moved beyond those dark days."[312]

Did you hear that from the top lawmaker in the USA? Male and female is a distinction without a difference. In May 2016 Obama then broadened the offensive, directing all 96,000 public schools in America "to allow transgender students to use bathrooms matching their gender identity".[313] Again Ms Lynch pontificated: "There is no room in our schools for discrimination of any kind, including discrimination against transgender students on the basis of their sex." No thought that perhaps her moral preening might infringe the wellbeing of girls forced to share bathrooms with disturbed young men?

A moment of sweet sanity broke through when a card-carrying 'progressive', Maya Dillard Smith, resigned as the head of the Georgia chapter of the American Civil Liberties Union (which is the organisational enforcer of ideological correctness in the USA). In June we read,

> Ms Smith explained that the last straw for her was when her young daughters ran into three transgender adults in the women's bathroom. "I have shared my personal experience of having taken my elementary school age daughters into a women's restroom when shortly after three transgender young adults over six feet with deep voices entered," she wrote. "My children were visibly frightened, concerned about their safety and left asking lots of questions for which I, like many parents, was ill-prepared to answer."[314]

Here in Australia those were the same questions asked by Victorian mother of four, Cella White, when she imagined her vision-impaired daughter having to share toilets with high school trans-boys. In a moving short video filmed in June 2016 and viewed half a million times on Facebook in 5 days, Mrs White said, "She'd be in year seven and a year twelve boy might walk in. That's frightening to me. I'm not saying that the boy's going to attack her or anything like that, but who would know where it leads?"[315] This concern was one of Mrs White's reasons, as we saw in Chapter 5, for withdrawing her children from the high school that was running the Safe Schools programme. Safe for whom?

Not to be outdone by Obama, the ultra-correct Canadian PM, Justin Trudeau, brought in his own bathroom bill that same month and spiced it with threats of prosecution for transgender "hate propaganda" (which would no doubt put Barry and Germaine in jail):

> Marking the International Day Against Homophobia, Transphobia and Biphobia [Trudeau] said the proposed law would "help ensure transgender and other gender-diverse people can live according to their gender identity, free from discrimination, and protected from hate propaganda and hate crimes ... Everyone deserves to live free of stigma, persecution and discrimination - no matter who they are or whom they love." [316]

In the lands where gay/trans/bisexual 'marriage' reigns, love is love, and love knows no boundaries, and anyone who thinks the boundary between sanity and delusion matters will be punished by the state. Because - pardon me if I have said this already - if we normalise gay 'marriage' we normalise the entire LGBTQ worldview in the culture and in our schools with the full force of anti-discrimination law.

IV. Transgender conditions: 'A mental disorder'

We cannot form a sound judgement on the strange claims of gender theory unless we understand the two phenomena of transgender and intersex conditions. Only then will we be able to respond with informed compassion to individuals while rejecting the demands of ideologues.

Two men tell of being a 'woman'

I met one such individual in America in 2015. Walt Heyer is a quietly spoken gentleman in his seventies. For many years he passed himself off as a woman before regretting that move and reverting, as best one can with a surgically damaged body, to his natural male sex. What led Walt to want to be a woman? He explains the strange form of abuse that messed with a little boy's sense of self:

> My mom and dad didn't have any idea that when they dropped their son off for a weekend at Grandma's that she was dressing their boy in girls' clothes. Grandma told me it was our little secret. My grandmother withheld affirmations of me as a boy, but she lavished delighted praise upon me when I was dressed as a girl. Feelings of euphoria swept over me with her praise, followed later by depression and insecurity about being a boy. Her actions planted the idea in me that I was born in the wrong body. She nourished and encouraged the idea, and over time it took on a life of its own.[317]

How common is that sort of experience in confusing a child's gender identity? One of the most famous transsexuals, "Renee" Richards, a male tennis professional and eye surgeon, established US legal precedent in 1977 by being declared a woman. He was born Richard Raskind. In his autobiography, *Second Serve*,[318] we learn that his older sister used to dress him in girls' underwear and try to push in his penis so that he looked more like a girl – a version of the above-mentioned "penis tucking", perhaps. In an interview with the *New York Times* in 2007 he recalled his "psychiatrist mother who occasionally dressed him in a slip."[319] And an interview with *People* magazine confirmed this formative experience:

> From the age of 9, Richards felt an "unsettling urge" to dress as a girl, a predilection she traces in part to her mother and older sister Jo's love of draping her in frills. Her mother, Richards remembers, "once forced me into a Halloween outfit so perfectly female that the parents who gave the party inquired discreetly why the pretty little girl was not in costume."[320]

Little Richard invented a female identity, Renee, to go with this cross-dressing game that had been pushed on him, which he continued to play at in secret. Likewise, Walt Heyer kept his split identity secret throughout a successful engineering career and even into a marriage, but it became too hard to suppress:

> After thirty-six years, I was still unable to overcome the persistent feeling I was really a woman. The seeds sown by Grandma developed deep roots. Unbeknownst to my wife, I began to act on my desire to be a woman. I was cross-dressing in public and enjoying it. I even started taking female hormones to feminize my appearance.

His wife did find out, and divorce ensued. That freed Walt to pursue his happiness, find a supportive "gender psychologist" and undergo surgical transition to "Laura Jensen", age 42. As is typical with gender reassignment surgery, the relief lasted for several years, but the underlying conflicts remained:

> The reprieve provided by surgery and life as a woman was only temporary. Hidden deep underneath the makeup and female clothing was the little boy carrying the hurts from traumatic childhood events, and he was making himself known. Being a female turned out to be only a cover-up, not healing.

Eight years into his life as Laura, Walt reached a deep low of alcoholism and depression. The psychiatrist he saw this time delved into his childhood and gave him a different explanation for his conflicted identity:

> Now it was apparent that I had developed a dissociative disorder in childhood to escape the trauma of the repeated cross-dressing by my grandmother and the sexual abuse by my uncle. That should have been diagnosed and treated with psychotherapy. Instead, the gender specialist never considered my difficult childhood... It was a quick jump to prescribe hormones and irreversible surgery.

And so began the painful journey back to being the Walt Heyer I met in 2015:

> Coming back to wholeness as a man after undergoing unnecessary gender surgery and living life legally and socially as a woman for years wasn't going to be easy... My full genitalia could not be restored - a sad consequence of using surgery to treat psychological illness. Intensive psychotherapy would be required to resolve the dissociative disorder that started as a child.

And then a gentle word of counsel from Walt to parents of gender-confused children:

> Changing genders is short-term gain with long-term pain. Its consequences include early mortality, regret, mental illness, and suicide. Instead of encouraging them to undergo unnecessary and destructive surgery, let's affirm and love our young people just the way they are.

And "Renee" Richards? More complicated. He seems to feel he could never have done anything but become a transgender woman, but he advises others to try to find different solutions to their cross-dressing compulsion. He told the *New York Times* in 2007, "Better to be an intact man ... than to be a transsexual woman who is an imperfect woman." A fuller reflection dates to 1999:

> I get a lot of inquiries from would-be transsexuals, but I don't want anyone to hold me out as an example to follow. Today there are better choices, including medication, for dealing with the compulsion to cross-dress and the depression that comes from gender confusion. As far as being fulfilled as a woman, I'm not as fulfilled as I dreamed of being. I get a lot of letters from people who are considering having this operation ... and I discourage them all.[321]

One would-be transsexual who is glad he didn't do it is gay British actor Rupert Everett. He told the *Sunday Times* in June 2016 that, for a period of childhood, he dressed exclusively as a girl: "I really wanted to be a girl. Thank God the world of now wasn't then, because I'd be on hormones and I'd be a woman. After I was 15, I never wanted to be a woman again."[322]

A medical opinion

A leading authority on the psychiatric dimension of transgenderism, Professor Paul McHugh, would agree with the words of caution from Richards and Heyer and Everett. Johns Hopkins University medical school led the world in surgery for transgender adults back in the sixties; they also led the world in rejecting the practice in the seventies, and McHugh was in the midst of it as senior psychiatrist. As recently as August 2016, *The New Atlantis* ("A Journal of Technology and Society") called McHugh "arguably the most important American psychiatrist of the last half-century".[323]

McHugh explains that Johns Hopkins stopped doing the transgender surgery that they themselves had pioneered, because the adults who had undergone surgery "were little changed in their psychological condition." He reports,

> The hope that they would emerge now from their emotional difficulties to flourish psychologically had not been fulfilled. We saw the results as demonstrating that just as these men enjoyed cross-dressing as women before the operation so they enjoyed cross-living after it. But they were no better in their psychological integration or any easier to live with. With these facts in hand I concluded that Hopkins was fundamentally cooperating with a mental illness. We psychiatrists, I thought, would do better to concentrate on trying to fix their minds and not their genitalia.[324]

Writing in the *Wall St Journal* in 2014, McHugh notes recent research showing that surgical intervention appears to give several years of relief but then worsening depression and despair:

> It now appears that our long-ago decision was a wise one. A 2011 study at the Karolinska Institute in Sweden produced the most illuminating results yet regarding the transgendered, evidence that

should give advocates pause.[325] The long-term study – up to 30 years – followed 324 people who had sex-reassignment surgery. The study revealed that beginning about 10 years after having the surgery, the transgendered began to experience increasing mental difficulties. Most shockingly, their suicide mortality rose almost 20-fold above the comparable non-transgender population.[326]

The essence of the troubled transgender mindset, McHugh says, is a disorder of "assumption". Writing in 2015, he gives an illuminating analogy with anorexia – another condition where the young person is utterly convinced that she is obese and needing to diet, when in fact she is dangerously thin and suffering a delusion of body perception:

> Gender dysphoria – the official psychiatric term for feeling oneself to be of the opposite sex – belongs in the family of similarly disordered assumptions about the body, such as anorexia nervosa and body dysmorphic disorder. Its treatment should not be directed at the body as with surgery and hormones any more than one treats obesity-fearing anorexic patients with liposuction. The treatment should strive to correct the false, problematic nature of the assumption and to resolve the psychosocial conflicts provoking it.[327]

A young woman who struggled with the "disordered assumption" of anorexia, Moira Fleming, wonders why a transgender delusion is treated differently:

> I approach this topic with a wrenching awareness of what it feels like to be disconnected from your body, to hate with every fiber of your being the way you look in the mirror, and to be willing to undergo great feats of self-mutilation to achieve a vision that is always just out of grasp ... As a person who has struggled with anorexia nervosa since puberty, the transgender anguish resonates with me. The similarities between the two illnesses are striking. Yet one is an identity, and the other is a disorder. Why?[328]

She suffered a delusional state but came out of it; she is in a position to warn against the gnostic fallacy of letting "feelings" trump reality:

> We *cannot* rely on our "feelings," as strong as they are. If I relied on my feelings, I'd be dead. Why? Because my feelings tell me that eating food means gaining weight, and gaining weight is intolerable.

Transgender children are apparently absolutely sure they were born in the wrong body. It is a belief held so deeply that we throw out all the entrenched knowledge of psychology and mental illness to appease it.

A truthful diagnosis, based on knowledge of psychology and mental illness, has to be made even when it's unwelcome. That is the service McHugh provides:

> "Sex change" is biologically impossible. People who undergo sex-reassignment surgery do not change from men to women or vice versa. Rather, they become feminized men or masculinized women. Claiming that this is civil-rights matter and encouraging surgical intervention is in reality to collaborate with and promote a mental disorder.[329]

As for the most famous "feminised man" of recent years, the 1976 Olympic decathlon champion Bruce Jenner, McHugh sees features that are typical of one type of transgender mindset:

> I have not met or examined Jenner, but his behavior resembles that of some of the transgender males we have studied over the years. These men wanted to display themselves in sexy ways, wearing provocative female garb. More often than not, while claiming to be a woman in a man's body, they declared themselves to be "lesbians" (attracted to other women). The photograph of the posed, corseted, breast-boosted Bruce Jenner (a man in his mid-sixties, but flaunting himself as if a "pin-up" girl in her twenties or thirties) on the cover of Vanity Fair[327] suggests that he may fit the behavioral mold that Ray Blanchard has dubbed an expression of "autogynephilia" – from gynephilia (attracted to women) and auto (in the form of oneself).[331]

The research from Johns Hopkins University in the seventies identified another transgender mindset: "conflicted and guilt-ridden homosexual men who saw a sex-change as a way to resolve their conflicts over homosexuality by allowing them to behave sexually as females with men".[332] Gender confusion in children arises for different reasons. Some, like the young Walt Heyer, might be initiated into cross-dressing confusion by adults. For other children, distress arises from developmental issues, as McHugh notes:

> Most young boys and girls who come seeking sex-reassignment are utterly different from Jenner. They have no erotic interest driving their quest. Rather, they come with psychosocial issues - conflicts over the prospects, expectations, and roles that they sense are attached to their given sex – and presume that sex-reassignment will ease or resolve them.[333]

A good reason not to offer children surgical and hormonal sex-reassignment is that the vast majority of young people who assert that they are "in the wrong body" will simply get over their confusion if left to themselves – as did Rupert Everett. He said, "I think a lot of children have an ambivalence when they're very young to what sex they are or what they feel about everyone ... It's nice to be allowed to express yourself, but the hormone thing, very young, is a big step."[334] McHugh points out, "When children who reported transgender feelings were tracked without medical or surgical treatment at both Vanderbilt University and London's Portman Clinic, 70%-80% of them spontaneously lost those feelings."[335] So if three quarters of young 'transgenders' (higher, in other studies) will no longer think of themselves as transgender a few years later, why the pressure by Safe Schools to affirm them and facilitate their transition? McHugh spoke up for the children most likely to suffer harm at the hands of gender ideologues in schools:

> Another subgroup consists of young men and women susceptible to suggestion from "everything is normal" sex education, amplified by Internet chat groups. These are the transgender subjects most like anorexia nervosa patients: They become persuaded that seeking a drastic physical change will banish their psycho-social problems. "Diversity" counselors in their schools, rather like cult leaders, may encourage these young people to distance themselves from their families and offer advice on rebutting arguments against having transgender surgery.[336]

The susceptibility to suggestion at that age is profound - recall from Chapter 5 the report of skyrocketing cases of transgender confusion presenting to Melbourne's Royal Children's Hospital that so strangely coincided with the Victorian rollout of Safe Schools: "From one patient in 2003, the hospital expects to see 200 children and adolescents this year."[337] With the uncensored version of Safe Schools to be made compulsory in every state high school in Victoria by 2018, what hope is there for impressionable children to escape the suggestive power of "everything is normal" sex education?

The only hope is to sweep away the gender-ideology muddle and restore sound clinical insight. As McHugh puts it, "What is needed now is public clamor for coherent science – biological and therapeutic science – examining the real effects of these efforts to 'support' transgendering."[338] But is that likely to happen any time soon, when the forces of political correctness intimidate clinicians and teachers and even parents from speaking their mind? McHugh describes the situation in some states of the USA where clinicians are deterred from giving the necessary help to troubled youngsters:

> The grim fact is that most of these youngsters do not find therapists willing to assess and guide them in ways that permit them to work out their conflicts and correct their assumptions. Rather, they and their families find only "gender counselors" who encourage them in their sexual misassumptions. There are several reasons for this absence of coherence in our mental health system. Important among them is the fact that both the state and federal governments are actively seeking to block any treatments that can be construed as challenging the assumptions and choices of transgendered youngsters ... In two states, a doctor who would look into the psychological history of a transgendered boy or girl in search of a resolvable conflict could lose his or her license to practice medicine. By contrast, such a physician would not be penalized if he or she started such a patient on hormones that would block puberty and might stunt growth.[339]

And not just in America. Dr Ken Zucker, a world expert in childhood gender issues who had run the largest gender identity clinic in Canada for thirty years, was sacked in December 2015 and his clinic closed because it was no longer "in step with the latest thinking":

> In the transgender community, Dr. Zucker's dismissal was celebrated – he had long been controversial for research suggesting children should be steered away from becoming transgender adults ... [Colleagues called it] a deplorable end to a fine career, wrought by political correctness and a misguided, but vocal, band of protesters with a flawed understanding of science.[340]

It is chilling to read of Zucker's PC assassination, a man in the sensible middle of clinical practice for decades but now washed away by a flood of sex-change fundamentalism. He had cared for some 650 troubled children over the years, about 10% of whom he helped to transition as adolescents, but his clinic's conservative views on younger children were unacceptable to the new gender enforcers:

> All else being equal, clinicians [at Zucker's centre] viewed it as preferable for a child to become comfortable with his or her natal gender rather than for them to socially transition ... If the child was probably going to desist [lose their transgender feelings] anyway, why nudge them prematurely toward accepting a cross-gender identity?[341]

Another voice of reason is Dr Lawrence Mayer, a physician, a Professor of biostatistics at Arizona State University and a scholar in residence in the Department of Psychiatry at Johns Hopkins University Medical School. In an excellent recent clinical review (recommended reading) of "Sexuality and Gender: Findings from the Biological, Psychological, and Social Sciences", co-authored with McHugh, he says,

> In the course of their development, many children explore the idea of being of the opposite sex. Some children may have improved psychological well-being if they are encouraged and supported in their cross-gender identification, particularly if the identification is strong and persistent over time. But nearly all children ultimately identify with their biological sex. The notion that a two-year-old, having expressed thoughts or behaviors identified with the opposite sex, can be labeled for life as transgender has absolutely no support in science. Indeed, it is iniquitous to believe that all children who have gender-atypical thoughts or behavior at some point in their development, particularly before puberty, should be encouraged to become transgender.[342]

A theme in this book is to 'think of the child' living in an era of genderless 'marriage' and PC genderless madness; Dr McHugh thinks also of the parents of gender-confused kids:

> Overlooked amid the hoopla ... stand many victims. Think, for example, of the parents whom no one - not doctors, schools, nor even churches - will help to rescue their children from these

strange notions of being transgendered and the problematic lives these notions herald.³⁴³

Kids like the young Walt Heyer will be abandoned by the enforced normalisation of all things transsexual. We fail such patients "by treating their confusions as a right in need of defending rather than as a mental disorder that deserves understanding, treatment and prevention."³⁴⁴ And yet even as I write this, news comes through that the World Health Organisation is considering removing transgenderism from the list of mental illnesses!³⁴⁵ Another bastion of reason might fall before the onslaught of gender theory.

V. Intersex conditions: no basis for abolishing male & female

Finally, we should try to understand the rare but tragic afflictions categorised as "intersex". Biology is always frayed around the edges. While the human species, along with all mammals, is fundamentally divided into male and female, a tiny number of babies are affected by genetic and hormonal disorders that disturb their sexual development. Such variation at the edges occurs in every other body system, too, whether of circulation, nerves, digestive tract or limbs, but there is no system that affects a person so intimately as a disorder of sexual form and function.

Safe Schools gets it wrong

The first thing to understand is just how rare intersex occurrences are amidst the male-female norm of human biology. Writing in the *Journal of Sex Research* (2002), Leonard Sax sums up:

> The available data support the conclusion that human sexuality is a dichotomy, not a continuum. More than 99.98% of humans are either male or female ... The birth of an intersex child ... is actually a rare event, occurring in fewer than 2 out of every 10,000 births.³⁴⁶

That is 0.02% of babies born. One in every five thousand. As with all areas of science that have political implications, attempts have been made to exaggerate the numbers of intersex cases to create the illusion of a larger constituency to drive public policy. The Safe Schools publication, *All of Us*, boldly asserts that the figure for intersex individuals is 1.7%, which is a hundred-fold exaggeration.[347] Such a bloated claim is clinically implausible, since it includes categories of people who are not, in any rigorous sense, intersex. Sax critiques the study[348] that is relied upon by the Safe Schools publication:

> Anne Fausto-Sterling's suggestion that the prevalence of intersex might be as high as 1.7% has attracted wide attention in both the scholarly press and the popular media. Many reviewers are not aware that this figure includes conditions which most clinicians do not recognize as intersex, such as Klinefelter syndrome, Turner syndrome, and late-onset adrenal hyperplasia. If the term intersex is to retain any meaning, the term should be restricted to those conditions in which chromosomal sex is inconsistent with phenotypic sex, or in which the phenotype is not classifiable as either male or female. Applying this more precise definition, the true prevalence of intersex is seen to be about 0.018%, almost 100 times lower than Fausto-Sterling's estimate of 1.7%.[349]

Another researcher, Carrie Hull, is just as critical: "the numerous errors and omissions made [by Fausto-Sterling et al] suggest that they were too keen to find a relatively high incidence of sexual nondimorphism."[350] In response, Fausto-Sterling graciously admitted her figure needed further work.[351] When I think of past patients with Turner's or Klinefelter's syndrome, as mentioned near the start of this chapter, they are obviously woman and man, and any impairment of their physical development and their fertility does not make them any less woman and man. They are not "intersex" in the way a child with cloacal exstrophy, for example, is intersex. Yet Safe Schools and other advocacy groups include such individuals, and ignore the "numerous errors and omissions" and Fausto-Sterling's concession, in promoting their 100-fold exaggeration. We await, as taxpayers, Safe Schools correcting its figure in the *All of Us* document.

'Intersex' individuals don't want to abolish male and female

The second thing to understand about "intersex" is that people affected by rare anomalies of ambiguous sex typically have no wish to abolish the natural dichotomy of male and female for everyone else. Here we have to listen to the individuals involved. One of their largest representative organisations is the Intersex Society of North America, ISNA, and it provides an information sheet, "Why doesn't ISNA want to eradicate gender?"

> At ISNA, we've learned that many intersex people are perfectly comfortable adopting either a male or female gender identity and are not seeking a genderless society or to label themselves as a member of a third gender class ... In fact, many of the people with intersex we know – both those subjected to early surgeries and those who escaped surgery – very happily accepted a gender assignment of male or female (either the one given them at birth or one they chose later for themselves later in life). Instead, adults with intersex conditions who underwent genital surgeries at early ages most often cite those early genital surgeries and the lies and shame surrounding those procedures as their source of pain.[352]

ISNA makes clear that the organisation is supportive of any gender identification, but that the public should not think that people with intersex conditions are wanting to pull the binary structure down. ISNA's pressing concern is to stop the surgical practice of imposing an acceptable genital appearance on a baby and instead wait until the individual is old enough to make his or her own decision.

How best to care for such babies?

So what should the medical profession be doing? Again, we take the counsel of Professor Paul McHugh, because he was head of psychiatry at Johns Hopkins University when that institute led the world in surgery for intersex conditions. He reflects on the individual children and families that he worked with over many years:

> I have witnessed a great deal of damage from sex-reassignment. The children transformed from their male constitution into female roles suffered prolonged distress and misery as they sensed their natural attitudes. Their parents usually lived with guilt over their decisions – second-guessing themselves and somewhat ashamed of the fabrication, both surgical and social, they had imposed on their sons.[353]

He concludes with the "best practice" policy that resulted from his team's experience and research at Johns Hopkins:

> For children with birth defects the most rational approach at this moment is to correct promptly any of the major urological defects they face, but to postpone any decision about sexual identity until much later, while raising the child according to its genetic sex ... Proper care, including good parenting, means helping the child through the medical and social difficulties presented by the genital anatomy but in the process protecting what tissues can be retained, in particular the gonads. This effort must continue to the point where the child can see the problem of a life role more clearly as a sexually differentiated individual emerges from within. Then as the young person gains a sense of responsibility for the result, he or she can be helped through any surgical constructions that are desired.[354]

The Johns Hopkins approach is consistent with ISNA's "patient-centred" model of care, which concludes:

> Following diagnostic work-up, newborns with intersex should be given a gender assignment as boy or girl, depending on which of those genders the child is more likely to feel as she or he grows up. Note that gender assignment does *not* involve surgery; it involves assigning a label as boy or girl to a child ... Surgeries done to make the genitals look "more normal" should not be performed until a child is mature enough to make an informed decision for herself or himself.[355]

Gender theory is put to the test – and fails

If only that cautionary approach had been taken in the case of David Reimer, the baby boy mentioned near the start of this chapter. At Johns

Hopkins, where Reimer was treated, McHugh observed that babies who had been surgically assigned a genital appearance that did not correspond with their actual chromosomal sex typically grew up confused and distressed. Many (like Reimer) later elected to have further surgery to return as close as possible to their true sex. In what seems to be a dig at John Money's gender theory, McHugh noted that this observation was at odds with "the opinion in psychiatric circles that one's 'sex' and one's 'gender' were distinct matters, sex being genetically and hormonally determined from conception, while gender was culturally shaped by the actions of family and others during childhood." So McHugh and colleagues, being inquisitive scientists, set out to test the gender/genetics question. He said, "I wanted to see whether male infants with ambiguous genitalia who were being surgically transformed into females and raised as girls did, as the theory (again from Hopkins) claimed, settle easily into the sexual identity that was chosen for them."[356]

The genital deformity selected for study was cloacal exstrophy in males, a grave malformation that could not be restored to a male appearance. The important point is that these poor infant boys, who were surgically castrated to a female appearance, had nevertheless made normal male hormones during the formative months in the womb. McHugh asked, "Would the fact that they had had the full testosterone exposure in utero defeat the attempt to raise them as girls?" A convenient colleague, William Reiner, was both a psychiatrist and former paediatric urologist, so he was ideally placed to conduct the study:

> [Reiner] discovered that such re-engineered males were almost never comfortable as females once they became aware of themselves and the world. From the start of their active play life, they behaved spontaneously like boys and were obviously different from their sisters and other girls, enjoying rough-and-tumble games but not dolls and "playing house." Later on, most of those individuals who learned that they were actually genetic males wished to reconstitute their lives as males (some even asked for surgical reconstruction and male hormone replacement) - and all this despite the earnest efforts by their parents to treat them as girls...[357]

The boys' genetic sex broke through in the end, contrary to the expectations of gender theory. After years of this research, and other studies, McHugh reported,

> We in the Johns Hopkins Psychiatry Department eventually concluded that human sexual identity is mostly built into our constitution by the genes we inherit and the embryogenesis we undergo. Male hormones sexualize the brain and the mind. Sexual dysphoria - a sense of disquiet in one's sexual role - naturally occurs amongst those rare males who are raised as females in an effort to correct an infantile genital structural problem.[358]

So much for the fallacy of gender theory – that being male or female is not a biological reality rooted in our genes and hormones, but a social construct that we can shape at will. So much for the ideologues trying to teach our kids that gender is a spectrum, exploiting that tiny number of infants, two in ten thousand, who are born with ambiguous sex. The care of children with such afflictions requires our best skill and compassion, above all respecting their later autonomy to choose how to manage their condition. These rare and tragic anomalies should not be misused by gender radicals to cast doubt on the timeless and true male-female structure of human nature.

VI. Clinging to reality

The subversive idea that two men can 'marry' is contained within the bigger lie that male and female are merely social constructs and we can define our own gender. That is gnostic mysticism, not science, and that way madness lies. We must cling to sanity in these surreal times and that means clinging to nature. By the standard of nature, a human being with male chromosomes and genitalia is a male no matter what other traits he exhibits. He is male even if he is an exquisitely effeminate boy, like my first patient, or a traumatised transvestite man, like my second patient, or a man with an extra X chromosome like my third. He is male if he is an effete poet or a heavyweight boxer. He is male if he wants to play with dolls rather than trucks. He is male if he is sexually attracted to men rather than women. There is indeed a rainbow spectrum of ways of being male, but nowhere on that spectrum from the most refined to the most brutal are we anything but male. That is where gender realists part ways with gender gnostics: we accept that we are defined by nature while affirming the vast variety of ways to be male; they do not accept that we are defined by nature and insist the identities of male or female or genderqueer or agender are fluid and free and all in our mind.

When we sit with a gender-confused child, gender realism sounds like tough love while gender gnosticism sounds compassionate. But it is false compassion to affirm a gender-confused boy in his mistaken assumption that he is a girl; he is not, he is an effeminate boy – and we still love him. Tough love requires understanding the sources of his confusion, helping heal any emotional wounds, keeping him company as he finds his way through puberty – at which time most young people get over their confusion.

It is false compassion to affirm a grown man's delusion that he is a woman; he is not, he is a feminised man – and we still love him. If he seeks the sexual excitement of permanent cross-dressing, that is a private fetish that we have no duty to affirm. If he does it out of conflicted homosexuality, wanting to see himself as a "heterosexual woman", that is a task for sensitive counselling, not surgery. And if he is unshakably deluded in his belief that he truly *is* a woman, in the same way as an anorexic schoolgirl is unshakably deluded that she truly *is* obese, then he is no longer a man in charge of his mind, and we should not collaborate with his delusion.

It is false justice to legislate that schools and public toilets and change rooms and sports teams and beauty pageants have to treat gender-confused males as females; they are not. Their private needs can be addressed by the responsible authorities with discretion, with not a whisper of unkindness, and everyone can get quietly on with their lives – as they always did until the recent ideological frenzy. But it is unjust and irrational to validate a transgender fetish or confusion or delusion to the detriment of others – of the female athletes forced to compete with cross-dressing males; of the schoolgirls confronted in the bathrooms by trans-males.

And it is a capitulation to craziness to buy the idea that boys and girls are "socially constructed" and therefore we should make girls plays with trucks and boys play with dolls to overcome society's gender stereotyping. We are mammals, and nobody suggests the differences between stag and doe are socially constructed. We are male and female, equal but different. The abolition of male and female is a sinister gnostic enterprise that will eventually fail, because nature says it must. But it will do grave damage to our children and our culture before it is tossed on the scrap heap of inhuman ideologies. To reprise the Hon. Mark Latham, "As parents we need to make our views known to election candidates and school leaders alike. Anyone who has researched this issue will know we are fighting for the future of our civilisation."[359]

On the duty of resistance to this onslaught of gender ideology, let us give the last word to the man who has been our guide for much of this chapter, a voice of reason, Paul McHugh:

> The idea that one's sex is fluid and a matter open to choice runs unquestioned through our culture and is reflected everywhere in the media, the theater, the classroom, and in many medical clinics. It has taken on cult-like features: its own special lingo, internet chat rooms providing slick answers to new recruits, and clubs for easy access to dresses and styles supporting the sex change. It is doing much damage to families, adolescents, and children and should be confronted as an opinion without biological foundation wherever it emerges.[360]

9

CHILDREN OF THE STATE

Gay marriage chimes brilliantly with these governments' insatiable desire to diminish the sovereignty of the family and intervene more in our personal lives, and to police what we think.
Brendan O'Neill

What danger has Brendan O'Neill seen in 'marriage equality' that others have missed – and how is it serious enough to make a libertarian leftie like him swim against the tide? He understands the Orwellian power of words. He alerts us to the consequences of giving government definitional power over our deepest bonds of kinship:

> The gay-marriage campaign grants the state a new, unprecedented authority over how we define our personal relationships and family lives … The ruling elites of Canada, the UK and elsewhere have rewritten public documents to excise mentions of "mothers", "fathers", "husbands" and "wives" in favour of a more neutral language to suit their homogenisation of all relationships as "marriage".[361]

Writing in *Spiked*, which he edits, he warns of a top-down disruption of organic social structures:

> In gay marriage's great rewriting and renaming of various communal identities that have been a core part of our societies for generations – from mother to wife to child - we can see the implicit diminishing of the value of a certain, more traditional way of life, with the old-style family unit itself being robbed of moral meaning and reduced to a business-like collection of partners and 'Parent 1' and 'Parent 2'. Here, too, there's a coercive component,

an attempted top-down refashioning of identities that emerged from within communities over a great period of time.[362]

When this self-described "godless Brit" writes of "these governments' insatiable desire to diminish the sovereignty of the family", he is not speaking of past dictatorships but of our own soft tyrannies. The soft socialists who command the high ground of our culture are different to their hard-edged forebears, but with genderless 'marriage' they will further a century-long quest to deconstruct the family and subject it to the authority of the state.

In sketching that century-wide backdrop, my hope is that readers will realise there is a lot more at play with 'marriage equality' than just rainbows and niceness and happy wedding days. Let us learn what company we keep, historically, if we give our support to the "breathtakingly subversive idea" of same-sex marriage; let us decide if we are happy to be, in Lenin's phrase, "useful idiots" in the service of ideological forces we hardly understand.

Into the hands of Big Government

In the genderless new world, neither spouse nor parent is defined by nature anymore; these words become a legal fiction defined by government. From Canada, law professor Margaret Somerville confirms that redefining marriage automatically redefines parenting for *all* parents and *all* children:

> Marriage is a compound right in both international and domestic law: it's the right to marry and to found a family. Giving the latter right to same-sex couples necessarily negates the rights of *all* children with respect to their biological origins and natural families, not just those born into same-sex marriages ... The Canadian Civil Marriage Act 2005, which legalised same-sex marriage, demonstrates this in providing that in certain legislation the term "natural parent" is to be replaced by "legal parent". In short, the adoption exception - that who is a child's parent is established by legal fiat, not biological connection - becomes the norm for all children.[363]

Somerville confirms that "some Canadian provincial legislation replaces the words 'mother' and 'father' on a birth certificate with 'Parent

1' and 'Parent 2'."³⁶⁴ Likewise, in socialist Spain, same-sex 'marriage' in 2005 led straight to the abolition of 'mother' and 'father':

> Spain has taken another step in its journey from conservative to liberal bastion by creating new birth certificates to avoid discrimination against same-sex couples. According to an announcement in the Official Bulletin of State, "The expression "father" will be replaced with "Progenitor A", and "mother" will be replaced with "Progenitor B". The head of the national Civil Register, Pilar Blanco-Morales, told the newspaper *ABC* that the change took account of a new law on same-sex marriages passed by the socialist government in July.³⁶⁵

True, other socialist states like the Australian Capital Territory have tried to get with the genderless agenda by using "parent 1 and parent 2" on birth certificates. Reactionary heteronormative parents who want "mother and father" on their baby's birth certificate must specifically opt in.³⁶⁶ The difference here is that parents have the power to sack the Labor-Green ACT government and restore sanity to birth certificates. Spanish parents do not, because a law for same-sex 'marriage' negates the legal argument that a biological mother and father have any special relationship with their child; the logic of 'marriage equality' denies the truth of the natural family and gives the power of definition to the state.

In Spain and other gay 'marriage' jurisdictions, the eyes of government look down with indifference at the genderless relationship of all parents and all children. My child is no longer "my child" in any primal sense that government must keep the hell clear of. Parenting is now defined by government, not by nature; and what Big Government gives, Big Government can take away.

Just spend a moment imagining yourself at your child's end of year assembly. Look around at all the married couples with their children. Right now, such a family constitutes "the natural and fundamental group unit of society, deserving of protection by society and the state" according to the Universal Declaration of Human Rights, Article 16. This primal unit predates all government and all laws and pulls rank on secondary institutions like the government. No more. Look around the assembly hall once the law has redefined marriage as a relationship of any two adults of any gender. Sitting over there are two men with wedding rings and the child they created by surrogacy. Next to them sit a married man and woman with their own biological daughter; the family resemblance is obvious. The law now says there is nothing special about a man and woman getting married versus two men getting 'married'; likewise the law says there is nothing special about a child being raised by her biological mother and father versus a surrogate baby being raised by two men.

This is what excites those who favour Big Government. They understand that abolishing the natural truth of man-woman marriage abolishes the natural truth of mother, father and child; with that natural structure demolished in law, the state moves in to fill the void.

The longest war

For more than a century, collectivists of every stripe have identified the family as the one rival centre of authority to the state and have long sought its subjugation. Obviously, most of the kind souls who support 'marriage equality' have no such motive. Yet ordinary people in Western countries today are unwittingly serving the cause of generations of anarchists, communists, and sexual decadents. At the end of his remarkable book, *Takedown: From communists to progressives, how the left has sabotaged marriage and family*, Paul Kengor writes,

> An utterly fascinating aspect of the general public's support of same-sex marriage is that this is the only time that a majority of everyday Americans have agreed with communists in one of their sharp, atheistic stances against marriage and the family. When Marx and Engels and Kollontai and Trotsky and Lenin and Lukács and Marcuse and Millett and Mao and Castro and Reich and Ayers and Dohrn and their assorted comrades pushed fringe ideas on infidelity and free love, on new motherhood, on full-time nursery care for children as wards of the state, on polymorphous perversity, on smashing monogamy, and so forth, they were far outside the mainstream. Not anymore. Today, CPUSA [Communist Party of the USA] and the American majority at long last finally agree, and they agree on a nontraditional marriage/family matter that does nothing less than irreversibly redefine marriage. It is a breathtaking development to behold.[367]

Few people know how the main characters listed by Kengor have agitated for the destruction of marriage and natural family and how the stroke of radical genius which is homosexual 'marriage' would have astounded them all. Few people understand that the move to homosexual 'marriage' has not just popped up out of nowhere, from a sudden fit of fairness amongst our gentle generation; it stands in a long tradition of Marxist and anarchist subversion which has sickened our culture almost to the point of death. A quick backward glance will help us understand how we got to where we are. It might make us uneasy about the company we are in if we go along with deconstructing marriage.

Communist rage: religious hatred

In the late nineteenth century the communists cried "Abolition of the family!" and committed themselves to breaking up that bourgeois capitalist enterprise, advocating wives in common and children raised by the state. Always the family was the enemy of the state, because the family was a rock so solid, a moral community so private and out of reach of the ideologues, that it had to be smashed if the state was to become all in all.

From the start, this demolition of the family required the severing of the mother-child bond. For communists this was achieved in two ways. First, by putting the woman in the factory and giving the offspring to the commune to look after, as children of the Party. Second, by making it easy for the woman to shake off the shackles of husband and child through easy divorce laws and unrestricted abortion. In exchange, communism would offer her the pride of work on a par with men and the liberation of "unconstrained sexual intercourse". Friedrich Engels, co-author of the *Communist Manifesto*, summed up this plan for collectivising children and liberating women in his 1884 book, *The Origin of the Family*,

> With the transfer of the means of production into common ownership, the single family ceases to be the economic unit of society. Private housekeeping is transformed into a social industry. The care and education of the children becomes a public affair; society looks after all children alike, whether they are legitimate or not. This removes all the anxiety about the consequences which

today is the most essential social-moral as well as economic factor that prevents a girl from giving herself completely to the man she loves. Will not that suffice to bring about the gradual growth of unconstrained sexual intercourse and with it a more tolerant public opinion in regard to a maiden's honor and a woman's shame? [368]

His comrade and co-author Karl Marx kept his focus on the related task of destroying religion. "Communism begins where atheism begins", said Marx, and communist animosity to bourgeois marriage was heightened by the perception that family and religion were intertwined in Western culture. After all, the dominant iconic image of Christianity was the mother and baby. Marx wrote, "Therefore after, for example, the earthly family is discovered as the secret of the holy family, the former must itself be theoretically and practically destroyed."[369] The great atheist saw that there is something quasi-sacred about the human trinity of father, mother and child, and it had to be destroyed as part of the destruction of religion.

And so began the great struggle for hearts and minds between communism and the church, with Pope Pius IX decrying "the unspeakable doctrine of Communism" in an 1846 encyclical published two years before the *Communist Manifesto*.[370] His successor, Pope Leo XIII, maintained a prolific critique of that "fatal plague" and on the question of communists and marriage wrote in *On Socialism* (1878), "They debase the natural union of man and woman, which is held sacred even among barbarous peoples; and its bond, by which the family is chiefly held together, they weaken, or even deliver up to lust."[371] Decades later in 1937 at the height of Stalin's power, Pope Pius XI wrote *On Atheistic Communism*, describing "the vast campaign of the Church against world Communism" and warning of that ideology's violation of the bond between parent and child:

> [The woman] is withdrawn from the family and the care of her children, to be thrust instead into public life and collective production under the same conditions as man. The care of home and children then devolves upon the collectivity. Finally, the right of education is denied to parents, for it is conceived as the exclusive prerogative of the community, in whose name and by whose mandate alone parents may exercise this right.[372]

The church was the one relentless enemy of the totalitarians from the days of Marx until the visit of Pope John Paul II to communist Poland in 1979, which tipped the first domino that brought down the Berlin wall a decade later. The enmity was always mutual, so when the Bolshevists took power in Russia in October 1917, Lenin first terrorized the Russian church into silence and then deployed two legal weapons against marriage and family: easy divorce and abortion. Kengor observes,

> The dramatic combined effect of an immediate full liberalization of divorce laws and institution of "red weddings" became especially acute with the corresponding complete legalization of abortion in 1920, which was an unprecedented action anywhere in the world at the time. With those changes and the squashing of the Russian Orthodox Church and its guidance in marriage and families and children and education and more, Lenin and his allies dealt a severe blow to marital and family life in traditionally religious Russia.[373]

The message was clear: the Total State needs to subjugate its one rival centre of moral authority, the family, if a collectivist utopia is to be achieved, and that task involved the parallel destruction of religion. That dual objective has not wavered in over a century. A snapshot of some of this movement's main advocates will help us understand the relentless effort to deconstruct the norms of marriage and family, which has brought us to our present crisis.

Feminist rage: marriage as prostitution

The prototype hybrid communist-feminist was Aleksandra Kollontai, appointed by Lenin to head his Women's Department in 1919. From there she spoke to women in the communist world about the need for both economic and sexual liberation, because "The shackles of the family, of housework, of prostitution still weigh heavily on the working woman". Marriage, to Kollontai, was a form of "prostitution". She assured the working mothers, newly liberated to factory work, that their children would be looked after: "Communist society will take upon itself all the duties involved in the education of the child," and "The worker-mother must learn not to differentiate between yours and mine."[374]

Children who are neither "yours nor mine" but all of ours still has a modern ring to it: compare that to the sentiments of American TV host Melissa Harris-Perry in 2013:

> We have never invested as much in public education as we should have because we've always had kind of a private notion of children. Your kid is yours and totally your responsibility. We haven't had a very collective notion of 'these are our children' ... So part of it is we have to break through our kind of private idea that kids belong to their parents, or kids belong to their families, and recognize that kids belong to whole communities.[375]

Children of the collective are most effectively created through state education, as Ms Harris-Perry implies. As with Australia's quasi-Marxist Safe Schools programme, subverting the relationship of parent and child in many ways, education is the key to shifting the loyalty of the child from family to state. And it takes a village, whether Soviet or inner city USA, to teach us "that kids belong to whole communities" (not to their families) and to relieve parents of their "private notion of children". Homosexual 'marriage' and parenting will be the hammer blow to the notion of a private, natural, inviolable bond between parents and their biological progeny. Once children are routinely created artificially for same-sex couples with the blessing of our law, formally disregarding the natural kinship bonds of parent and child, there is no longer any logic in defining the family as "the natural and fundamental group unit of society". Children of same-sex parented families will indeed belong to the "whole community" – from the technicians who did the artificial fertilisation to the officials who issued false birth certificates excluding the genetic and surrogate mothers to the lawyers resolving the competing interests of up to five adults who all have a claim as 'parent' of the child of same-sex couples. It just about takes a village to bring such a child to life, and kinship bonds are mangled in the process.

Kate Millett: "destroying monogamy"

In the century that passed between the ferocious communism of Kollontai and the well-heeled collectivism of Harris-Perry, Marxist feminism made its long march through western institutions. If one figure were to be chosen to illustrate this movement's assault on marriage and sexual norms, it would be Kate Millett. She was featured on the cover of *Time* magazine in August 1970 as "the Mao Tse-Tung of Women's Liberation".[376] As a student in the sixties at America's hothouse of cultural Marxism, Columbia University, Millett came to prominence with her doctoral thesis, *Sexual Politics*. She made her intentions quite clear about the importance of unconstrained sexuality, including homosexuality, in bringing down "patriarchal monogamous marriage":

> A sexual revolution would require, perhaps first of all, an end of traditional sexual inhibitions and taboos, particularly those that most threaten patriarchal monogamous marriage: homosexuality, 'illegitimacy,' adolescent, pre-and extramarital sexuality.[377]

If you want an insight into the world of the sixties sexual revolutionaries, and their marination in Marxist dogma, there is a remarkable account by Millett's sister, Mallory, of a visit to New York where Millett was meeting with her fellow student radicals.

> It was 1969. Kate invited me to join her for a gathering at the home of her friend, Lila Karp. They called the assemblage a "consciousness-raising-group," a typical communist exercise, something practiced in Maoist China. We gathered at a large table as the chairperson opened the meeting with a back-and-forth recitation, like a Litany, a type of prayer done in Catholic Church. But now it was Marxism, the Church of the Left, mimicking religious practice: "Why are we here today?" she asked. "To make revolution," they answered. "What kind of revolution?" she replied. "The Cultural Revolution," they chanted. "And how do we make Cultural Revolution?" she demanded. "By destroying the American family!" they answered. "How do we destroy the family?" she came back. "By destroying the American Patriarch," they cried exuberantly. "And how do we destroy the American Patriarch?" she replied. "By taking away his power!" "How do we do that?" "By destroying monogamy!" they shouted. "How can we destroy monogamy?" Their answer left me dumbstruck, breathless, disbelieving my ears. Was I on planet earth? Who were these people? "By promoting promiscuity, eroticism, prostitution and homosexuality!" they resounded. They proceeded with a long discussion on how to advance these goals by establishing The National Organization of Women. It was clear they desired nothing less than the utter deconstruction of Western society.[378]

And their programme has worked out pretty well in the subsequent half century, with homosexual 'marriage' just the final blow to "patriarchal monogamous marriage". For as Australia's most eminent gay activist, Denis Altman, has made clear, "one of the things about gay male culture is that it is not a monogamous culture".[379] We have seen that gay 'marriage' is going to be "monogamish" at best, since by its nature it is not inclined to be monogamous. Accepting 'marriage equality', therefore, is to tacitly abandon the sexual exclusivity of marriage; a quiet final nail in the coffin of monogamy.

From Marcuse to Denis Altman

Millett stood in the tradition of the Frankfurt School of communist intellectuals, many Jewish, who fled Germany when Hitler came to power and found refuge at America's most radical university, Columbia. The influence of Herbert Marcuse, Wilhelm Reich, Max Horkheimer, Erich Fromm, Georg Lukács and others is felt in our schools and universities to this day, including the inspiration they gave to the cause of homosexual radicalism. Kengor relates the insights of a student at Columbia at that time, Ralph de Toledano:

> These Freudian-Marxists (Toledano wrote) realized that sex could be a devastating instrument if permitted to run rampant, and so they advocated the elimination of all sexual restraints along with the destruction of the family, religion, and 'bourgeois' morality ... Their so-called "Critical Theory" would spout everything and anything from "compulsory promiscuity" (Toledano's apt description) to one-parent families, premarital sexual activity, and also homosexuality, "since it struck at the family and childbearing." Marxist-communist fundamental transformation of society would ultimately come not through economic changes – which were dismally failing to produce their goals and win converts – but through vast cultural-sexual changes directly relating to family and married life.[380]

Each of the Frankfurt School's leading figures played their role in fomenting the sexual revolution of the 1960s on American campuses, whose toxic spillage still poisons our culture. Herbert Marcuse remains the towering figure among them and he best illustrates the zeitgeist's lust for cultural destruction. He is honoured with an extensive article at the *GLBTQ Encyclopedia*:

> Marcuse had an enormous influence on theories of sexual liberation, particularly in the early post-Stonewall gay movement and on the left. Many young people in the 1960s adopted Marcuse-like sexual politics as the basis for the counter-culture's radical transformation of values.[381]

In his memoir of that tumultuous era, Ralph de Toledano felt less honour was due, describing Marcuse as "the guru of the New Left in its war on education, religion and the family in the 1960s and its call for violence against all authority".[382] Still, one man's violence is another man's liberation, and the *GLBTQ Encyclopedia* dwelt on Marcuse's formula for liberation in lurid detail:

> Marcuse proposed sexual liberation through the cultivation of a "polymorphous perverse" sexuality (which includes oral, anal, and genital eroticism) that eschews a narrow focus on genital heterosexual intercourse. Marcuse believed that sexual liberation was achieved by exploring new permutations of sexual desires, sexual activities, and gender roles – what Freud called "perverse" sexual desires, that is, all nonreproductive forms of sexual behavior, of which kissing, oral sex, and anal sex are familiar examples. Marcuse was himself heterosexual, but he identified the homosexual as the radical standard bearer of sex for the sake of pleasure, a form of radical hedonism that repudiates those forms of repressive sexuality organized around genital heterosexuality and biological reproduction. "Against a society which employs sexuality as a means for a useful end," Marcuse argued, "the perversions uphold sexuality as an end itself ... and challenge its very foundations."

Australia's own Denis Altman, who told us earlier that there are no monogamous gay relationships, is cited in similarly explicit form in the Marcuse review:

> Dennis Altman's *Homosexual: Oppression and Liberation* (1971), one of the earliest theoretical discussions of gay liberation and sexual politics, reflected the same assumption and relied extensively on Marcuse's work ... Like Marcuse, Altman also emphasized "polymorphous perversity," the undifferentiated ability to take

pleasure from all parts of the body. "Anatomy," Altman noted, "has forced the homosexual to explore the realities of polymorphous eroticism." Thus, homosexual sex represented an expression of pleasure and love "free of any utilitarian ends."[383]

From Reich to Roz Ward

Just one more snapshot of a leading figure from the Frankfurt school, which will link back to present day Australia. Wilhelm Reich coined the term "sexual revolution" and brought to his life's work a deeply damaged childhood, a clinical apprenticeship with Sigmund Freud and a determination to marry Marxism with Freudianism. The flavour of that heady blend can be captured in this passage from his 1940s work, *The Function of the Orgasm*:

> The structuring of masses of people to be blindly obedient to authority is brought about not by natural parental love, but by the authority of the family. The suppression of the sexuality of small children and adolescents is the chief means of producing this obedience ... The unity and congruity of culture and nature, work and love, morality and sexuality, longed for from time immemorial will remain a dream as long as man continues to condemn the demand for natural (orgiastic) sexual gratification.[384]

The sexuality of small children oppressed by "the authority of the family". Does that passage ring any faint bells? "Children are sexual beings and it's a strong part of their identity," we were told in the last chapter by Early Childhood Australia spokeswoman Clare McHugh, who said "rigid views on gender" were associated with domestic violence.[385] Or set the rhapsodic urgings of Reich's second paragraph alongside Roz Ward's equally effusive paean to sexual Marxism which we met in an earlier chapter:

> Programs like the Safe Schools Coalition are making some difference but we're still a long way from liberation ... Marxism offers the hope and the strategy needed to create a world where human sexuality, gender and how we relate to our bodies can blossom in extraordinarily new and amazing ways that we can only try to imagine today.[386]

Sentiments like these do not arise from nowhere; they develop within a long tradition. Ward's speech at the 2015 Marxism Conference in Melbourne was entitled, "The Role Of The Left For LGBTI Rights", and she stood squarely alongside Kollontai, Marcuse and Millett in her militancy: "LGBTI oppression and heteronormativity are woven into the fabric of capitalism" she said, and "it will only be through a revitalised class struggle and revolutionary change that we can hope for the liberation of LGBTI people".[387]

"Part of something bigger"

So what does this backward glance over a dismal century of barbarian invasion teach us about the present question of redefining marriage? Only that there is a recognisable mindset that spans the century, a sustained hostility to things that our culture has held dear. Central to our culture – any culture – is family and faith. In order to subjugate them both, the atheist weapon of state tyranny was first deployed and, when that proved unable to break the spirit of these two institutions, the weapon of sexual mayhem. It appears the latter weapon may prevail.

As Paul Kengor cautions near the start of his history, joining the dots in a long ideological pedigree like this is instructive but must not be simplistic:

> Same-sex marriage is hardly a Marxist plot, a latent communist conspiracy. It is, however, a crucial final blow to marriage - the only blow that is enabling a formal legal definition that will unravel the institution. It has distinct origins traceable to the far-left's initial thrusts at this once unassailable monogamous, faithful male-female institution.[388]

These sexual revolutionaries will be cheering from their graves as the mums and dads of Australia cast their vote for the homosexualisation of natural marriage, and so unknowingly usher in the final stage of the long campaign to deconstruct the family. For if the word "marriage" is emptied of its natural meaning, so is the word "family". So are the words husband, wife, mother, father. All is a genderless, government-defined chaos, which is exactly the objective. Remember Brendan O'Neill's warning: "Those who say "They're only words, who cares?" clearly don't know their Orwell." Kengor notes near the end of his history:

> Advocates of gay marriage have no idea how what they want to do so closely conforms to today's communist agenda ... They are not intending harm, nor do they realize how and where they are part of something bigger, a larger movement using and exploiting them for a purpose they cannot imagine ... Nonetheless, the far left couldn't care less how the rest of the culture and everyone else gets there, with whatever slogans or well-intended notions, so long as they get there and assist the grand takedown.[389]

This brief review of the far left's long war on natural marriage and family might help us make sense of the things we hear from Roz Ward and other academics who seem to live in a different cultural world from us. Their worldview derives from the likes of Millett and Marcuse, Engels and Reich and so many luminaries of the great degraded socialist venture of the last century. It is up to us as parents and citizens to decide whether their worldview will prevail today. Our only choice, whether at the local P&C meeting discussing Safe Schools or in the plebiscite booth deciding on same-sex 'marriage', is whether or not we acquiesce in the world they would create for our children.

PART IV

PILLAGING THE VILLAGE

10

THE SILENCE OF THE SHEPHERDS

> *Changing the definition of marriage, which has lasted for time immemorial, is not an exercise in human rights and equality; it is an exercise in de-authorising the Judaeo-Christian influence in our society, and any who pretend otherwise are deluding themselves.*
> The Hon. John Howard, former Prime Minister of Australia.[390]

They say it takes a village to raise a child. That means, in order to raise tomorrow's child according to the values of the LGBT revolution, it will be necessary to purge the village of reactionary moral leaders. That means faithful pastors, priests and rabbis.

A law for homosexual 'marriage' will strike the shepherds and the sheep will be scattered. It will intimidate religious leaders (and their insurers) with the relentless threat of anti-discrimination lawsuits; traditional moral teaching will become something to be whispered in private. There ain't room in this village for both state-enforced homosexual orthodoxy and Christian moral orthodoxy.

The revolution's strategists know that once homosexual 'marriage' is the law of the land, the power of anti-discrimination law to silence conscientious objectors and indoctrinate children (including those from religious homes) into approved LGBT views will be complete. In this way, the entire moral community surrounding a child will be harassed into ideological correctness by 'human rights' laws: blatant cultural tyranny. Every revolution knows there are two conditions for success:

first, obtain control of a child's education; second, suppress dissidents. A law for 'marriage equality' makes that possible, at last.

Canadian Queen's Counsel, Barbara Findlay, declared years ago: "The legal struggle for queer rights will one day be a showdown between freedom of religion versus sexual orientation." Law professor and "activist for LGBT rights",[391] Chai Feldblum, was asked about such a showdown. Her views matter because she is an Obama-appointee to the US Equal Employment Opportunity Commission. She answered, "In almost all cases sexual liberty should win, because that's the only way that the dignity of gay people can be affirmed in any realistic manner."[392] The editorial of America's leading journal on religion and public life, *First Things*, responded to Feldblum's comment, "It's a frank statement that clarifies how few restraints progressives feel once they are convinced that they are fighting for 'the great civil-rights issue of our times'."[393]

Laws normalising gay 'marriage' will be the big stick needed for "queer rights" to beat religious freedom into legal submission. And any who pretend otherwise are deluding themselves.

The Bishop before the Inquisition

Consider a local example of this showdown. In June 2015, Rodney Croome, the head of the gay lobby group Australian Marriage Equality, took offence at the Pastoral Letter from Australia's Catholic Bishops entitled "Don't Mess with Marriage".[394] This gracious, beautifully written booklet conveyed traditional Catholic teaching on marriage to students in Catholic schools, but that was unacceptable to the homosexual lobby. Croome issued a media release: "I urge everyone who finds [the Catholic booklet] offensive and inappropriate, including teachers, parents and students, to complain to the Anti-Discrimination Commissioner."[395] In response to his incitement, a transgender Tasmanian Greens candidate took Hobart's Archbishop Julian Porteous to the Anti-Discrimination Commission. Presciently, the Bishops' Pastoral Letter included this passage: "People who adhere to the perennial and natural definition of marriage will be characterised as old-fashioned, even bigots, who must answer to the law." The Tasmanian Anti-Discrimination Commissioner, Robin Banks, was inclined to agree: she judged that the Bishops had a case to answer. Columnist for *The Australian*, Angela Shanahan, wrote at the time,

> Since when has teaching your children what you and most of the world's population believe to be right, been a thought crime? Since when have those beliefs, enshrined in the law of the land, and always seen as positive and good, suddenly been deemed harmful? Since when has a well-liked member of the church's hierarchy been told when and where he should disseminate fundamental Christian doctrine, and threatened with being hauled up to an anti-discrimination body? Since last week, that's when.[396]

And consider: this harassment is happening while we have no law for same-sex 'marriage'. What level of intimidation might the church expect once homosexual 'marriage', and therefore homosexual behaviour, is enshrined in the law as normal and right? To quote a pertinent saying from the Good Friday narrative: "If men do these things when the wood is green, what will they do when the wood is dry?"

When I met Archbishop Porteous in Hobart in 2015 I said, "Your Grace, remember that you are not the problem. The existence of laws that suppress free argument on matters of public importance – that is the problem." I made the same point to Mr Croome in a debate on Hobart ABC radio: "You don't set government lawyers onto people that you disagree with, Rodney. You don't take the Archbishop to the Thought Police because you don't like his tone in his book. That is not how men in a free society settle disputes."[397] But increasingly it is, as the homosexual juggernaut uses the force of law to crush foundational liberties of speech and conscience.

The existence of 'human rights' commissions is a central part of the problem. These 'progressive' institutions exist primarily, IMHO, to impose the views of Australia's social elite upon the rest of us. Their effective role is to police unacceptable opinion, those old-fashioned, conservative, patriotic or Christian voices that jar against inner-city sensibilities. So how apt that a former Anti-Discrimination Commissioner for NSW and homosexual-rights advocate Chris Puplick should also put the boot into the Bishops.

Puplick wrote in *The Australian* that the Porteous case was about "vilification and hate speech".[398] Among several false assertions about

Church teaching, Puplick claimed that "homosexual people are described as 'intrinsically disordered'." That is not so and the booklet does not say that. The official teaching in the Catholic Catechism reads: "Basing itself on sacred scripture ... tradition has always declared that homosexual acts are intrinsically disordered".[399] The acts are described as "disordered"; the individuals are described as "created in the image of God and loved by Him", as the booklet says. There is a big difference between calling a person "disordered" and an act "disordered", and Puplick would know that. The Catechism takes pains to be pastorally sensitive, noting that individuals "do not choose their homosexual condition; for most of them it is a trial. They must be accepted with respect, compassion, and sensitivity. Every sign of unjust discrimination in their regard should be avoided." Puplick also plays the child abuse card, a predictable but nasty tactic which seeks to smear the whole church at every opportunity with the filth of a few. He writes,

> Even more egregiously, at a time when the whole nation is shocked and scandalised by the revelations of widespread child abuse (especially in the churches themselves), supporters of marriage equality are accused by the bishops of "messing with kids".

Does that accusation sound remotely plausible? Are supporters of same-sex 'marriage' really accused by the Bishops of sexually interfering with children, as Puplick suggests? Consider the injustice of his insinuation, when you read the actual paragraph from the Bishops' booklet:

> Sometimes people claim that children do just fine with two mums or two dads and that there is "no difference" between households with same-sex parents and heterosexual parents. But sociological research, as well as the long experience of Church and society, attests to the importance for children of having, as far as possible, both a mother and father. 'Messing with marriage', therefore, is also 'messing with kids'. It is gravely unjust to them.

So the Bishops make a comment about the injustice of messing with a child's optimal family structure; Puplick ignores their point and twists it into a chance to shame the church on paedophilia. Such an uncivil response comes from a man who has spent his professional life as a Commissioner urging civility on others – on pain of punishment.

It is important to call justice-crusaders like Puplick to account for unjust comments, but he is not the only offender. Returning to my Hobart ABC radio debate, Rodney Croome told thousands of listeners that the Catholic booklet says homosexual people "are a grave threat to others".[400] Not so, I replied: "I've read that booklet and nowhere does it say that homosexuals are a grave threat to others. That is simply false."[401] As with Puplick, Mr Croome seems to feel free to invent Church teaching if that helps foment outrage against the Bishops. Despite my call for him to retract and apologise, Croome has never (to my knowledge) withdrawn that false and inflammatory accusation. And the media do not seem interested in calling him to account. The media, on the whole, occupy the same self-satisfied moral high ground as the gay activists, acting as if there is clearly one side of this debate to be framed sympathetically and one to be smeared. Anyone who dares assert that a child should have, where possible, both a mother and father will be labelled a bigot; anyone who dares believe that homosexual acts are wrong must be shamed and silenced by any means necessary.

Archbishop Porteous was tied up for the best part of a year in expensive, time-consuming legal proceedings before a decision was made (for strategic reasons, in my view) to drop the case, just as the federal election was called.[402] The transgender Green, Delaney, did not retract the substance of the complaint at all, but this assault on freedom of speech and religion was playing badly in the media – so the claws of ideological coercion were temporarily sheathed. Porteous pointed out that, while the Church had stood its ground, nothing had been resolved:

> What we don't know is whether myself or somebody else who makes another public statement in support of traditional marriage could actually have a complaint registered against them. It leaves those who want to speak out about the traditional relationship of marriage feeling somewhat intimidated (and it creates) an unfair advantage for those who support a change in the definition of marriage.[403]

The trashing of religious liberty

Ah yes, you say, but if 'marriage equality' became law, surely our legislators are clever enough to write in protections for religious people? If only. Any talk of authentic religious freedom under a regime of homosexual 'marriage' is naïve. The same week in 2015 as the Bishops' booklet was published, Ireland voted for 'marriage equality' while promising to protect religious freedom. That truce lasted six months. Under Ireland's Employment Equality Act, a church school can no longer dismiss homosexual activists who defy church teaching on marriage. That effectively negates the church's liberty to educate their children according to their values and beliefs.

A few months later, a court in Canada (which has same-sex 'marriage') ruled that law graduates from a private Christian University, Trinity Western, cannot be registered to practice as lawyers because of a pledge they make to uphold man-woman marriage:

> At the heart of the dispute was Trinity Western's "community covenant" or code of conduct, which all students are required to agree to. It includes requiring students to abstain from gossip, obscene language, prejudice, harassment, lying, cheating, stealing, pornography, drunkenness and sexual intimacy "that violates the sacredness of marriage between a man and a woman." "The part of TWU's Community Covenant in issue in this appeal is deeply discriminatory to the LGBTQ community, and it hurts," the appeal court ruling said. "The Law Society of Upper Canada's decision not to accredit TWU was indeed a reasonable conclusion." The appeal court also noted that while the university might find it more difficult to operate a law school without accreditation in Ontario, it wasn't prevented from running the facility in accordance with its beliefs.[404]

Yes, it would be quite difficult to operate a law school when your graduates are unemployable, one might think. Note that last contemptuous comment from the court, for that is the flavour of things to come: "You can have your disgusting reactionary beliefs, but don't let them outside your disgusting church walls into the public square, or we will shut you down." And this is happening in Canada, our sister country in the family of once-free English-speaking nations. Commenting on this case, former federal Labor Minister Gary Johns writes,

> Just contemplate that for a moment. Staff and students of the university freely enter into a covenant that deems that only married heterosexual couples may have sex. The Law Society argues that discriminates against LGBTQ couples and withholds accreditation. Young graduates from the law school will be unemployable in the profession. How is that reasonable or of public benefit? Does the covenant make these graduates bad lawyers? LGBTQ couples could, of course, attend another university.[405]

He's right, but he misses the political point: the hard-won LGBTQ victory for 'marriage equality' has given that lobby the legal high ground to command the rest of the culture war, including shutting down Christian colleges that won't get with the programme. Let nobody be so trivial, so condescending, as to pretend we can have religious liberty under a 'marriage equality' law that is hostile to traditional values on sex and marriage. Listen to the top legal mind in the US, Supreme Court Chief Justice John Roberts. He and three of his fellow justices were scathing about the prospects for authentic religious liberty after 'marriage equality' was imposed on the entire USA by their five fellow unelected judges in March 2015.[406] Chief Justice Roberts was particularly discouraged by the way the majority judges went out of their way to classify opponents of homosexual 'marriage' as "bigoted":

> Unfortunately, people of faith can take no comfort in the treatment they receive from the majority today ... The most discouraging aspect of today's decision is the extent to which the majority feels compelled to sully those on the other side of the debate ... These apparent assaults on the character of fair-minded people will have an effect, in society and in court. Moreover, they are entirely gratuitous ... It is one thing for the majority to conclude that the Constitution protects a right to same-sex marriage; it is something else to portray everyone who does not share the majority's 'better informed understanding' as bigoted.[407]

Fellow dissenter, Justice Alito, pointed out that the majority's contemptuous opinion put opponents of homosexual 'marriage' on a moral par with the racists of an earlier era:

> It will be used to vilify Americans who are unwilling to assent to the

new orthodoxy. In the course of its opinion, the majority compares traditional marriage laws to laws that denied equal treatment for African-Americans and women. The implications of this analogy will be exploited by those who are determined to stamp out every vestige of dissent ... I assume that those who cling to old beliefs will be able to whisper their thoughts in the recesses of their homes, but if they repeat those views in public, they will risk being labeled as bigots and treated as such by governments, employers, and schools.[408]

Chief Justice Roberts is astonished at the majority's trivial notion of religious liberty, as if it were merely the freedom to hold private beliefs and did not extend to living out one's life in accordance with those beliefs: "The majority graciously suggests that religious believers may continue to 'advocate' and 'teach' their views of marriage." But as Roberts points out, the First Amendment is not just about ideas but actions; it "guarantees ... the freedom to 'exercise' religion. Ominously, that is not a word the majority uses." His colleague, Justice Thomas, expanded on this critique of religious liberty-lite:

> Religious liberty is about more than just the protection for "religious organizations and persons ... as they seek to teach the principles that are so fulfilling and so central to their lives and faiths." Religious liberty is about freedom of action in matters of religion generally, and the scope of that liberty is directly correlated to the civil restraints placed upon religious practice.[409]

Here in Australia there are reassuring noises about guaranteeing religious liberty within a regime of 'marriage equality'. Believe that by all means if you are a trusting soul and it gives you comfort, but you do not understand that the sexual ideologues are playing for keeps. There should be no pretence in our Parliament that churches and their associated institutions will have lasting exemption from anti-discrimination law. Such pretence serves as a sugar coating for the passage of a gay 'marriage' pill, but the sweetness will soon pass.

The Bishops' booklet records a few of many other examples of harassment of religious people who fall foul of rainbow politics:

- The City of Coeur d'Alene, Idaho, ordered Christian ministers to perform same-sex weddings under pain of

180 days' imprisonment for each day the ceremony is not performed.
- The City of Houston, Texas, has subpoenaed pastors to submit sermons to legal scrutiny when discussing sexuality.
- Church-based adoption agencies in Britain and some American states have been forced to close for not placing children with same-sex couples: for example, Evangelical Child Family Services in Illinois (US) was shut down for its refusal to do so.
- The Chief Rabbi of Amsterdam has been threatened with prosecution for 'hate speech' merely for restating the position of his religious tradition.[410]

And the examples keep rolling in. A British Conservative MP, Mark Spencer, said in 2015 that the laws used to clamp down on terrorist hate-speech "should be used against Christian teachers who teach children that gay marriage is wrong".[411] What more chilling example could there be of the intention of the elite to expunge unacceptable views on homosexuality? And it shows that the totalitarian itch is found in people of all political stripes: a willingness to use the force of law to abolish from the public square, and ultimately from the private mind, any moral or religious objection to homosexual acts or homosexual 'marriage'.

In June 2016, in a country with 'marriage equality', another church leader has been threatened with legal action for criticising the homosexual agenda and its consequences for the family. We read that Spanish Cardinal Antonio Cañizares "is under fire for issuing warnings about a "gay empire" and denouncing the perils of "gender theory" in a recent homily, with pro-LGBT associations threatening to sue him for being homophobic."[412] The offending comments, made to Catholics to mark the end of the school year in Spain, seem fair enough to me:

> We have legislation contrary to the family, the action of political and social forces, with added movements and actions of the gay empire, of ideas such as radical feminism, or the most insidious of all, gender theory.

The report noted a similarly strong stand by Pope Francis:

> "Gender theory is an error of the human mind that leads to so

much confusion," [the Pope] said in March 2015, when visiting the southern Italian city of Naples. Later in that speech he said "the family is under attack" because of it.

Far from caving in to threats of prosecution, the elderly Spanish Cardinal ramped up his defiance against the "most insidious and destructive ideology of humanity in all its history, which is gender ideology, which global powers try to impose upon us through more or less covert innocuous legislations, which mustn't be obeyed". Go, Antonio!

The "gay empire" referred to by the Cardinal seems intent on splitting the church off from the rest of our culture, creating an impassable divide between western civilisation and the institution that nurtured it for more than a millennium. The end game of the "empire" is to compel acquiescence from all of society in all matters homosexual/bisexual/transsexual, and that means above all "de-authorising the Judaeo-Christian influence in our society". Any who pretend that churches and people of faith will be allowed to uphold and live out their beliefs in their schools and hospitals and businesses under a regime of rainbow enforcement are deluding themselves.

Some religious people are starting to understand the threat and consider their response. We read in *The Australian* in June 2016,

> The Presbyterian Church will halt all co-operation with the state on the matter of marriage if same-sex marriage is legalised. It will refuse to conduct any state marriages and some of its pastors will encourage Presbyterians to live outside the legal institution of marriage. They would live in de facto relationships as far as civil law is concerned.[413]

The proposal will be presented to the Presbyterian General Assembly in September by a senior Victorian pastor, Rev. Darren Middleton:

> Mr Middleton believes it is only a matter of time before anti-discrimination laws are wielded as a blunt club against religious freedom. "Those who seek to redefine marriage will seek to redefine freedom of speech and freedom of religion, as surely as night follows day," he said.

I'm with Rev. Middleton. By all means, let the 'progressives' and sexual ideologues do their worst to "de-authorise the Judaeo-Christian influence in our society" by trashing the truth of marriage, but spare us the patronising line that it will be business as usual for the churches. The radicals want destruction of Christian culture, as they have since the days of Marx, and with the cultural wrecking ball of homosexual 'marriage' they will get it.

Let the Shepherds speak

In this twilight of religious liberty, before gentle "haters" like Archbishop Porteous and Cardinal Cañizares and other faithful Christians are silenced by anti-discrimination law, there is poignancy in the fading voices of pastors teaching their flock about marriage, family and sexual right and wrong. There is also curiosity as to what sort of hateful things they teach. To quench that curiosity, I have gathered a few statements from a remarkable colloquium of four hundred religious leaders and scholars in 2014, guests of Pope Francis at the *Humanum* conference in Rome.[414] To these excerpts I will add passages from the Australian Catholic Bishops' booklet *Don't Mess with Marriage (DMWM)*[415] that so offended Mr Croome and also the recent publication from Pope Francis, *Amoris Laetitia* (March 2016).[416] And no, I am not a Catholic, but I recognise words that are wise and beautiful. Here are some important themes in their teaching:

1. Marriage is founded on a natural, timeless reality:

Australian Catholic Bishops:

> The word 'marriage' isn't simply a label that can be attached and transferred to different types of relationships as the fashion of the day dictates. It has an intrinsic or natural meaning prior to anything we may invent or the state may legislate. *(DMWM)*

Rev Dr Russell D. Moore is president of the (USA) Southern Baptist Ethics & Religious Liberty Commission:

> We recognize that marriage, and the sexual difference on which

it is built, is grounded in a natural order bearing rights and responsibilities that was not crafted by any human state, and cannot thus be redefined by any human state. (*Humanum*)

Pope Francis:

Family is an anthropological fact – a socially and culturally related fact. We cannot qualify it with concepts of an ideological nature that are relevant only in a single moment of history and then pass by. (*Humanum*)

2. Marriage is built around the rights and needs of the child:

Rabbi Lord Jonathan Sacks is former chief rabbi of the UK and the Commonwealth and Professor of Judaic Thought at New York University:

The family – man, woman, and child – is not one lifestyle among many ... For any society, the family is the crucible of its future, and for the sake of our children's future, we must be its defenders. (*Humanum*)

Pope Francis:

The family is the foundation of coexistence and a guarantee against social fragmentation. Children have a right to grow up in a family with a father and a mother capable of creating a suitable environment for the child's development and emotional maturity. (*Humanum*)

Australian Catholic Bishops:

The decision to commit permanently and exclusively to sharing the whole of one's life with someone of the opposite sex and to raise any children that are the fruit, embodiment and extension of that union, is good in itself, even if no children are conceived. But because children are the natural result of marital life and are best reared within the commitment of marriage, this makes marriage also an essential part of the propagation and nurturing of the human family. (*DMWM*)

3. Other relationships are not marriage:

Pope Francis:

> In discussing the dignity and mission of the family, the Synod Fathers observed that, "as for proposals to place unions between homosexual persons on the same level as marriage, there are absolutely no grounds for considering homosexual unions to be in any way similar or even remotely analogous to God's plan for marriage and family." (*Amoris Laetitia*, 252)

Australian Catholic Bishops:

> To say that other friendships are not marriages is not to demean those other friendships or the individuals concerned, but merely to recognise that marriage is the covenant of a man and a woman to live as husband and wife, exclusively and for life, and open to the procreation of children. (*DMWM*)

4. Opposition to same-sex 'marriage' is entirely consistent with love for same-sex attracted people:

Rev Dr Rick Warren gave the invocation at President Obama's first inauguration. He is founder and senior pastor of Saddleback Church, California:

> Our culture has accepted two lies: that if you disagree with someone's lifestyle you must hate them or are afraid of them, and that to love someone means that you must agree with everything they believe or do. Both are nonsense. (*Humanum*)

Australian Catholic Bishops:

> We all know and love people with same-sex attraction. They are our brothers and sisters, sons and daughters, friends and neighbours. They need love and support like anyone else. But pretending that their relationships are 'marriages' is not fair or just to them. As Christians we must be willing to present the truth about marriage, family and sexuality and to do so charitably and lovingly. (*DMWM*)

Rabbi Lord Jonathan Sacks:

> No one, surely, wants to go back to the narrow prejudices of the past ... But our compassion for those who choose to live differently should not inhibit us from being advocates for the single most humanizing institution in history. (*Humanum*)

Jacqueline C. Rivers PhD (Harvard) is director of the Seymour Institute for Black Church and Policy Studies:

> To insist on the truth that neither mothers nor fathers are expendable is not to dishonour anyone's dignity. Every human being is beloved and precious in God's sight. The mere issue of an individual's sexual inclinations (or even sinful practices) cannot alter this. God loves all of us, and reaches out in love to sinners. Furthermore, as Christians and people of faith we are commanded to love each of our neighbors as ourselves. Therefore, we embrace all people, regardless of their struggles. However, though all people are created equal, all sexual practices are not. (*Humanum*)

5. Denying the true meaning of marriage will have grave consequences:

Rabbi Lord Jonathan Sacks:

> It will go down in history as one of the tragic instances of what Friedrich Hayek called "the fatal conceit" that somehow we know better than the wisdom of the ages, and can defy the lessons of biology and history. (*Humanum*)

Australian Catholic Bishops:

> If the civil definition of marriage were changed to include 'same-sex marriage' then our law and culture would teach that marriage is merely about emotional union of any two (or more?) people. All marriages would come to be defined by intensity of emotion rather than a union founded on sexual complementarity and potential fertility. Husbands and wives, mothers and fathers, will be seen to be wholly interchangeable social constructs as gender would no longer matter. (*DMWM*)

Jacqueline C. Rivers:

> Black children have suffered the most as a result of the decline of marriage in the black community. The deleterious effects of being raised in female-headed households have been well documented … Today, marriage faces new threats as the divinely established order of marriage between one man and one woman is challenged … The unavoidable message is a profoundly false and damaging one: that children do not need a mother and a father in a permanent, complementary bond. (*Humanum*)

6. The church will not abandon its teaching on sexual right and wrong:

Australian Catholic Bishops:

> Christians believe that all people including those with same-sex attraction are called by God to live chastely and that, by God's grace and the support of friends, they can and should

grow in fulfilling God's plan. (*DMWM*)

Rev Dr Russell D. Moore:

> Many would tell us that contemporary people will not hear us if we contradict the assumptions of the sexual revolution. We ought to conceal, or at least avoid mentioning, the specifics of what we believe about the definition of marriage, about the limits of human sexuality, about the created and good nature of gender, and speak instead in more generic spiritual terms ... To jettison or to minimize the Christian sexual ethic is to abandon the message Jesus handed to us, and we have no authority to do this. Moreover, to do so is to abandon our love for our neighbors. We cannot offer the world the half-gospel ... which exempts from God's judgment those sins we fear are too fashionable to address. (*Humanum*)

Rev Rick Warren:

> The church cannot be salt and light in a crumbling culture if it caves in to the sexual revolution and fails to provide a countercultural witness. It is a myth that we must give up biblical truth on sexuality and marriage in order to evangelize ... I warn those flirting with this myth that it would be a terrible mistake for the church. (*Humanum*)

7. The church stands firm against state intimidation on same-sex 'marriage':

Pope Francis:

> It is unacceptable "that local Churches should be subjected to pressure in this matter and that international bodies should make financial aid to poor countries dependent on the introduction of laws to establish 'marriage' between persons of the same sex." (*Amoris Laetitia, 252*)

Jacqueline C. Rivers:

> Christians who stand against these developments are in some cases under threat of losing their jobs and their businesses. Those who promote what they call marriage equality have unjustly appropriated the language and the mantle of the black struggle in the United States, the civil rights movement. But there can be no equivalence between blacks' experience of slavery and oppression and the circumstances of homosexuals ... God is calling us to stand, in humility and love, against the movement to destroy marriage. God is calling us to defend innocent children whose futures are at risk. (*Humanum*)

Rev Rick Warren:

> Every church leader needs training in how to represent Christ when attacked. But it's a fact: if you stand courageously for the truth, you will be attacked. How do you stay winsome under attack? First, remember your reward: "Blessed are you when people insult you, persecute you and falsely say all kinds of evil against you because of me. Rejoice and be glad, because great is your reward in heaven..." We must be willing to be ridiculed, and even to suffer, for the truth ... Second, live for an audience of One. Remember who we answer to at the end of the day ... As Saint Peter has said, "We must obey God rather than men." (*Humanum*)

8. Marriage reflects cosmic order and divine purpose and is not for changing:

N.T. Wright, former Bishop of Durham in the Church of England:

> Right there at the start of the whole Bible ... we have this rich symbolic account of God's good creation in which, at its very heart, the coming together of male and female is itself

a signpost pointing to that great complementarity of God's whole creation, of heaven and earth belonging together. When we then jump in a huge sweep to the very end of the Bible … we find in Revelation 21 and 22 substantially the same thing … the new Jerusalem is coming down from heaven like a bride adorned for her husband. This symbolism of marriage, of male and female coming together (only now it is the church which is the new Jerusalem, coming together with Christ as the bridegroom), tells us that here we find the very heart of God's intended creation … That is why, I believe, the biblical picture of man and woman together in marriage is not something about which we can say, "Oh well, they had some funny ideas back then. We know better now"… Marriage is a sign of all things in heaven and on earth coming together in Christ. That's why it is a tough calling. But that is why, also, it is central and non-negotiable. (*Humanum*)

Rev Rick Warren:

Ephesians 5 explains that marriage is a metaphor, a model of the mystery of Christ's love for his bride and body:

"For this reason a man will leave his father and mother and be united to his wife, and the two will become one flesh." This is a profound mystery – but I am talking about Christ and the church. However, each one of you also must love his wife as he loves himself, and the wife must respect her husband.

This is the deepest meaning of marriage. This is the most profound purpose of marriage. This is the strongest reason marriage can only be between a man and a woman. No other relationship, including the parent-child relationship, can portray this intimate union. To redefine marriage would destroy the picture that God intends for marriage to portray. We cannot cave on this issue. (*Humanum*)

Rev Dr Russell D. Moore:

> One key aspect of this unveiled mystery is that the family structure is not an arbitrary expression of nature or of the will of God. Marriage and family are instead archetypes, icons of God's purpose for the universe. When the apostle appealed to the Genesis 2 account of the creation order, explaining why a man leaves his father and mother to cleave to his wife, and that they become one flesh (Eph. 5:31), he wrote of something that every human being can see, even without divine revelation ... We are not created as "spouse A" and "spouse B," but as man and woman, and in marriage as husband and wife, and in parenting as father and mother. (*Humanum*)

Rabbi Lord Jonathan Sacks:

> As they were about to leave Eden and face the world as we know it, a place of darkness, Adam gave his wife the first gift of love, a personal name. And at that moment, God responded to them both in love, and made them garments to clothe their nakedness, or as Rabbi Meir put it, "garments of light." And so it has been ever since, that when a man and woman turn to one another in a bond of faithfulness, God robes them in garments of light, and we come as close as we will ever get to God himself, bringing new life into being, turning the prose of biology into the poetry of the human spirit, redeeming the darkness of the world by the radiance of love. (*Humanum*)

'The darkness drops again...'

Rabbi Sacks turns our mind to the world's most poignant dreamtime story. The archetypal belonging-together of man and woman; the drama of passion and compassion, joy and shame; the tragic vocation of begetting life but only at the risk of the beloved woman's death and all sustained only by the sweat of the man's brow; death and a return to dust that makes our fleeting existence so puzzling and precious.

Above all, this most ancient story is an assertion of the deep sanity of the love of man and woman, an archetype of primal nature and blessed by God as "very good". Historically, the culture of man-woman faithfulness that flowed from Genesis and was reaffirmed so forcefully by the Jewish Rabbi Jesus was a radical rebuke to the unconstrained sexual practices of the surrounding nations of the ancient world. And if we are to understand the moral and spiritual consequences of the move to deconstruct man-woman marriage and re-create a culture without sexual boundaries, it would help to take a brief look back at those societies.

In the view of that great secular Jew, Sigmund Freud, civilisational vitality could only be achieved by the discipline of widespread sexual repression: the imposition of boundaries. A Jewish author, Dennis Prager, makes the same observation when comparing the progress of Judaeo-Christian civilisation with pagan society of the ancient world:

> Man's nature, undisciplined by values, will allow sex to dominate his life and the life of society ... It is not overstated to say that the Torah's prohibition of non-marital sex made the creation of Western civilization possible. Societies that did not place boundaries around sexuality were stymied in their development. The subsequent dominance of the Western world can, to a significant extent, be attributed to the sexual revolution initiated by Judaism and later carried forward by Christianity.[417]

In Judaism, the assertion of marital faithfulness was a revolt against the idolatrous sexual polymorphism of pagan tribes. Psychiatrist, Dr Jeffrey Satinover, links the cultural with the psychological:

> The idolatry warned against in both Hebrew and Christian Scripture is not some vague intellectual nodding to a wood or stone model, but rather the repeated attraction to an ecstatic, pagan, orgiastic form of nature-worship—involving both male and female ritual prostitution in an unlimited variety of sexual forms. The overwhelming power of sexual gratification is what makes it so susceptible to becoming a true compulsion. The Bible therefore most often condemns ritualized sexual compulsion as a quintessential act of idolatry ... Thus the Apostle Paul cried out to all those in the Roman Empire who would listen, calling them away from the sexual worship of their many gods to the worship of

the Holy One of Israel. These "gods" were but the multicultural variants of the same Baal and Astarte and Molech against whose worship the earlier Israelite prophets had similarly cried out to the Jewish people, making clear the link between idolatry and unconstrained sexuality.[418]

"Idolatry" seems a quaintly archaic word, but the psychological force it represents is undiminished, based on the addictive and corrupting power of unconstrained sexuality. The ancient Judaic sexual revolution away from pagan polymorphism to closely constrained monogamy was the antithesis of our own counter-revolution of the last fifty years. Our own revolt has, in Satinover's view, brought our culture closer to the unconstrained sexuality (the essence of idolatry) of the pagan world: "A biblically informed perspective on our own era would consider it to be similarly idolatrous: dominated by materialistic sexual hedonism undergirded by a secularized, skeptical, or pop-spiritual, quasi-occult theology."[419]

Of course, most of the "materialistic sexual hedonism" he refers to is heterosexual in our society, but his professional understanding of the homosexual drive is one of an often-supercharged form of sexual compulsion. It is an additional powerful impulse towards a culture of unconstrained sexuality. He explains the demoralising power of any compulsive / addictive behaviour:

> The compulsions are neither simple choices nor true illnesses. They are a category unto themselves that includes elements of both choice and disease. They are a process, a way or path by which a life – a free, moral life – is progressively, not all at once, undone. It is this erosion of moral capacity that makes these pre-eminently spiritual conditions ... Thus we identify a whole class of non-illnesses that nonetheless make people sick at heart. This is what the Bible calls "idolatry," the central sin that wrought the destruction of ancient Israel – as it does of all people and nations.[420]

His depiction of ancient idolatry energised by compulsive sex-without-boundaries has a strange resonance with the slogan for genderless 'marriage', "Love knows no boundaries". As he notes, "the hallmark of a society in which all sexual constraints have been set aside is that finally it sanctions homosexuality as well."[421] Satinover gives historical context to our present struggle over the normalisation of homosexuality – and beyond that, as we now know, of pansexuality and total gender fluidity. He sees it is a recrudescence in modern times of the ancient confrontation between a moral/spiritual culture of man-woman faithfulness and a culture of unconstrained sexuality:

> Because it is not really a battle over mere sexuality, but rather over which spirit shall claim our allegiance, the cultural and political battle over homosexuality has become in many respects the defining moment for our society. It has implications that go far beyond the surface matter of "gay rights." And so the more important dimension of this battle is not the political one, it is the one for the individual human soul.[422]

Perhaps, like me, you feel out of your depth at this point. But the battle for the individual human soul is core business for the pastors considered in this chapter, and they are the ones who understand the dark things of a culture in archetypal, spiritual terms. That is why their potentially powerful voices must be silenced by force of law if the new (but ancient) creed of unconstrained sexuality is to successfully "de-authorise the Judaeo-Christian influence in our society." Once that creed prevails, the primal warp in the human psyche that gave us the soul-destroying rites of Baal and Molech will manifest in a modern way; the raging spirit of idolatrous Nero, chief persecutor of first-century Christians and pioneer of gay 'marriage', can make a contemporary comeback. The gentle, sexually constrained truth of marriage and family will be banished again to the catacombs; the faith founded on Bethlehem, on the near-sacred love between mother and baby and devoted dad, will be persecuted with two millennia of pent-up hatred. William Yeats, the mystical Irish poet, sensed the 'second coming' of an ancient darkness:[423]

> ...A shape with lion body and the head of a man,
> A gaze blank and pitiless as the sun,
> Is moving its slow thighs, while all about it
> Reel shadows of the indignant desert birds.
> The darkness drops again; but now I know
> That twenty centuries of stony sleep
> Were vexed to nightmare by a rocking cradle,
> And what rough beast, its hour come round at last,
> Slouches towards Bethlehem to be born?

11

BIGOTS, BAKERS AND THE THOUGHT POLICE

"Pro-traditional marriage doctor cops vandalism spray"
ABC Southern Queensland, June 2, 2015.[424]

How bracing it is to be on the wrong side of history! Bernard Keane, political editor at *Crikey*, tweets his forty thousand followers that my friend Lyle Shelton, managing director of the Australian Christian Lobby is "a nauseating piece of filth" for his opposition to same-sex 'marriage'.[425] I am declared a "bigot" in big red painted letters on the wall of my medical centre, courtesy of a local anarchist.[426] On the same day as the vandalism, a gent called Joel emails to inform me that "all the people in my circles would like to punch you in the face".[427] Just one of dozens of such charming messages.

What an honour it is to cop this sort of abuse for the sake of something so nearly sacred: the life between mother, father and child. And yet, how contemptible that a mature society like ours seeks to silence and demonise defenders of natural marriage – of the law of the land as it has always been. In a powerful article, "Gay marriage: coercion dolled up as human rights", the editor of *Spiked*, Brendan O'Neill, shares this disdain:

> There is a morally coercive streak to the gay-marriage movement, which seems to desire not just tolerance of its ideas, but 'psychological acceptance and positive affirmation' of them by everyone. To this end, businesses run by individuals who are less than keen on gay marriage have found themselves boycotted against, protested against, demonised by Twittermobs. Individuals who have voted in favour of traditional marriage in referendums have been denounced as 'hateful', 'brainwashed', 'knuckle-draggers' ... The impact of all these shrill assaults on opponents of gay marriage, of this often media-led branding of critics of gay marriage as 'phobic' and irrational, has been to chill debate, to encourage one side in the discussion to shut the hell up or risk 'ostracism from public life'.[428]

Censorship by the media

The ostracism and bias is evident even with government owned media like SBS and the Australian Broadcasting Corporation (ABC), which are legally obliged to be impartial. The ABC's own *Media Watch* programme, the High Court for all journalistic mischief, admitted this bias against our side of the marriage debate in a remarkable episode on August 17, 2015.

Paul Barry issued the judgement:

> Are opponents of marriage equality getting an equal run in the media? Or at least a fair hearing? We don't think they are ... For example, none of the commercial TV stations covered the launch of the Marriage Alliance campaign. And major one-on-one interviews on radio and TV have also been out of kilter with two key spokespeople for marriage equality, Rodney Croome and Christine Forster, scoring 32 interviews between them in the first 12 days of August and by our count, two key speakers against – Sophie York and David van Gend – scoring a grand total of only 12 ... I am a supporter of marriage equality. But, as we're constantly being reminded, this is a conscience issue and an important change that's being proposed, and surely both sides of the debate have an equal right to be heard.[429]

Indeed we do, but will Their ABC be professional enough to show impartiality, even through gritted teeth, during the national plebiscite debate on marriage? Will their partner in crime, SBS? For Paul Barry reached his judgement without even mentioning the grossest act of bias by taxpayer-funded media against our side of the marriage debate, the act of ideological censorship committed by SBS under its openly gay CEO, Michael Ebeid.

SBS had booked and confirmed the Australian Marriage Forum TV ad, "What about equality for kids?" for broadcast during their coverage of the Sydney Gay and Lesbian Mardi Gras in 2015. The Mardi Gras Parade is a protest march, which had its usual 'Marriage Equality' float and political messages in 2015. Our ad was a gentle but direct counter-protest, standing as it were in the path of the Mardi Gras saying "Stop! It's not just about you adults. Think of the child!" The 30 second pitch (which had no professional actors, just me and a few friends) ran like this:

> *Mother:* We hear a lot about 'Marriage Equality', but what about equality for kids?
>
> *Doctor:* Children have an equal right, wherever possible, to both a mum and a dad. So-called 'marriage equality' forces a child to miss out on a mother, or a father. That's not 'equality' for the kids who miss out. That's not marriage.

Mother: Give every child their chance of a mum AND a dad.[430]

Two commercial channels in Sydney showed the ad as the parade got underway, but with one day's notice, SBS pulled the ad without any reason given.[431] This became a big issue of free speech, covered in all national media. To their credit, prominent people who disagreed with the Australian Marriage Forum's position nevertheless defended our right to be heard and condemned SBS for their censorship. Tim Wilson, the openly gay human rights commissioner; Senator David Leyonhjelm who was proposing a same-sex 'marriage' Bill in the Senate; even the head of *Get Up!* all agreed the ad should not have been banned.[432]

This news story marked the moment at which, in principle at least, we won the battle for free speech: the right for our side of this great matter to have its say, not to be demonised and silenced.[433] Admittedly, we did not win over the CEO of SBS to this more civil and open-minded position. An unrepentant Mr Ebeid was grilled two months later at a Senate estimates hearing by Queensland Senator Matt Canavan, whose office issued this statement:

> In evidence to the estimates hearing, SBS confirmed that in fact they would have put to air an advertisement in favour of same-sex marriage, while refusing to air an advertisement in favour of traditional marriage. That admission directly demonstrates interference in free speech, self-censorship and political selectivity – in other words, bias. Senator Canavan told Mr Ebeid "You are a public broadcaster using public money and clearly favour one side of the argument over the other. You are meant to be fair and balanced."[434]

It is not my intention to document the many and varied episodes of bias and abuse, of vanishing Facebook sites and mass-attacks on our web page and tedious threats of violence, since that is only to be expected from the torchbearers of tolerance, but I mention the ABC and SBS because they are publicly funded by both sides of the marriage debate and they have been found guilty of political bias. These public institutions must now suppress the ideological itches of their journalists and management and fulfil their statutory duty to be impartial in this national debate.

Censorship by the elite

On the subject of public institutions and ideological itches, we think back to the previous chapter and the decision of an Anti-Discrimination Commissioner to call an Archbishop to account for teaching Catholic doctrine on marriage. The effect, and possibly the purpose, of 'human rights' tribunals is to undermine the human right of free speech, limiting expression of public opinion to that deemed acceptable by our betters. Hold the approved 'progressive' attitudes and you will be free to speak your mind; hold unacceptable attitudes, and you will be harassed all the way to the Anti-Discrimination Tribunal. And so the machinery of political censorship is constructed under the guise of preventing offense.

Remember John Milton's cry to the English Parliament in 1644: "Give me the liberty to argue freely according to conscience, above all liberties."[435] Free speech, free argument, is at the heart of a self-governing society, and yet that liberty is being constricted throughout the developed world in the name of a new and bogus 'right not to be offended'. The greatest free-speech warrior of the West, Canadian writer Mark Steyn, speaks from experience: "In Canada, I committed the crime of 'offending' certain approved identity groups. And there is no defense to that: truth, facts, evidence are all irrelevant. If someone's 'offended', that's that: You're guilty."[436] Thanks to Steyn's magnificent push-back against the Canadian 'human rights' establishment, the Canadian Parliament repealed the vilification law under which he was harassed. In Australia that remains unfinished business.

Under the Queensland anti-vilification laws,[437] I too had a minor altercation with the thought-police for offending an approved identity group. *The Courier-Mail* in Brisbane published a forum in June 2011 entitled "Gay marriage: the case for and against".[438] I was asked to give the case against, and I opened:

> If you hold to the old-fashioned idea that a baby deserves both a mother and a father, the president of the Queensland branch of the Labor Party, Andrew Dettmer, calls your views "abominable" ... Dettmer slurred opponents [of same-sex marriage] as being no better than racists: "Discrimination against people on the basis of their gender or their sexual orientation is just as abominable as discrimination on the basis of race."

Those on my side of the marriage debate just shrug off the 'racist' slander, but those on the other side are more diligent in taking offense: my next paragraph was cited by a gay activist as "vilifying the homosexual community". These were my exact words, my very first crime against humanity:

> Yes, it is discrimination to prohibit the 'marriage' of two men, but it is just and necessary discrimination, because the only alternative is the far worse act of discrimination against children brought artificially into the world by such men, compelled to live their whole lives without a mother. Now that approaches the abominable.

That was it. For that heinous paragraph saying that a child should not be deprived of a mother and for alluding to the Labor president's archaic choice of words, an invited participant in a newspaper forum is compelled under section 124A of the Queensland Anti-Discrimination Act 1991 to attend "conciliation". Of course I had nothing to conciliate. I said to the complainant: "You are a gay activist; I am a family activist – so we disagree! Free men in a self-governing society argue their case; they don't set government lawyers onto their opponent."

Senator Ron Boswell made a speech in federal Parliament the night before my "compulsory conciliation":

> If people like Dr van Gend are forced to appear before the Anti-Discrimination Commission of Queensland, that is a threat to one of Australia's greatest freedoms: the right to free speech. It is a major disincentive to people making a contribution to debate. How has a country like Australia come to this? Anti-discrimination bodies should not be used as star chambers by those who simply do not like what someone else says.[439]

The activist's worthless complaint was withdrawn unconditionally, but not until the process had cost me time and money – and as Steyn points out, that is the whole point: "the process is the punishment". I relished this opportunity to push back against such contemptible and repressive laws, but for many people the experience would have been distressing. And so the chilling of free speech, the intimidation of free conscience, spreads and saps the vigour of the body politic.

These state and federal vilification laws are unnecessary as well as unworthy of a free people. Where free speech strays into personal attack we already have laws against defamation and, ultimately, against incitement to violence. That is enough. Free public argument is the birthright of free citizens – especially argument that offends elitist orthodoxy on matters like homosexual 'marriage'. Will speech be 'free' in the coming plebiscite debate, or will the side of the argument that displeases the elite be demonised and censored as per usual?

Crushing conscientious objectors

"Won't somebody please think of the bakers?" is the mocking line from gay activists, but it is no joke for father of five, Aaron Klein of Oregon. He was fined $135,000 and lost his livelihood as a baker because a lesbian couple demanded he bake them a wedding cake and he, in sincere conscience, declined. He had happily sold cakes to these clients for other events, but he did not want to take payment for a same-sex wedding cake, because that would go against what he believed to be right and true. The lesbian couple could have shown neighbourly tolerance and got their cake from the bakery down the road, but they preferred to take Klein to court. There they obtained a six figure payout as compensation for nearly two hundred ailments they claimed were related to the cake-refusal, including "impaired digestion," "loss of appetite," "migraine headaches," "pale and sick at home after work," "shock" and "weight gain".[440] All that without eating a mouthful!

Labor Senator Penny Wong, in her 2015 National Press Club debate with Senator Cory Bernardi,[441] said that lesbian couples would simply avoid bakers who did not want to bake them a cake, but of course the opposite is true: the whole objective is to identify those bakers, or florists, or photographers, or wedding venue proprietors who are not compliant with the gay agenda and force them to comply – or break them. Her leader, Bill Shorten, vowed before the 2016 election that there would be no conscientious liberty under a government he leads; well, not those Gillardesque words exactly, but close enough: "We don't need to water down anti-discrimination law to keep some people [who oppose same-sex marriage] happy."[442] Consider some examples of what that coercion of conscience will mean.

In May 2014, gay activist Gareth Lee walked into an Ashers bakery in Belfast and ordered a cake to be decorated with the slogan "Support gay marriage" along with the "Queer Space" logo and an image of Bert and Ernie from *Sesame Street* as the happy homosexual couple.[443] The owners, Karen and Colin McArthur, are devout Christians who politely declined the job, not wanting to provide their labour to make such a political statement. There is no shortage of bakers in Belfast but the gay activist took the young couple to the Equality Commission. A court ruling in March 2015 found them guilty of discrimination. At appeal in May 2016, the Attorney General of Northern Ireland made a memorable intervention on the young couple's behalf, saying "No one should be forced to be the mouthpiece for someone else's views when they are opposed to their own – whether in print or in icing sugar."[444] At the time of writing the outcome of their appeal is pending, but who can doubt the intimidating effect this case will have on any other baker who is asked to be a mouthpiece for LGBT activism.

Back in the US, just two months after the Supreme Court imposed same-sex 'marriage' on the nation, we read, "A suburban Denver baker who wouldn't make a wedding cake for a same-sex couple cannot cite his religious beliefs in refusing them service because it would lead to discrimination, the Colorado Court of Appeals ruled Thursday. The decision is the latest victory for gay couples, who have won similar cases in other states."[445] Indeed they have. Jack Phillips, the baker, says he gladly serves gays and lesbians in his family business but he could not in good conscience design a wedding cake for a same-sex couple when, as a Christian, he believes that marriage is the union of a man and a woman. Too bad, says the Court. Bend the knee to what you believe to be wrong, or the State will break you.

I could list a baker's dozen of such cases, but for variety consider Mrs Barronelle Stutzman, a florist in Washington State. She gently explained to a long-term gay friend and customer that she could give him flowers for any other occasion, but could not violate her faith by decorating his same-sex 'wedding'. She reflected, "As much as I loved Rob, I couldn't be a part of that".[446] The State Attorney General heard of her refusal to get with the agenda and took her to court, where she was found guilty and ordered to pay fines and costs. At the time of writing, the appeal to the Washington State Supreme Court is pending.[447] The legal expenses and toxic publicity will no doubt put this gentle Christian grandmother out of business.

It's the same with photographers. In Albuquerque, New Mexico, Elaine Huguenin and her husband, Jon, declined a job covering a same-sex ceremony. Their company, Elane Photography was happy to take pictures of gay and lesbian individuals, but a same-sex ceremony went against their belief that marriage can only be the union of a man and a woman. As always, there were plenty of other photographers willing to do the job, but the young couple was taken to the New Mexico Human Rights Commission, which ruled that the Huguenins had discriminated on the basis of sexual orientation. An appeal to the New Mexico Supreme Court in 2013 found against them, with Justice Richard Bosson ruling that the Huguenins needed to set aside their religious convictions as "the price of citizenship."[448]

And to round out the picture of this uncivil enforcement of the new LGBT 'normal', consider an elderly Mennonite Christian couple in Iowa, artists who used to hire out their art gallery for wedding functions. We read in July 2015,

> Charged with discriminating against a gay couple, the owners of another Christian family-run business are being forced to shut their doors … On August 3, 2013, a gay couple from Des Moines asked to rent Görtz Haus for their wedding. Because of their Mennonite faith, the Odgaards told the couple they could not host their wedding. Within 24 hours, the couple filed a discrimination complaint through the Iowa Civil Rights Commission … If they continued to offer wedding-related services, the Odgaards knew they could be subject to another discrimination complaint. "We didn't have a choice," Betty, 63 said. "We would be targets..." Betty said the situation drove her into a "really dark depression" – so bad, that she had to seek the help of professionals. "I'm a melancholy artist and no stranger to depression, but this took me down to the darkest I've ever been before," she said.[449]

Once again, "the price of citizenship" for people who think homosexual marriage is a desecration of true marriage is to betray that conscientious conviction or go out of business. Not because they are inconveniencing the gay clients – there are always plenty of other venues, florists, bakers or photographers who would happily take the job – but because they do the unforgivable: they conscientiously refuse to affirm all things LGBTQ. We should understand that the goal for the hard-heads of the 'marriage equality' movement is not marriage, but obtaining the legal power to compel social approval of sexual behaviour previously considered immoral. Only then will we comprehend the ruthlessness and spitefulness of these attacks on gentle citizens who only want to run their businesses according to their values and beliefs.

How ironic that the creative gifts of Christian people are now excluded from the wedding culture that they themselves nurtured over centuries. But if people think the target of gay enforcement is always overtly Christian business, think again. No less a figure than the founder of Mozilla, the creator of JavaScript, Brendan Eich, was strung up by this lynch mob. As soon as he was elevated to CEO of Mozilla Corporation on March 24, 2014, gay activists started tweeting that Eich had donated a thousand dollars to the plebiscite campaign in California in 2008 that had successfully opposed same-sex marriage. Boycott threats by *OKCupid* and widespread abuse ensued and within ten days Eich had resigned.[450] To their credit, the civilised faction of the gay lobby warned that this was a step too far, but by then Eich's career was dangling by that rainbow noose. Andrew Sullivan, wrote in "The hounding of a heretic",

> The whole episode disgusts me – as it should disgust anyone interested in a tolerant and diverse society. If this is the gay rights movement today – hounding our opponents with a fanaticism more like the religious right than anyone else – then count me out. If we are about intimidating the free speech of others, we are no better than the anti-gay bullies who came before us.[451]

Sullivan's defence of free speech was echoed by other gay activists like Conor Friedersdorf, who wrote in *The Atlantic*,

> Most vexing of all is Mozilla's attempt to present this forced resignation as if it is consistent with an embrace of diversity and openness ... Mozilla's actions will undercut tough conversations by making fewer people willing to engage in them. If you believe that an open, robust public discourse makes the world better, as they purport to, they've made the world worse.[452]

Such hand-wringing did not impress Brendan O'Neill, who told Sullivan and others, "Stop treating Brendan Eich as a one-off – gay marriage is inherently illiberal".

> Anyone who over the past few years has paid attention to the moral delegitimation of critics of gay marriage, to the state attacks on anti-gay marriage protesters, to the social ostracism of those who favour traditional marriage, to the attempt to force religious schools to teach about gay marriage, and to the Orwellian airbrushing from history of the words and identities cleaved to by the already married, cannot have been surprised by what happened to Eich. His fate wasn't the product of a handful of zealous campaigners going too far on Twitter – it was the end result of an intolerant culture, sometimes mob-like, sometimes state-enforced, that has been gaining ground for years, and which showed long before the elbowing aside of Eich that it was more than happy to ostracise, punish, criminalise and censor anyone who dared raise a peep of opposition to gay marriage. Coercion is built into gay marriage. They used to say love and marriage went together – in the gay-marriage movement, it's authoritarianism and marriage that are bedfellows.[453]

Any law normalising homosexual marriage will be a truncheon in the fist of the thought police, enforcing approved opinion on sexuality in schools, churches and businesses via their 'Human Rights' Commissions. It will be a major cultural triumph for advocates of state authority over individual conscience, and, to reprise Mr Howard, "any who believe otherwise are deluding themselves".

SETTLEMENT

Here then is the conundrum we face ... On the one hand we must decide how best to counter the tactics of intimidation and refute the false claims of a group that operates in the hostile mode of raw, power politics. On the other hand we must retain the profound compassion and fellow-feeling toward individual homosexuals that we ourselves need and yearn for from others. We must respect as fellows the very individuals whom we may reject as claimants in the public square.
Dr Jeffrey Satinover, Homosexuality and the Politics of Truth.[454]

There's politics, and then there's people, as Dr Satinover says. As I started this book I understood how difficult it would be to defend what I, and millions of Australians, hold to be true without offending and angering other citizens. So be it. There is no avoiding such anger, no matter how sincere one's arguments or how faultless one's personal dealings with those offended. I face any hostility with the indestructible confidence that is only possible for someone who has never in his life been discourteous to a gay person or laughed at a gay joke, who even as a schoolboy defended those who were being teased and has been a strong arm of trust for gay, lesbian and transgender patients for decades. That is a private confidence, and I do not intend to parade it further, but I state it in calm defiance of the demonising that always comes from a movement "that operates in the hostile mode of raw, power politics".

This book is just one citizen's contribution to the plebiscite debate, but there are voices of "raw power politics" trying to stop that debate in its tracks. A man who has seen it all in Australian politics, Paul Kelly of *The Australian*, has never seen it like this before:

> Consider the fierce opposition to the government's proposed

plebiscite on same-sex marriage ... that it should be opposed because it will offend the lesbian, gay, bisexual, transgender and intersex community. This constitutes a seismic shift in our politics and testifies to the power of identity politics. An expression of popular will and democratic sentiment cannot be conducted because it will give offence. The nation has never been in such a situation before. The power of the argument is immense – witness Shorten railing in the campaign against the plebiscite, saying it would release hate and homophobia ... In this climate the spirit of Orwell and Voltaire face a slow but sure death. Let's hope there is still sufficient left of the old Australian character and courage to turn back the tide.[455]

The fine art of taking offence

There is something in this book to offend everyone, but it is the reader's choice whether to respond with adult-centred grievance or child-centred grace.

The central judgement of this book – that a child must not be deliberately deprived of her mother or father – offends some gay couples. Other gay people are gracious enough to acknowledge that the project of marriage must remain a man-woman thing, for the sake of the child. As Paddy Manning put it: "A same-sex relationship is different to a marriage, because marriage is at its heart about children, and providing those children with their biological parents. Recognising difference is not discrimination."[456]

This central thesis about the rights of the child even offends some single parents, which puzzles me; we only do wrong if we "deliberately" deprive a child of her mother or father, and no single parent I know has ever "deliberately" done that. They never wanted their child to miss out on the other parent – things just happened, with no harm intended. No doubt this book also offends transgender men who don't like being told the problem lies with their mind not their body. It might even offend a lesbian throuple or loving incestuous couple. The list goes on, but there is a more fundamental offence that will certainly be taken, and which deserves to be addressed.

On normal and abnormal

The spirit of the age insists that there is no "right and wrong", even "normal and abnormal", in sexual acts between consenting adults. So the PC hounds start baying when they sniff out a forbidden judgement: that somebody somewhere is suggesting there's something wrong about homosexuality. Such a judgement is taken to be a slur on the deepest "self" of the person who experiences same-sex attraction, but I disagree. A journalist from the *Sydney Morning Herald* asked me, "What are your thoughts on homosexuality?" and I responded, "My thoughts are that homosexuality does not define a person: he or she is a unique, transient and beloved creature like anyone else, and if a person happens to experience same-sex impulses that is merely a puzzling aspect of their emotional makeup; it is not who they are."[457] The journalist then focussed her question on the behaviour itself, "Do you believe it is a normal expression of human sexuality?" and I replied:

> Homosexuality is clearly not normal in a statistical sense, since only 1.2% of the Australian population identify as homosexual while 97.4% identify as heterosexual.[458] In a clinical sense I agree with Dr Robert Spitzer, the gay-friendly psychiatrist who led the campaign to delete homosexuality from the American Psychiatric Association's *Diagnostic & Statistical Manual* in 1973, who described homosexuality as "a form of irregular sexual development".[459] It is not a mental illness, but nor is it normal, and for many years Spitzer argued against "the acceptance of the view that homosexuality is a normal variant." We should not form public policy on marriage or sex-education based on the false view that homosexuality is normal.

The most offensive question touches on "normal" in the moral sense. Just days before the 2016 federal election, Roy Morgan Research published a poll asking Australians if they agree that "homosexuality is immoral".[460] That is an unsatisfactory question, of course. It fails to make the vital distinction between homosexual orientation – which is nobody's choice, nobody's fault, and carries no moral culpability at all – and homosexual acts, which are a choice like any sexual act. The poll found that a third of people in my federal electorate of Groom agree with the statement, "homosexuality is immoral", and forty per cent in the neighbouring electorate of Maranoa. That figure drops to twenty one per cent nationwide, but it still represents three million voters. Judgements will differ on homosexual behaviour and whether it should be taught in school as being normal and right. What matters on such disputed questions is that we agree to differ, coexist courteously and don't force each other's conscience. So I heartily defend the liberty of consenting adults to engage in any lawful sexual acts in private. I defend the liberty of activist educators to teach our children that wrong acts are right, provided we parents are at liberty to push back and get rid of the activists. One of the biggest problems with a law for homosexual 'marriage' is that it takes away the liberty of parents. It *institutionalises* homosexual acts as normal and right – no further discussion will be entered into – and gives activists the big stick of anti-discrimination law to disempower parents and silence pastors who hold contrary moral values. That is the coercion of conscience that comes with same-sex 'marriage'. This aspect of the debate is not about the rights or wrongs of homosexuality; it is about the rights or wrongs of giving one group in society the legal clout to compel acquiescence in a disputed moral question.

The settlement sought in this book is a return to the civil coexistence that prevailed prior to the long LGBT march on marriage. Society has given everything possible to our fellow citizens who are same-sex attracted: full equality under the law as individuals and as couples, with no discrimination whatsoever; affectionate treatment in the media and popular culture; genuine camaraderie in our workplaces and clubs; exhortations in our churches that "they must be accepted with respect, compassion, and sensitivity."[460] We only ask that the generals of the gender movement do not usurp the one institution that is built around the child and her kinship bonds; that is founded on a truth of nature, not a fashion of ideology; that cannot be rendered 'gender-neutral' without violating the deepest moral and spiritual convictions of millions of their fellow citizens. It is not too late for more men and women who are same-sex attracted to stand up and say, "Not in my name!" to this deeply hostile deconstruction of marriage, this violation of a child's birthright, this coercion of conscience. If this book has provoked, irritated, encouraged and inspired any such people, I will be glad.

Summing Up

All that remains in this extended prosecution of the injustice of 'marriage equality' is the summing up. The opening indictment in this book was threefold, and the proposition of same-sex 'marriage' is found guilty on all three counts: it is untrue, unjust and unnecessary. Untrue to nature, which alone defines the male-female reality underlying marriage; unjust to children, since the institution of same-sex 'marriage' destines future kids to a motherless or fatherless life; unnecessary for civil equality, since that has already been achieved completely in our current law.

To that, the offence of fraud must be added, since what purports to be a very small change to the definition of marriage turns out to be a very large change – indeed a radical change – to key elements of society: to the education of children, the liberties of speech, conscience and religion, the power balance between family and government, and the very meaning of male and female.

A further conviction, to be served concurrently with the above, is made for dealing in narcotic slogans like "love is love" and "love makes a family": dangerous shots of emotion that would justify aberrations like group marriage, incestuous marriage, and others yet unimagined.

We are advised there is no crime on the statute books for being seen in the vicinity of Marx, Marcuse, Millett and Ms Ward, but that is the ideological company we keep if we vote to deliver them the long-sought prize of the deconstruction of marriage and family. Nor is it an indictable offence to be Premier Daniel Andrews, but he embodies the coercive character of rainbow politics: smearing opponents of gay 'marriage' as bigots;[462] subjecting all Victorian public school children to the corrupting "Safe Schools" programme; appointing a full-time Thought Policewoman to ensure Victorians only hold approved attitudes on LGBT matters.[463]

The privacy of the booth

My hope is that this book has given readers both a comprehensive warning and an encouragement as they approach the marriage plebiscite.

They should be encouraged that we can preserve the natural meaning of marriage without unjust discrimination, since gay and lesbian couples already have exactly the same legal status and benefits as any other couple. Voters might remind themselves how few same-sex couples actually want to 'marry', and recall the voices of gay people who oppose gay 'marriage'.

Voters should be encouraged that children of same-sex households already have exactly the same legal status and security as any other child. It is worth recalling that most same-sex attracted or gender-confused children will get over that phase in just a few years. We can also have confidence that there are good ways to manage bullying and depression for all children, for all causes. We can help young people through difficult times without overturning the foundation of society.

What will be in the back of our minds as we make our pencil mark? For me, it will always be the image of father, mother and baby; the triple-bond at the heart of human life. That is the Real Thing, the beautiful thing, at stake in this plebiscite; defending that is the last ditch to die in. In addition, my fighting spirit will rise at the thought of the genderless madness that will be imposed on our children or grandchildren at school under a regime of genderless 'marriage'. Likewise, my defiance of the 'progressive' elite who would use the legal power that comes with 'marriage equality' to harass dissenters into silence. And no way will I have the words 'husband' and 'wife' demeaned as in other countries to 'Partner A and B' just to meet the requirements of genderless couples.

At the front of our minds as we stand in that booth is the choice we cannot avoid: will we give priority "to children's rights or to homosexual adults' claims"? Faced with that choice, my hope and confidence is that Australians will stand with the child.

Acknowledgements

My thanks to Connor Court Publishing for their patience during the nine-month gestation of this book. Particular appreciation to four editors whose online journals yielded the most valuable articles: Ryan Anderson at *Public Discourse*; Joy Pullman at *The Federalist*; Michael Cook at *Mercatornet*; Brendan O'Neill at *Spiked*. Of the books listed in the select bibliography, special mention must be made of Dr Jeffrey Satinover's *Homosexuality and the Politics of Truth*, Paul Kengor's *Takedown: From Communists to Progressives, How the Left Has Sabotaged Family and Marriage* and Ryan T. Anderson's *Truth Overruled: the Future of Marriage and Religious Freedom*. Recommended reading to all.

Thanks to my colleagues (and patients) for bearing with my frequent absences. Even more so to my wife, Jane; it has encroached on our gardening time. To son Robert for formatting the endnotes to his scholarly standard; my first collection was a schmozzle... (could you just check the spelling on that one, Rob?)

Thanks to co-workers around the country who read the draft and improved it. And to the board of the Australian Marriage Forum: thank you for supporting me in this task. It has been a labour of love, first and foremost to defend the right of future children to know the love of both mother and father.

Select Bibliography

Alvare, Helen and Lopes, Steven (ed.) *Not Just Good but Beautiful: The Complementary Relationship between Man and Woman*. Walden NY: Plough Publishing House 2015.

Anderson, Ryan. *Truth Overruled: the Future of Marriage and Religious Freedom*. Washington DC: Regnery Publishing 2015.

Bayer, Ronald. *Homosexuality and American Psychiatry: the Politics of Diagnosis*. Princeton University Press 1981.

Blankenhorn, David. *The Future of Marriage*. New York: Encounter Books 2009.

Chesterton, Gilbert Keith. *The Superstition of Divorce*. London: Chatto and Windus 1920.

Colapinto, John. *As Nature Made Him: The Boy Who Was Raised as a Girl*. Harper Perennial 2001.

De Haan, Linda and Nijland, Stern. *King & King*. Berkeley: Tricycle Press 2002.

De Toledano, Ralph. *Cry Havoc! The Great American Bring-down and How it Happened*. Washington DC: Anthem 2006.

Healy, Gráinne et al. *Ireland Says Yes: The Inside Story of How the Vote for Marriage Equality Was Won*. Merrion Press 2015.

Hirst, Jo. *The Gender Fairy*. Oban Road Publishing 2015.

Jones, Stanton and Yarhouse, Mark. *Homosexuality: The Use of Scientific Research in the Church's Moral Debate*. Downers Grove IL: Intervarsity Press 2000.

Kengor, Paul. *Takedown: From Communists to Progressives, How the Left Has Sabotaged Family and Marriage*. Washington DC: WND Books 2015.

Kirk, Marshall and Madsen, Hunter. *After the Ball*. New York: Plume 1990.

Levi-Strauss, Claude. *The View from Afar*. Chicago: The University of Chicago Press 1992.

Millett, Kate. *Sexual Politics*. Urbana and Chicago: University of Illinois Press 1969.

Muehlenberg, Bill. *Strained Relations: The Challenge of Homosexuality*. Melbourne: Freedom Publishing 2011.

Reilly, Robert. *Making Gay OK: How Rationalizing Homosexual Behavior is Changing Everything*. San Francisco: Ignatius 2014.

Ritchie, Paul. *Faith, Love & Australia: the Conservative Case for Same-sex Marriage*. Redland Bay: Connor Court 2016.

Satinover, Jeffrey. *Homosexuality and the Politics of Truth*. Grand Rapids MI: Baker Books 1996.

Selmys, Melinda. *Sexual Authenticity: an Intimate Reflection on Homosexuality and Catholicism*. Huntington IN: OSV 2009.

ENDNOTES

1. Somerville M., "It's all about the children, not selfish adults," *The Australian*, July 23, 2011, accessed July 1, 2016, http://www.theaustralian.com.au/opinion/its-all-about-the-children-not-selfish-adults/story-e6frg6zo-1226099613917

2. O'Neill B., "Same-sex marriage: coercion dolled up as human rights," *Spiked*, April 30, 2014, accessed July 1, 2016, http://www.spiked-online.com/newsite/article/same-sex-marriage-coercion-dolled-up-as-civil-rights/14967#.V3mEQSN96Cc

3. *Universal Declaration of Human Rights*, Article 16.

4. Graff E.J., "Same-sex marriage is a radical feminist idea", *The American Prospect*, June 28, 2012, http://prospect.org/article/same-sex-marriage-radical-feminist-idea

5. Chesterton G.K., *The Superstition of Divorce* (London: Chatto and Windus, 1920).

6. Wroe D., "Amid the madness, Gillard shines with mother apology," *The Sydney Morning Herald,* March 22, 2013, http://www.smh.com.au/federal-politics/political-news/amid-the-madness-gillard-shines-with-mother-apology-20130321-2gixj.html

7. Levi-Strauss C., "Introduction," in Andre Burguiere et al. (eds.), *A History of the Family: Distant Worlds, Ancient Worlds* (1996).

8. Russell B., *Marriage and Morals* (London: Allen & Unwin, 1929), 96.

9. Davis, K. (ed.), *Contemporary Marriage: Comparative Perspectives on a Changing Institution* (New York: Russell Sage Foundation, 1985), 7.

10. Obergefell v. Hodges , 576 U. S. (2015), https://www.supremecourt.gov/opinions/14pdf/14-556_3204.pdf

11. Levi-Strauss C., *The View from Afar* (The University of Chicago Press: Chicago, 1992) 40-41.

12. Ibid.

13. Tacitus, *Annals* XV, 37-41. https://facultystaff.richmond.edu/~wstevens/history331texts/tacitus3.html

14. Australian Bureau of Statistics, 2013, "Same-Sex Couples," accessed July 1, 2016, http://www.abs.gov.au/AUSSTATS/abs@.nsf/Lookup/4102.0Main+Features10July+2013

15. Osbourne P., "Labor to introduce bill legalising gay marriage," *The New Daily*, May 26, 2015, accessed July 1, 2016, http://thenewdaily.com.au/news/2015/05/26/labor-brings-gay-marriage-laws/

16. Faust K, interview by Tony Jones, *ABC Lateline*, August 12, 2015, http://www.abc.net.au/news/2015-08-12/interview-katy-faust-who-serves-on-the-academic/6693296

17. "Reflecting on 12 years of gay marriage in the Netherlands," *Euronews*, April 1, 2013, accessed July 1, 2016, http://www.euronews.com/2013/04/01/reflecting-on-12-

years-of-gay-marriage-in-the-netherlands/

[18] van Gend D. and Croome R., interviewed by Melanie Tait, *ABC Hobart*, radio, August 31, 2015, https://soundcloud.com/936-abc-hobart/for-and-against-the-same-sex-marriage-debate

[19] Ritchie P., *Faith, Love and Australia: the conservative case for same-sex marriage* (Redland Bay: Connor Court, 2016), 32.

[20] Ibid.

[21] Sullins D.P., "The Unexpected Harm of Same-sex Marriage: A Critical Appraisal, Replication and Re-analysis of Wainright and Patterson's Studies of Adolescents with Same-sex Parents," *British Journal of Education, Society & Behavioural Science* 11, no. 2 (2015): 1-22, http://dx.doi.org/10.2139/ssrn.2589129

[22] Healy G. et al, *Ireland Says Yes: The Inside Story of How the Vote for Marriage Equality Was Won* (Merrion Press, 2015).

[23] Ibid.

[24] Van Onselen P., "Same-sex marriage plebiscite is a ruse to delay decision," *The Australian*, August 13, 2016, http://www.theaustralian.com.au/opinion/columnists/peter-van-onselen/samesex-marriage-plebiscite-is-a-ruse-to-delay-decision/news-story/d2a7f88f5003018c53a5f6a3843fe233

[25] Faust K., "Dear Justice Kennedy: An Open Letter from the Child of a Loving Gay Parent," *Public Discourse*, February 2, 2015, http://www.thepublicdiscourse.com/2015/02/14370/

[26] *Wikipedia*, "LGBT adoption and parenting in Australia," last updated June 13, 2016, https://en.wikipedia.org/wiki/LGBT_adoption_and_parenting_in_Australia

[27] Cook M., "Marriage leads to children – gay marriage leads to surrogacy," *Sydney Morning Herald*, July 19, 2012, accessed July 1, 2016, http://www.smh.com.au/federal-politics/political-opinion/marriage-leads-to-children--gay-marriage-leads-to-surrogacy-20120718-22aco.html#ixzz4DJy7iKf0

[28] Ibid.

[29] Somerville M., "Submission to the Senate enquiry into the Marriage Equality Amendment Bill 2010," March 13, 2012, http://www.aph.gov.au/Parliamentary_Business/Committees/Senate/Legal_and_Constitutional_Affairs/Completed_inquiries/2010-13/marriageequality2012/submissions

[30] "Why I Stay Quiet," Anonymous Us, March 30, 2016, accessed July 1, 2016, https://anonymousus.org/why-i-stay-quiet/

[31] "I need to know my father," Anonymous Us, April 12, 2016, accessed July 1, 2016, https://anonymousus.org/need-know-father/

32 Ellis B., "Timing of Pubertal Maturation in Girls: An Integrated Life History Approach," *Psychology Bulletin* 130 (2004): 920-958; Ellis B.et al., "Does Father Absence Place Daughters at Special Risk for Early Sexual Activity and Teenage Pregnancy?" *Child Development* 74 (2003): 801-821.

33 Karp P., "Penny Wong says homophobic election slurs show perils of plebiscite," *The Guardian*, July 12, 2016, https://www.theguardian.com/australia-news/2016/jul/12/penny-wong-homophobic-election-slurs-perils-marriage-equality-plebiscite

34 Somerville, "Submission to the Senate Enquiry."

35 van Gend D., "A dad does matter to a child," *The Australian*, August 29, 2011, accessed July 1, 2016, http://www.theaustralian.com.au/opinion/a-dad-does-matter-to-a-child-whether-gay-couples-like-it-or-not/story-e6frg6zo-1226124001348

36 Keim S., "Equality in eyes of law, love and marriage," *Courier Mail*, February 15, 2012 accessed July 1 2016, http://www.couriermail.com.au/news/equality-in-eyes-of-law-love-and-marriage/story-e6frerdf-1226271862297

37 Nathan S., "Revealed: the surrogacy clinic to the stars used by Elton John," *Daily Mail Australia*, December 30, 2010, http://www.dailymail.co.uk/femail/article-1342346/Elton-Johns-baby-2-mothers-required-produce-heir.html#ixzz4HfR6uDlN

38 "New Galaxy Poll for AMF: reframes the same-sex marriage debate," Australian Marriage Forum, accessed July 1, 2016, http://australianmarriage.org/new-galaxy-poll-for-amf-reframes-the-same-sex-marriage-debate/

39 Somerville, "Submission to the Senate Enquiry."

40 Somerville, "It's all about the children, not selfish adults," *op.cit.*

41 Barwick H., "Dear gay community, your kids are hurting," *The Federalist*, March 17, 2015, accessed July 1, 2016, http://thefederalist.com/2015/03/17/dear-gay-community-your-kids-are-hurting/

42 Ibid.

43 Walton B., "The Kids Are Not Alright: A Lesbian's Daughter Speaks Out," *The Federalist*, April 21, 2015 http://thefederalist.com/2015/04/21/the-kids-are-not-alright-a-lesbians-daughter-speaks-out/

44 Faust K., interview by Tony Jones, *ABC Lateline*, August 12, 2015, http://www.abc.net.au/news/2015-08-12/interview-katy-faust-who-serves-on-the-academic/6693296

45 Faust K., "Dear Justice Kennedy: An Open Letter from the Child of a Loving Gay Parent," *Public Discourse*, February 2, 2015, http://www.thepublicdiscourse.com/2015/02/14370/

46 "RADIO: 'Amy' re childhood in lesbian household. AMF 2015," YouTube video, from talkback radio 96.5FM Brisbane on March 22, 2015 (abridged and edited excerpt), posted by "Australian Marriage Forum," March 28, 2015, https://youtu.be/43P9Xd2t9Ug

47. "The real issue with same-sex parenting from a child's perspective," YouTube video, posted by "Millie Fontana," March 9, 2015, https://youtu.be/FCrzKsrZ1eg
48. "Child of Gays, Millie Fontana, speaks at Parliament House, Canberra," YouTube video, address at Parliament House, Canberra, August 2015, posted by "Millie Fontana," September 23, 2015, https://youtu.be/7g4vphO1SkE
49. Faust K., Amicus Curiae brief, US Court of Appeal of the Fifth Circuit, August 2014, https://www.scribd.com/doc/240312274/Katy-Faust-Amicus-Briefs
50. Lopez R., "Growing up with two mums: the untold children's view," *Public Discourse*, August 6, 2012, http://www.thepublicdiscourse.com/2012/08/6065/
51. Ibid.
52. Klein B.N., Amicus Curiae brief, US Court of Appeal of the Fifth Circuit, August 2014, https://www.scribd.com/doc/240312276/B-N-Klein-Amicus-Brief
53. Stefanowicz D., Amicus Curiae brief, US Court of Appeal of the Fifth Circuit, August 2014, https://www.scribd.com/doc/240313523/Dawn-Stefanowicz-Amicus-Brief
54. Barwick, "Dear gay community."
55. Faust, Amicus curiae.
56. Barwick, "Dear gay community."
57. Faust, Amicus Curiae.
58. Barwick, "Dear gay community."
59. "Child of gays," YouTube video, Millie Fontana-Fox.
60. Lopez, "Growing up with two mums."
61. Stefanowicz, Amicus curiae.
62. Stefanowicz, D., "My father was gay. Why I oppose legalising same-sex marriage," *The Daily Signal*, April 13, 2015, accessed July 1, 2016, http://dailysignal.com/2015/04/13/my-father-was-gay-why-i-oppose-legalizing-same-sex-marriage/
63. "Supporters," Gayby Baby, accessed July 1, 2016, http://thegaybyproject.com/supporters/
64. "Child of gays," YouTube video, Millie Fontana-Fox.
65. Klein, Amicus Curiae brief.
66. Lopez, R., Amicus Curiae brief, US Court of Appeal of the Fifth Circuit, August 2014, https://www.scribd.com/doc/251078014/Robert-Oscar-Lopez-Amicus-Brief

67 Stefanowicz, "My father was gay".

68 Barwick, "Dear gay community."

69 Faust, "Dear Justice Kennedy."

70 "I'm gay and I'm voting No. Here's why," YouTube video, Paddy Manning and Keith Mills Irish referendum video, posted by "Mothers and Fathers Matter," May 16, 2015, https://youtu.be/Q6HD8KLQBvA

71 ibid.

72 "AMF on ABC - Gay family-law barrister says "NO" to gay parenting," YouTube video, interview on Peter Goers show with Joe the barrister, ABC radio 891 Adelaide, 16 March 2015, posted by "Australian Marriage Forum," March 17, 2015, https://youtu.be/EI-73uAoipk

73 Pearson P., "Gay marriage demands should be left on shelf," *The Australian*, November 20, 2010, accessed July 1, 2016, http://www.theaustralian.com.au/opinion/gay-marriage-demands-should-be-left-on-shelf/story-e6frg6zo-1225956787304

74 Ward, V., "Sir Elton John boycotts Dolce & Gabbana after row over same-sex families," *The Telegraph*, March 15, 2015, accessed July 1, 2016, http://www.telegraph.co.uk/news/celebritynews/11473198/Sir-Elton-John-calls-for-Dolce-and-Gabbana-boycott-after-row-over-same-sex-families.html

75 "Dolce and Gabbana Interview", *Panorama,* March 2015, http://www.panorama.it/news/cronaca/dolce-gabbana-lunica-famiglia-quella-tradizionale/

76 "Gay designer Gabbana is against same-sex parents," *Daily Mail,* December 10, 2006, accessed April 8, 2016, http://www.dailymail.co.uk/femail/article-421672/Gay-designer-Gabbana-sex-parents.html

77 "Dolce & Gabbana and Victoria Beckham join Elton John in 'synthetic' baby debate," *The Australian,* March 17, 2015, accessed April 8, 2016, http://www.theaustralian.com.au/news/world/the-times/dolce-amp-gabbana-and-victoria-beckham-join-elton-john-in-synthetic-baby-debate/news-story/20d29ae4810c457a25e2ba1a5d669bbc?=

78 Mainwaring, D., "Nature vs Synthetics: What's at stake in the Dolce and Gabbana Controversy?" *Public Discourse,* March 19, 2015, http://www.thepublicdiscourse.com/2015/03/14663/

79 Mainwaring, D., "I'm gay and I oppose gay marriage," *Public Discourse,* March 8, 2013, http://www.thepublicdiscourse.com/2013/03/9432/

80 Ibid.

81 Ibid.

[82] Ibid.

[83] Mainwaring, D., "Hearts, Parts and Minds," *Public Discourse*, March 9, 2015, http://www.thepublicdiscourse.com/2015/03/14510/

[84] Ibid.

[85] Ibid.

[86] "Homosexuals Against Gay Marriage – part 5 of 5," YouTube video, posted by "AdamAndEveNotSteve," July 31, 2011, https://youtu.be/cUADJnfAK_U. See 6.09 mins.

[87] Popenoe D., *Life without Father: Compelling New Evidence That Fatherhood and Marriage Are Indispensable for the Good of Children and Society* (New York: The Free Press, 1996), 197.

[88] Links to reviews of the settled science. *Marriage and the Public Good: Ten Principles* Princeton, NJ): The Witherspoon Institute, 2008), http://winst.org/wp-content/uploads/WI_Marriage_and_the_Public_Good.pdf ; Kristin Anderson Moore, Susan M. Jekielek, Carol Emig. "Marriage from a Child's Perspective: How Does Family Structure Affect Children, and What Can be Done about It?" *Child Trends* (2002): 6, http://www.childtrends.org/wp-content/uploads/2013/03/MarriageRB602.pdf; W. Bradford Wilcox et al. 2005, *Why Marriage Matters, Second Edition: Twenty-Six Conclusions from the Social Sciences* (New York: Institute for American Values http://www.healthymarriageinfo.org/research-and-policy/other-resources/download.aspx?id=1259 ; McLanahan S., Donahue E., and Haskins R., "Introducing the Issue," *The Future of Children* 15 (2005): 3-12.; Mary Parke, M., *Are Married Parents Really Better for Children?* (Washington, DC: Center for Law and Social Policy, 2003)

[89] Moore K., Jekielek S., Emig C., "Marriage from a Child's Perspective: How Does Family Structure Affect Children, and What Can be Done about It?" *Child Trends* (2002): 6, http://www.childtrends.org/wp-content/uploads/2013/03/MarriageRB602.pdf

[90] Scholars of marriage, Amicus Curiae brief, Supreme Court of the USA, *Obergefell* 2015, 9 http://sblog.s3.amazonaws.com/wp-content/uploads/2015/04/14-55614-56214-57114-574bsac100ScholarsOfMarriage.pdf

[91] Marks L., "Same-sex parenting and children's outcomes: A closer examination of the American psychological association's brief on lesbian and gay parenting," *Social Science Research* 41, no. 4, (2012): 735–751. http://www.sciencedirect.com/science/article/pii/S0049089X12000580

[92] Moore et al, "Marriage from a Child's Perspective," op.cit.

[93] Sullins D.P., "Emotional Problems among Children with Same-Sex Parents: Difference by Definition," *British Journal of Education, Society and Behavioural Science* 7, no. 2 (2015):

99-120, http://papers.ssrn.com/sol3/Papers.cfm?abstract_id=2500537

[94] Londregan J., "Same-sex parenting: unpacking the social science," *Public Discourse*, February 24, 2015, www.thepublicdiscourse.com/2015/02/14465/

[95] McLanahan S., Sandefur G., *Growing Up with a Single Parent* (Cambridge: Harvard University Press, 1994), quoted in The Witherspoon Institute, *Marriage and the Public Good: Ten Principles,* op.cit.

[96] Allen D., "High school graduation rates among children of same-sex households," *Review of Economics of the Household* 635 (2013) http://www.terpconnect.umd.edu/~pnc/allen-ss-grad.pdf

[97] Regnerus M., "New research on same-sex households reveals kids do best with Mom and Dad," Public Discourse (Witherspoon Institute), Feb 10, 2015, www.thepublicdiscourse.com/2015/02/14417/

[98] Sullins, "Emotional problems," 115.

[99] Sullins, "Unexpected Harm."

[100] Ibid, 20.

[101] American College of Pediatricians et al, Amici Curiae brief, Supreme Court of the USA, April 2015, http://www.supremecourt.gov/ObergefellHodges/AmicusBriefs/14-556_American_College_of_Pediatricians.pdf

[102] "History: 1997 Overview," Victorian Gay & Lesbian Rights Lobby, accessed July 1, 2016, http://www.vglrl.org.au/about/history/1997-overview

[103] Dempsey D., "Same-sex Parented Families in Australia," AIFS (2013), https://aifs.gov.au/cfca/publications/same-sex-parented-families-australia/introduction

[104] Marks, "Same-sex parenting and children's outcomes."

[105] Wainright J. et al, "Psychosocial adjustment, school outcomes, and romantic relationships of adolescents with same-sex parents," *Child Development* 75, no.6 (2004): 1886-1898.

[106] Stacey J., Biblarz T., "Does the sexual orientation of parents matter?" *American Sociological Review* 66, no.2 (2001): 159, 166.

[107] "Public Interest Directorate," American Psychological Association, accessed July 1, 2016, http://www.apa.org/pi/index.aspx

[108] Cummings N. and Wright R. eds., *Destructive trends in mental health: the well-intentioned path to harm* (Routledge, 2005), 14.

[109] "Australian Study of Child Health in Same-Sex Families (ACHESS)," University of Melbourne, 2012-2014 http://www.achess.org.au/

[110] "Children raised by same-sex couples healthier and happier, research suggests,"

ABC Radio AM, July 7, 2014 http://www.abc.net.au/news/2014-07-05/children-raised-by-same-sex-couples-healthier-study-finds/5574168

[111] Crouch S.R., McNair R, Waters E and Power J, "The health perspectives of Australian adolescents from same-sex parent families: a mixed methods study," *Child: Care, Health and Development* 41, no. 3 (2015): 356-364, http://onlinelibrary.wiley.com/doi/10.1111/cch.12180/full

[112] Dempsey, "Same-sex parented families," op.cit.

[113] Patterson C, "Lesbian and gay parenting, Summary of research findings," American Psychological Association (1995), http://www.felgtb.org/rs/648/d112d6ad-54ec-438b-9358-4483f9e98868/a85/filename/apsa-lesbian-and-gay-parenting.pdf and subsequent papers.

[114] Wainright J, Patterson C, "Delinquency, victimization, and substance use among adolescents with female same-sex parents," *Journal of Family Psychology* 526 (2006); Wainright J, Patterson C, "Peer relations among adolescents with female same-sex parents," *Developmental Psychology* 117 (2008); Wainright J. et al, "Psychosocial adjustment, school outcomes, and romantic relationships of adolescents with same-sex parents," *Child Development* 75, no.6 (2004): 1886-1898.

[115] Sullins D.P., "Child Attention-Deficit Hyperactivity Disorder (ADHD) in Same-Sex Parent Families in the United States: Prevalence and Comorbidities," *British Journal of Medicine and Medical Research* 6, no.10 (2015), http://www.sciencedomain.org/abstract/7834

[116] Rosenfeld M., "Nontraditional Families and Childhood Progress through School," *Demography* 47, no.3 (August 2010): 755-775, http://web.stanford.edu/~mrosenfe/Rosenfeld_ Nontraditional_Families_Demography.pdf

[117] Black D. et al., "The measurement of same-sex unmarried partner couples in the 2000 US Census," *California Centre for Population Research* (2007), https://escholarship.org/uc/item/72r1q94b#page-3

[118] Potter D, "Same-Sex parent Families and Children's Academic Achievement," *Journal of Marriage and Family* 74 (2012): 556 – 571, http://www.baylorisr.org/wp-content/uploads/Potter.pdf

[119] Regnerus M., "How different are the adult children of parents who have same-sex relationships? Findings from the New Family Structures Study," *Social Science Research* 41, no.4 (2012): 752, http://www.sciencedirect.com/science/article/pii/S0049089X12000610

[120] American College of Pediatricians et al, Amici Curiae.

[121] Sullins, "Unexpected Harm," 20.

[122] Marquardt E., *Between Two Worlds: The Inner Lives of Children of Divorce* (New York: Crown, 2005). Cited in Witherspoon op cit.

123 Weitoft G. et al, "Mortality, Severe Morbidity, and Injury in Children Living with Single Parents in Sweden: A Population-Based Study," *The Lancet* 361 (2003): 289-295.

124 McLanahan S., "Parent Absence or Poverty: Which Matters More?" in G. Duncan and J. Brooks Gunn eds., *Consequences of Growing Up Poor* (New York: Russell Sage, 1997). Cited in Witherspoon op cit.

125 Sullins, "Emotional Problems."

126 In a recent independent assessment of peer review at over three hundred scientific publishers by Science, the world's premiere scientific journal, the publisher of Sullins' studies attained the highest ranking possible for peer review rigor, a distinction earned by only the top 7% of journals worldwide. See Bohannon J., "Who's Afraid of Peer Review?" *Science* 342 no.6154 (October 2013): 64.

127 "The true objection of the APA and ASA to Sullins's articles has nothing to do with their scientific rigor, but with his findings, which do not conform to the ideology of harm denial," quoted in American College of Pediatricians et al, Amici Curiae brief, 20-29, http://www.supremecourt.gov/ObergefellHodges/AmicusBriefs/14-556_American_College_of_Pediatricians.pdf

128 Sullins, "Unexpected Harm."

129 Wainright, "Psychosocial adjustment."

130 Stern M., "The scientific debate over same-sex parenting is over," *Slate*, April 13, 2016, http://www.slate.com/blogs/outward/2016/04/13/scientific_debate_over_same_sex_parenting_is_over.html

131 Ford Z, "The conservative argument against same-sex parenting just fell apart," *Think Progress*, April 12, 2016, http://thinkprogress.org/lgbt/2016/04/12/3768442/same-sex-parenting-study-population-sample/

132 Bos H. et al, "Same-Sex and Different-Sex Parent Households and Child Health Outcomes: Findings from the National Survey of Children's Health," *Journal of Developmental & Behavioral Pediatrics* 37, no.3 (April 2016): 179– 187, http://journals.lww.com/jrnldbp/Fulltext/2016/04000/Same_Sex_and_ Different_Sex_Parent_Households_and.1.aspx

133 Ford, "The conservative argument."

134 Regnerus M, "Media gush over new study only to find same-sex parents more irritated with their children," *Public Discourse,* April 15, 2016, http://www.thepublicdiscourse.com/2016/04/16760/

135 American College of Pediatricians et al, Amici Curiae.

136 Sullins, "Unexpected Harm"; Regnerus, "How different are the adult children."

137 American College of Pediatricians et al, Amici Curiae.

[138] Sullins, "Unexpected Harm," 14,15.

[139] Australian Bureau of Statistics 2013, "How many same-sex couples have children?" http://www.abs.gov.au/AUSSTATS/abs@.nsf/Lookup/4102.0Main+Features10July+2013#children

[140] Klein B.N. testimony (excerpted and abbreviated), Case 14-50196 – August 15, 2014, US court of appeal for the fifth circuit, https://www.scribd.com/doc/240312276/B-N-Klein-Amicus-Brief

[141] American College of Pediatricians et al, Amici Curiae, 45-46.

[142] "FULL VIDEO: 'Safe Schools' is not about bullying, organiser admits!" Talk by Joel Radcliffe reportedly at "Safe Schools Coalition National Symposium 13th June 2014, Melbourne", posted by End Safe Schools, at 3:38, https://www.youtube.com/watch?v=j5uNocBCw3Q&feature=youtu.be

[143] Villarreal D., "Can we please just start admitting that we do actually want to indoctrinate kids?" *Queerty News*, May 12, 2011, accessed July 1, http://www.queerty.com/can-we-please-just-start-admitting-that-we-do-actually-want-to-indoctrinate-kids-20110512 ; see Villarreal profile at GLAAD http://www.glaad.org/profile/daniel-villarreal

[144] For references see George Christensen MP link below and others in this chapter.

[145] Bita N., "Safe Schools Coalition: sexual politics in the classroom," *The Australian*, February 13, 2016, http://www.theaustralian.com.au/news/inquirer/safe-schools-coalition-sexual-politics-in-the-classroom/news-story/bf58ff141ba0b08bf165e3d53cc8a055

[146] Cook H., "University suspends Safe Schools co-founder Roz Ward over Facebook post," *The Age*, June 1, 2016, http://www.theage.com.au/victoria/university-suspends-safe-schools-cofounder-roz-ward-over-facebook-post-20160601-gp9ezu.html#ixzz4D9uzhXOP

[147] Cook H., "Guard of honour greets Safe Schools founder Roz Ward as she returns to work," *The Age*, June 6, 2016, http://www.theage.com.au/victoria/guard-of-honour-greets-safe-schools-founder-roz-ward-as-she-returns-to-work-20160606-gpchiu.html

[148] "FULL VIDEO: 'Safe Schools' is not about bullying," op. cit., Roz Ward comments at 1:30.

[149] Hillier L., Jones T., et al., *Writing themselves in again*: *6 years on* (Melbourne: La Trobe University's Australian Research Centre in Sex, Health & Society, 2005), 2, http://www.glhv.org.au/files/writing_themselves_in_again.pdf

[150] Eacott A, "Anti-bullying programme PEACE pack reaching students across the globe," *ABC News Online*, June 30, 2016, http://www.abc.net.au/news/2016-06-

30/anti-bullying-peace-pack-reaching-students-across-the-globe/7557920

[151] See the following subsection as well as Chapter 6 section 'Born that way' and Chapter 8 for relevant studies.

[152] Fink M. et al., eds., OMG I'm Trans (MINUS18, 2015), 6, accessed June 19, 2016, https://minus18.org.au/omgit/omgit-web.pdf

[153] Korte A. et al., "Gender identity disorders in childhood and adolescence: currently debated concepts and treatment strategies," *Dtsch Arztebl Int.* 105, no.48 (November 2008): 834, http://www.ncbi.nlm.nih.gov/pubmed/19578420

[154] Cantor, J., "Do trans-kids stay trans when they grow up?" *Sexology Today* website, January 11, 2016, http://www.sexologytoday.org/2016/01/do-trans-kids-stay-trans-when-they-grow_99.html

[155] De Cuypere G., Knudson G. et al., *WPATH consensus process regarding transgender and transsexual-related diagnoses in ICD-11* (World Professional Association for Transgender Health, May 31, 2013), 55, https://dl.dropboxusercontent.com/u/7789275/ICD%20Meeting%20Packet-Report-Final-sm.pdf

[156] Korte, "Gender identity disorders", op.cit.

[157] Dhejne C. et al., "Long-Term Follow-Up of Transsexual Persons Undergoing Sex Reassignment Surgery: Cohort Study in Sweden," *PLoS ONE* 6, no.2 (2011): e16885, http://dx.doi.org/10.1371/journal.pone.0016885

[158] Legge, K., "Transgender children: what's behind the spike in numbers?" *The Australian*, July 18, 2015, accessed August 20, 2016, http://www.theaustralian.com.au/life/weekend-australian-magazine/transgender-children-whats-behind-the-spike-in-numbers/story-e6frg8h6-1227446188926

[159] Fink M., *All of Us* (Safe Schools Coalition Australia, 2016), 30, accessed July 29, 2016, http://www.safeschoolshub.edu.au/common/downloads/All-Of-US-Online-Version-May-2016-v3.pdf

[160] Ward R., Radcliffe J., Parsons M. et al., *Guide to supporting a student to affirm or transition gender identity at school* (Safe Schools Coalition Australia, 2015), accessed July 27, 2016, http://www.safeschoolshub.edu.au/common/downloads/guide-to-supporting-a-student-to-affirm-or-transition-gender-identity-at-school_oct-2015.pdf

[161] Scott M., ed., *OMG I'm Queer* (MINUS18) Uncensored version, 2014, 10, https://drive.google.com/open?id=0B-BTrWV2QzdbSHl3eWREYnJkams or https://www.dropbox.com/s/axzdt5uodgzuqbc/OMG%20I%27m%20Queer%20-%202014%20edition.pdf?dl=0 or ask Minus18 for a 2014 version (paid for by public money).

[162] Scott, M. ed., *OMG I'm Queer*, uncensored 2014 version at Golden Grove High School website http://www.goldengrovehs.sa.edu.au/our-school/learner-

support/access-centre-counseling-service.html and document at http://www.goldengrovehs.sa.edu.au/images/PDFS/OMG%20Im%20Queer.pdf accessed June, 24, 2016.

163 "Fury at school transgender lessons," Herald Sun, February 8, 2016, accessed August 20, 2016, http://www.heraldsun.com.au/news/national/mother-pulls-children-from-frankston-high-school-over-transgender-awareness-rules/news-story/40d51309df1386a55f7602f6e2e22bca

164 "Cella's Story," YouTube video, posted by "youreteachingourchildrenwhat?" June 21, 2016, https://youtu.be/rOmCyw9vRi4

165 "Steve's Story," YouTube video, posted by "youreteachingourchildrenwhat?" June 27, 2016, https://youtu.be/25-Y-4U_yag

166 George Christensen MP, Hansard 25th Feb 2016 http://parlinfo.aph.gov.au/parlInfo/search/display/display.w3p;query=Id%3A%22chamber%2Fhansardr%2F115c3603-d1aa-4e7e-8ec1-5ec3e40edc8a%2F0156%22

167 Australian Family Association, "Submission to Inquiry: Submission No.30," dated February 16, 2016, NSW Parliamentary enquiry into Sexualisation of children and young people, https://www.parliament.nsw.gov.au/committees/inquiries/Pages/inquiry-submission-details.aspx?pk=%2053009 or https://www.parliament.nsw.gov.au/committees/DBAssets/InquirySubmission/Body/53009/Submission%2030%20Australian%20Family%20Association.pdf A full version with graphics can be obtained from the enquiry secretary: childrenyoungpeople@parliament.nsw.gov.au

168 Fink, *All of Us,* op.cit.

169 *All of Us*, uncensored version (prior to May 2016) see https://drive.google.com/open?id=0B-BTrWV2QzdbcTJVdFc3cmtrQUk or https://www.dropbox.com/s/ojmjl4stxmnpx1g/Safe%20Schools%20-%20All%20of%20Us%20%28original%20version%29.pdf?dl=0 or request the original version, paid for by your taxes, from SSCA.

170 Ibid., 44.

171 "Victorian Premier guarantees future of Safe Schools program as Federal MPs call for scheme to be axed," ABC, March 16, 2016, accessed August 20, 2016, http://www.abc.net.au/news/2016-03-16/victorian-premier-guarantees-safe-schools-if-federal-funding-cut/7252272

172 Birmingham S., "Statement on Safe Schools Coalition," The Department of Education and Training Media Centre, March 18, 2016, https://ministers.education.gov.au/birmingham/statement-safe-schools-coalition

173 Fink, *All of Us*, op. cit., 30.

174 Ibid., 42.

175 De Haan L., Nijland S., *King & King* (Berkely: Tricycle Press, 2002).

176 "PARENTS OUTRAGED: Second-grade teacher (in David Parker's school!) reads "modern fairy tale" to class on homosexual romance and marriage!" Mass Resistance, April 19, 2006, accessed August 20, 2016, http://www.massresistance.org/docs/issues/king_and_king/index.html

177 Parker & Wirthlin v. Hurley, Ash et al., "Complaint and Jury Demand," United States District Court District of Massachusetts, (April 27, 2006), http://www.massresistance.org/docs/parker_lawsuit/filing_2006/complaint.html

178 "Yes on 8 TV Ad: Everything To Do With Schools," YouTube video, posted by "VoteYesonProp8," October 20, 2008, https://youtu.be/7352ZVMKBQM

179 Judge Lynch, quoted in "Federal court denies appeal in David Parker Civil Rights case on homosexual programs in elementary school," Mass Resistance, accessed August 20, 2016, http://www.massresistance.org/docs/parker_lawsuit/appeal_loss_013108/index.html

180 King M. et al., "Mental Health and Quality of Life of Gay Men and Lesbians in England and Wales," *British Journal of Psychiatry* 183, no.6 (2003): 552-558, http://bjp.rcpsych.org/content/183/6/552.full, Table 4.

181 Sullins P., "Emotional Problems among Children with Same-Sex Parents: Difference by Definition," *British Journal of Education, Society and Behavioural Science* 7, no.2 (2015): 99-120, http://papers.ssrn.com/sol3/Papers.cfm?abstract_id=2500537

182 Hillier L., Jones T., et al., *Writing themselves in again: 6 years on,* op.cit., 2.

183 "FULL VIDEO: 'Safe Schools' is not about bullying, organiser admits!" YouTube video, Roz Ward at SSC Symposium 2014, posted by "End SafeSchools," March 17, 2016, 1:30, https://youtu.be/j5uNocBCw3Q

184 Kirk M., Madsen H., *After the Ball* (New York: Plume, 1990) 183.

185 Questions and Answers, Legislative Council of New South Wales, Asked on May 26, 2015, answered on August 11, 2015, 264 *71, http://23.101.218.132/prod/lc/lcpaper.nsf/0/54512D75C8A028BFCA257E9E003A3C87/$file/QA_15_11_AUGUST_2015R.pdf

186 Devine M., "The thought police telling kids heterosexuality's not the norm," *Daily Telegraph*, October 17, 2012, accessed August 20, 2016, http://www.dailytelegraph.com.au/news/opinion/the-thought-police-telling-kids-heterosexualitys-not-the-norm/story-e6frezz0-1226497311742

187 Australian Covert Bullying Prevalence Study (ACBPS), *The nature of covert bullying from a student perspective: Qualitative research* (Edith Cowan University, 2009), 149. https://docs.education.gov.au/system/files/doc/other/australian_covert_bullying_prevalence_study_chapter_4.pdf

[188] ACBPS, ch. 2.5, 133, https://docs.education.gov.au/system/files/doc/other/australian_covert_bullying_prevalence_study_chapter_2.pdf

[189] Ibid., ch. 2, 26.

[190] Ibid., ch. 2, 48.

[191] Fink, *All of Us*, op. cit., 8.

[192] Hillier L., Jones T., et al., *Writing themselves in three: The 3rd national study on the sexual health and wellbeing of same sex attracted and gender questioning young people* (Melbourne: La Trobe University's Australian Research Centre in Sex, Health & Society, 2010), 2, http://glhv.org.au/files/wti3_web_sml.pdf

[193] Ibid., 39.

[194] Ibid., Fig. 11.

[195] Ibid., 15.

[196] Urban R., "Stereotype of 'bullied, at-risk' homosexual youth queried," *The Australian*, April 21, 2016, accessed August 20, 2016, http://www.theaustralian.com.au/national-affairs/stereotype-of-bullied-atrisk-homosexual-youth-queried/news-story/f4303adf020d0dfbd28ba787693d716d

[197] Jones T., "How sex education research methodologies frame GLBTIQ students," *Sex Education* 13, no.6 (2013): 687-701, http://dx.doi.org/10.1080/14681811.2013.806262

[198] Ibid., p.693

[199] Ibid., p.692

[200] Athanasou J., "A critical analysis of Writing Themselves in 3," *Occasional Paper 1*, March 2016.

[201] An example, as mentioned, is the PEACE Pack anti-bullying programme from Adelaide: Eacott A., "Anti-bullying program PEACE Pack reaching students across the globe," *ABC*, June 30, 2016, accessed August 20, 2016, http://www.abc.net.au/news/2016-06-30/anti-bullying-peace-pack-reaching-students-across-the-globe/7557920

[202] "Interview with Peter Van Onselen, Sky News, Canberra," Australian Government Treasury, August 12, 2015, http://bfb.ministers.treasury.gov.au/transcript/095-2015/

[203] AMF newspaper ad in *The Australian*, August 10, 2015, "Its.Not.Marriage." http://australianmarriage.org/wp-content/uploads/AMF_Australian.jpg

[204] Koziol M., "Same-sex marriage: LGBTI advocates fear harm from plebiscite," *Sydney Morning Herald*, August 15, 2015, accessed August 20, 2016, http://www.smh.com.au/national/samesex-marriage-lgbti-advocates-fear-harm-from-plebiscite-

20150812-gixdri.html

205 "'Marriage Equality? What about equality for kids?' – Australian Marriage Forum - March 2015 - YT," YouTube video, posted by "Australian Marriage Forum," March 6, 2015, https://youtu.be/s80wL5al5NA

206 Whitbourn M., "Backlash after anti-marriage equality ad debuts on Mardi Gras night," *The Sydney Morning Herald*, March 8, 2015, accessed August 1, 2016, http://www.smh.com.au/entertainment/tv-and-radio/backlash-after-antimarriage-equality-ad-debuts-on-mardi-gras-night-20150308-13y8yi.html

207 "2015 Annual Surveillance Report of HIV, viral hepatitis, STIs," The Kirby Institute, (for example, ~70% of new HIV cases are in 'men who have sex with men') http://kirby.unsw.edu.au/surveillance/2015-annual-surveillance-report-hiv-viral-hepatitis-stis

208 Satinover J., *Homosexuality and the Politics of Truth* (Grand Rapids, MI: Baker Books, 1996), 225.

209 2010 National Drug Strategy Household Survey report (Australian Institute of Health and Welfare, 2011), http://www.aihw.gov.au/WorkArea/DownloadAsset.aspx?id=10737421314

210 King et al., "Mental Health and Quality of Life of Gay Men and Lesbians in England and Wales," op. cit.

211 Human Rights Complaint against the Government of Canada, February 2009, http://web.archive.org/web/20090521102049/http://www.xtra.ca/BinaryContent/pdf/human%20rights%20complaint.pdf

212 Cover R., "Is same-sex marriage an adequate response to queer youth suicide?" *Online Opinion*, August 22, 2012, accessed August 20, 2016, http://www.onlineopinion.com.au/view.asp?article=14017

213 Pryor L. and Kealy-Bateman W., "Marriage equality is a mental health issue," *Australasian Psychiatry* 23, no.5 (October 2015): 540-543, http://apy.sagepub.com/content/23/5/540.abstract

214 Kealy-Bateman W., "Submission for Recognition of Foreign Marriages Bill 2014 Inquiry," Submission 139, July 9, 2014, http://www.aph.gov.au/DocumentStore.ashx?id=a89be407-21ed-4610-b718-36e83d90a98e&subId=300423

215 Scholars of Marriage, Brief of Amici Curiae, *Obergefell v Hodges* 2015, http://sblog.s3.amazonaws.com/wp-content/uploads/2015/04/14-55614-56214-57114-574bsac100ScholarsOfMarriage.pdf

216 Ibid., 3; see further 20-22 and Appendix B.

217 Ibid., 20-22 and Appendix B.

218 Ibid., 30.

[219] Jones T., "How sex education research methodologies frame GLBTIQ students," op cit, 692-3.

[220] Selmys M., *Sexual Authenticity, An intimate reflection on Homosexuality and Catholicism* (Huntington IN: OSV, 2009), 30.

[221] Koziol M., "Plebiscite 'yes' campaign takes shape," *The Sydney Morning Herald*, July 31, 2016, accessed August 1, 2016, http://www.smh.com.au/federal-politics/political-news/plebiscite-yes-campaign-takes-shape-amid-division-between-marriage-equality-supporters-20160728-gqfkbf.html

[222] "Position Statement on Issues Related to Homosexuality", American Psychiatric Association, December 2013, Accessed August 1, 2016, https://www.psychiatry.org/File%20Library/About-APA/Organization-Documents-Policies/Policies/Position-2013-Homosexuality.pdf

[223] "Sexual Orientation & Homosexuality," American Psychological Association, accessed August 20, 2016, http://www.apa.org/topics/lgbt/orientation.aspx

[224] Byrd D., "'Homosexuality Is Not Hardwired,' Concludes Head of The Human Genome Project," *Life Site News*, March 20, 2007, accessed August 20, 2016, https://www.lifesitenews.com/news/homosexuality-is-not-hardwired-concludes-head-of-the-human-genome-project

[225] "Identical Twin Studies Demonstrate Homosexuality is Not Genetic," NARTH Institute, accessed August 20, 2016, http://www.narth.com/#!gay---born-that-way/cm6x

[226] Bailey J. M., et al., "Genetic and Environmental Influences on Sexual Orientation and Its Correlates in an Australian Twin Sample," *Journal of Personality and Social Psychology* 78, no.3 (2000): 524–536, https://genepi.qimr.edu.au/contents/p/staff/CV261Bailey_UQ_Copy.pdf

[227] Bearman, P.S. and Bruckner H., "Opposite-sex twins and adolescent same-sex attraction," *American Journal of Sociology* 107, no.5 (March 2002): 1179–1205, http://www.soc.duke.edu/~jmoody77/205a/ecp/bearman_bruckner_ajs.pdf

[228] See also the summary of adolescent fluidity of sexual orientation: "Adolescents, Therapeutic Choice and Scientific Integrity," American College of Pediatricians, February 13, 2014, http://www.acpeds.org/adolescents-therapeutic-choice-and-scientific-integrity

[229] Mayer L., McHugh P., "Sexuality and Gender: Findings from the Biological, Psychological and Social Sciences", *The New Atlantis*, August 19, 2016, especially page 25 and following, http://www.thenewatlantis.com/docLib/20160819_TNA50SexualityandGender.pdf

[230] Official Committee Hansard, "Legal and Constitutional Affairs Legislation Committee on the Marriage Equality Amendment Bill 2010," Senate of the Parliament of Australia, May 4, 2012, http://parlinfo.aph.gov.au/parlInfo/search/display/display.

w3p;query=Id%3A%22committees%2Fcommsen%2Fc8e9db57-3acd-4c0f-a11a-96077dfac944%2F0000%22

[231] Denizet-Lewis B, New York Times, "My Ex-gay Friend," June 16, 2011 http://www.nytimes.com/2011/06/19/magazine/my-ex-gay-friend.html?_r=0

[232] "Interview With Former Gay Activist, Michael Glatze," Joseph Nicolosi website, February 2014, accessed August 20, 2016, http://www.josephnicolosi.com/interview-with-former-gay-acti/

[233] Mayer, McHugh, "Sexuality and Gender", op.cit. expecially page 50 and following.

[234] Savin-Williams R.C. and Ream G.L., "Prevalence and Stability of Sexual Orientation Components During Adolescence and Young Adulthood," *Archives of Sexual Behavior* 36, no.3 (2007): 385-394, http://link.springer.com/article/10.1007/s10508-006-9088-5. Note: for the drift from same-sex to opposite-sex attraction see Table 2 (Wave 1 to Wave 3, 71.7% male, 55.3% female) and for behaviour see Table 3 (Wave 1 to Wave 3, 71.6% male, 76.8% female).

[235] Ott M.Q., Corliss H.L., et al., "Stability and Change in Self-Reported Sexual Orientation Identity in Young People: Application of Mobility Metrics," *Archives of Sexual Behavior* 40, no.3 (June 2011): 519-532, http://link.springer.com/article/10.1007%2Fs10508-010-9691-3

[236] "National Health and Social Life Survey," Population Research Center of the University of Chicago, http://popcenter.uchicago.edu/data/nhsls.shtml Also reviewed in book form at Laumann E. et al., *The Social Organization of Sexuality: Sexual Practices in the United States* (University of Chicago Press, 2000).

[237] Dr Satinover's full testimony is reproduced with permission at: Satinover J., "Testimony Before the Massachusett's Senate Committee Studying Gay Marriage," Catholic Education Resource Center, accessed August 20, 2016, http://www.catholiceducation.org/en/marriage-and-family/sexuality/testimony-before-the-massachusetts-senate-committee-studying-gay-marriage.html

[238] Anthony M.A. et al, "Sex in Australia: Sexual identity, sexual attraction and sexual experience among a representative sample of adults," *Australian and New Zealand Journal of Public Health* 27, no.2 (2003): 138–145, http://www.blackwell-synergy.com/doi/abs/10.1111/j.1467-842X.2003.tb00801.x

[239] Fink, *All of Us*, op. cit. 8.

[240] For data obtained by the abuse of children see Table 34. Unruh B., "U.N. set to recognize Kinsey sex 'research'," *WND*, February 16, 2014, accessed August 20, 2016, http://www.wnd.com/2014/02/u-n-set-to-recognize-kinsey-sex-research/

[241] Leonhardt D., "John Tukey, 85, Statistician"(Obituary), *The New York Times*, July 28, 2000, http://www.nytimes.com/2000/07/28/us/john-tukey-85-statistician-coined-the-word-software.html?_r=0

242 Painton P., "The shrinking ten percent," *Time* magazine, April 26, 1993, http://content.time.com/time/magazine/article/0,9171,978345,00.html

243 Gallup Poll, "U.S. adults estimate that 25% of Americans are gay or lesbian," May 27, 2011, http://www.gallup.com/poll/147824/Adults-Estimate-Americans-Gay-Lesbian.aspx

244 Ward B. et al., "Sexual Orientation and Health among U.S. Adults," *National Health Statistics Report* no.77 (July 15, 2014), http://www.cdc.gov/nchs/data/nhsr/nhsr077.pdf

245 UK Office for National Statistics, "Integrated Household Survey: January to December 2014 (sexual identity)," October 1, 2015, http://www.ons.gov.uk/peoplepopulationandcommunity/culturalidentity/sexuality/bulletins/integratedhouseholdsurvey/2015-10-01

246 "Homosexuality isn't natural," Peter Tatchell website, June 24, 2008, accessed August 20, 2016, http://www.petertatchell.net/lgbt_rights/gay_gene/homosexualityisntnatural.htm

247 Graff E.J., "What's wrong with choosing to be gay?" *The Nation*, February 3, 2014, accessed August 20, 2016, https://www.thenation.com/article/whats-wrong-choosing-be-gay/

248 Paglia C., *Vamps and Tramps* (Knopf Doubleday, 2011).

249 Mayer, McHugh "Sexuality and Gender," op.cit.

250 Koziol M., "Are we winning the war on HIV?" *The Sydney Morning Herald*, September 18, 2015, http://www.smh.com.au/national/health/are-we-winning-the-war-on-hiv-20150916-gjo6oa See also "2015 Annual Surveillance Report of HIV, viral hepatitis, STIs," The Kirby Institute.

251 "Gay marriage debate: Penny Wong vs Cory Bernardi," YouTube video, Debate at the National Press Club in Canberra on July 29, 2015, posted by "porjo38," July 29, 2015, https://youtu.be/Vyqz5tuPhIw

252 Gessen M., interview by Annette Shun Wah, *Radio National*, June 11, 2012, Sydney Writer's Festival 2012, at 6.20min, http://www.abc.net.au/radionational/programs/lifematters/why-get-married/4058506

253 Signorile M., "Bridal wave" *Out*, December 1993, 161.

254 Willis E. et al, "Can marriage be saved?" *The Nation*, June 17, 2004, https://www.thenation.com/article/can-marriage-be-saved-0/

255 Graff E.J., "Same-sex marriage is a radical feminist idea," *The American Prospect*, June 28, 2012, accessed August 20, 2016, http://prospect.org/article/same-sex-marriage-radical-feminist-idea

256 Altman D., interview by Annette Shun Wah, *Radio National*, June 11, 2012, Sydney

Writer's Festival 2012, http://www.abc.net.au/radionational/programs/lifematters/why-get-married/4058506

257 Selmys M., *Sexual Authenticity, An intimate reflection on Homosexuality and Catholicism* (Huntington IN: OSV, 2009), 215.

258 McWhirter D. and Mattison A., *The male couple: how relationships develop* (Englewood Cliffs, N.J.: Prentice Hall, 1984).

259 Selmys, *Sexual Authenticity*, op.cit.

260 Brennan D., "Gay marriage: eight centuries of law obliterated overnight," *The Telegraph*, March 13, 2012, Accessed August 1, 2016, http://www.telegraph.co.uk/women/sex/9140790/Gay-marriage-Eight-centuries-of-law-obliterated-overnight.html

261 Supreme Court of the USA, *Obergefell v Hodges*, March 2015 at http://www.supremecourt.gov/opinions/14pdf/14-556_3204.pdf

262 Holehouse M., "Green Party 'open' to three-person marriage, says Natalie Bennett," *The Telegraph*, May 1, 2015, accessed August 1, 2016, http://www.telegraph.co.uk/news/general-election-2015/11576818/Greens-open-to-three-person-marriage-says-Natalie-Bennett.html

263 Willis, "Can marriage be saved?" op.cit.

264 Li D.K., "Married lesbian threesome expecting first child," *New York Post*, April 23, 2014, accessed August 20, 2016, http://nypost.com/2014/04/23/married-lesbian-threesome-expecting-first-child/

265 Haque F., "Meet the 'world's first' gay married throuple'," *New York Post*, February 27, 2015, accessed August 20, 2016, http://nypost.com/2015/02/27/thai-throuple-believed-to-be-worlds-first-gay-married-trio/

266 White R., Interview on Perth radio *6PR*, May 5, 2012.

267 Gill C., "Disgusted by Incest? Genetic Sexual Attraction is real and on the rise," *The Telegraph*, April 11, 2016, accessed August 20, 2016, http://www.telegraph.co.uk/women/family/disgusted-by-incest-genetic-sexual-attraction-is-real-and-on-the/

268 Williams R., "German incest couple lose rights ruling," *Independent*, April 12, 2012, accessed August 20, 2016, http://www.independent.co.uk/news/world/europe/german-incest-couple-lose-rights-ruling-7640247.html

269 Overton P., "Forbidden Love," *60 Minutes*, April 6, 2008, http://sixtyminutes.ninemsn.com.au/stories/peteroverton/441583/forbidden-love

270 Gill, "Disgusted by Incest?" op. cit.

271 Bergelson V., "Vice is Nice But Incest is Best: The Problem of a Moral Taboo," *Criminal Law and Philosophy* 7, no.1 (2013): 43-59, http://link.springer.com/article/10.1007/s11572-012-9158-9

272 Ibid.

273 Newton J., "In love British mother, 51, and son plan to have BABY after she broke up his marriage," *Daily Mail*, April 8, 2016, accessed August 20, 2016, http://www.dailymail.co.uk/news/article-3529572/I-m-love-son-want-baby-Mother-falls-son-gave-adoption-32-years-ago.html

274 Gill, "Disgusted by Incest?" op. cit.

275 O'Neill B., "Here's my beef with gay marriage," *Catallaxy Files*, August 24, 2015, http://catallaxyfiles.com/2015/08/24/guest-post-brendan-oneill-heres-my-beef-with-gay-marriage/

276 Hirst J., *The Gender Fairy* (Oban Road Publishing, 2015), see http://www.thegenderfairy.com

277 McHugh P., "Transgender Surgery isn't the Solution," *Wall St Journal*, June 12, 2014, http://www.wsj.com/articles/paul-mchugh-transgender-surgery-isnt-the-solution-1402615120

278 Westen J., "Pope Francis condemns gender theory a third time: 'The family is under attack'," *Life Site News*, March 23, 2015, accessed August 20, 2016, https://www.lifesitenews.com/news/pope-francis-condemns-gender-theory-a-third-time-the-family-is-under-attack; Kengor P., "Pope Francis vs. the 'Demon' of Gender Theory," *CNS News*, October 6, 2015, accessed August 20, 2016, http://cnsnews.com/commentary/dr-paul-kengor/pope-francis-vs-demon-gender-theory

279 Pope Benedict XVI, "Address of his Holiness Benedict XVI on the occasion of Christmas greetings to the Roman Curia," Vatican Publishing House, December 21, 2012, http://w2.vatican.va/content/benedict-xvi/en/speeches/2012/december/documents/hf_ben-xvi_spe_20121221_auguri-curia.html

280 Latham M., "From reason to radicalism: gender fluidity," *Daily Telegraph*, May 31, 2016, accessed August 1, 2016, http://www.dailytelegraph.com.au/news/opinion/from-reason-to-radicalism-gender-fluidity/news-story/832eb330f1e68c0af8ab37521dc402d7

281 Gergis S., "Obergefell and the New Gnosticism," *First Things*, June 28, 2016, http://www.firstthings.com/web-exclusives/2016/06/obergefell-and-the-new-gnosticism

282 Money J., "Hermaphroditism, Gender and Precocity in Hyperadrenocorticism: Psychological Findings," *Bulletin of the Johns Hopkins Hospital* 96 (1955).

283 Colapinto J., "The True Story of John/Joan," *The Rolling Stone*, December 11, 1997 http://web.archive.org/web/20000815095602/http://www.pfc.org.uk/news/1998/johnjoan.htm

284 Colapinto J., *As Nature Made Him: The Boy Who Was Raised as a Girl* (Harper Perennial, 2001).

285 Burkeman O. and Younge G., "Being Brenda," *The Guardian*, May 12, 2004,

accessed August 20, 2016, https://www.theguardian.com/books/2004/may/12/scienceandnature.gender

286 *Time* magazine, January 1973, quoted in Burkeman and Younge, "Being Brenda," op.cit.

287 Money J., "Preface" in Money and Ehrhardt A., *Man & Woman, Boy & Girl: Gender Identity from Conception to Maturity* (Northvale, NJ: Jason Aronson, 1996), xii.

288 Bita N., "Activists push taxpayer-funded gay manual in schools," *The Australian*, February 10, 2016, accessed August 20, 2016, http://www.theaustralian.com.au/national-affairs/education/activists-push-taxpayerfunded-gay-manual-in-schools/news-story/4de614a88e38ab7b16601f07417c6219

289 O'Brien S., "Toddlers to be taught about cross-dressing in controversial sex ed program," *Herald Sun*, March 6, 2016, accessed September 3, 2016, http://www.heraldsun.com.au/news/toddlers-to-be-taught-about-crossdressing-in-controversial-sex-ed-program/news-story/7b935bb2e1573c1b2e748755d0f18986

290 Urban R., "Call to study gay issues at preschool," *The Australian*, April 30, 2016, accessed August 20, 2016, http://www.theaustralian.com.au/national-affairs/education/call-to-study-gay-issues-at-preschool/news-story/b3e7ff84aa012df302424d7756741790

291 Fink M. et al., eds., *OMG I'm Trans* (MINUS18, 2015), 6, accessed June 19, 2016, https://minus18.org.au/omgit/omgit-web.pdf

292 Ibid., 24.

293 Ibid., 30.

294 Ward R., Radcliffe J., Parsons M. et al., *Guide to supporting a student to affirm or transition gender identity at school* (Safe Schools Coalition Australia, 2015), accessed August 20, 2016, http://www.safeschoolshub.edu.au/common/downloads/guide-to-supporting-a-student-to-affirm-or-transition-gender-identity-at-school_oct-2015.pdf

295 Korte A. et al., "Gender identity disorders in childhood and adolescence: currently debated concepts and treatment strategies," *Dtsch Arztebl Int*. 105, no.48 (November 2008): 834, http://www.ncbi.nlm.nih.gov/pubmed/19578420

296 Cantor, J., "Do trans-kids stay trans when they grow up?" *Sexology Today* website, January 11, 2016, http://www.sexologytoday.org/2016/01/do-trans-kids-stay-trans-when-they-grow_99.html

297 De Cuypere G., Knudson G. et al., *WPATH consensus process regarding transgender and transsexual-related diagnoses in ICD-11* (World Professional Association for Transgender Health, May 31, 2013), 55, https://dl.dropboxusercontent.com/u/7789275/ICD%20Meeting%20Packet-Report-Final-sm.pdf

298 Urban R., "Kids, 5, in sex-change stories research trial", *The Australian*, August 16, 2016,

http://www.theaustralian.com.au/national-affairs/education/kids-5-in-sexchange-stories-uni-research-trial/news-story/2a5f196e1609ec2541d0fee4dd3545e5?utm_source=The%20Australian&utm_medium=email&utm_campaign=editorial

299 *Guidelines for Best Practices: Creating Learning Environments that Respect Diverse Sexual Orientations, Gender Identities and Gender Expressions* (Alberta: Alberta Education, 2016), https://education.alberta.ca/media/1626737/91383-attachment-1-guidelines-final.pdf

300 "College Kids Say the Darndest Things: On Gender," YouTube video, posted by "Family Policy Institute of Washington," May 9, 2016, https://youtu.be/-4S0gHlKiho

301 McHugh, "Transgender Surgery isn't the Solution," op. cit.

302 "Congratulations to DCA Chair David Morrison AO – 2016 Australian of the Year!" Diversity Council of Australia, January 25, 2016, accessed August 20, 2016, https://www.dca.org.au/News/All/-Congratulations-to-DCA-Chair-David-Morrison-AO-%E2%80%93-2016-Australian-of-the-Year!/506

303 Power S., "Cate McGregor apologises for "weak" selection comments of Australian of the Year winner," January 27, 2016, accessed August 20, 2016, http://www.starobserver.com.au/news/national-news/cate-mcgregor-wants-to-train-new-australian-of-the-year-on-trans-issues/144998

304 Tacopino J., "Not using transgender pronouns could get you fined," *New York Post*, May 19, 2016, accessed August 20, 2016, http://nypost.com/2016/05/19/city-issues-new-guidelines-on-transgender-pronouns/

305 Duffy N., "Germaine Greer: Lopping off your d**k and wearing a dress doesn't make you a f***ing woman," *Pink News*, October 26, 2015, accessed August 20, 2016, http://www.pinknews.co.uk/2015/10/26/germaine-greer-lopping-off-your-dk-and-wearing-a-dress-doesnt-make-you-a-fing-woman/

306 "Barry Humphries angers transgender community," *Sky News*, January 6, 2016, accessed August 20, 2016, http://www.skynews.com.au/culture/showbiz/celebrity/2016/01/06/barry-humphries-angers-transgender-community.html

307 Denholm M., "Feminists decry sex change proposals on men who identify as women", The Australian, August 26, 2016, http://www.theaustralian.com.au/national-affairs/state-politics/feminists-decry-sex-change-proposals-on-men-who-identify-as-women/news-story/600466f4e420ad31dca556c23d863bbc

308 ibid.

309 ibid.

310 "Blues in the toilet," *The Washington Times*, April 25, 2016, accessed August 20, 2016, http://www.washingtontimes.com/news/2016/apr/25/editorial-gender-confusion-in-the-toilet/

311 Katz J.M., "Major Companies Press North Carolina on Law Curbing Protections

From Bias," *New York Times*, March 29, 2016, accessed August 20, 2016, http://www.nytimes.com/2016/03/30/us/north-carolina-governor-attacks-critics-of-law-curbing-protections-from-bias.html

312 Sterling J. et al., "North Carolina, U.S., square off over transgender rights," *CNN*, May 10, 2016, accessed August 20, 2016, http://edition.cnn.com/2016/05/09/politics/north-carolina-hb2-justice-department-deadline/

313 Grinberg E., "Feds issue guidance on transgender access to school bathrooms," *CNN*, May 14, 2016, accessed August 20, 2016, http://edition.cnn.com/2016/05/12/politics/transgender-bathrooms-obama-administration/

314 Chasmar J., "Ga. ACLU leader resigns over Obama's transgender bathroom directive," *Washington Times*, June 2, 2016, accessed August 20, 2016, http://www.washingtontimes.com/news/2016/jun/2/maya-dillard-smith-georgia-aclu-leader-resigns-ove/

315 "Cella's Story," YouTube video, posted by "youreteachingourchildrenwhat ?" June 21, 2016, https://youtu.be/rOmCyw9vRi4

316 Chasmar J., "Canadian Prime Minister Justin Trudeau seeks federal ban on anti-transgender speech," *The Washington Times*, May 23, 2016, accessed August 20, 2016, http://www.washingtontimes.com/news/2016/may/23/justin-trudeau-canadian-prime-minister-seeks-feder/

317 Heyer W., "I was a transgender woman," *Public Discourse*, April 1, 2015, http://www.thepublicdiscourse.com/2015/04/14688/

318 Richards R., *Second Serve* (New York: Stein & Day, 1984).

319 Wadler J., "The Lady Regrets," *New York Times*, February 1, 2007, accessed August 20, 2016, http://www.nytimes.com/2007/02/01/garden/01renee.html

320 Green M., "The world's most famous transsexual looks back," *People* Magazine, March 5, 2007, accessed August 20, 2016, http://www.people.com/people/archive/article/0,,20062902,00.html

321 Richards R., "The Liaison Legacy," *Tennis* Magazine, March 1999, cited in "Trouble in Transtopia," *The Federalist*, November 11, 2014, accessed August 20, 2016, http://thefederalist.com/2014/11/11/trouble-in-transtopia-murmurs-of-sex-change-regret/

322 "Rupert Everett: I really wanted to be a girl", *The Telegraph*, June 19, 2016, http://www.telegraph.co.uk/news/2016/06/19/rupert-everett-i-really-wanted-to-be-a-girl/

323 Editor's note, "Special Report, Sexuality and Gender", *The New Atlantis*, no.50, Fall 2016, 1.

324 McHugh P., "Surgical Sex: Why We Stopped Doing Sex Change Operations," *First Things*, November 2004, http://www.firstthings.com/article/2004/11/surgical-sex

325. Dhejne C. et al, "Long-Term Follow-Up of Transsexual Persons Undergoing Sex Reassignment Surgery: Cohort Study in Sweden," *PLoS ONE* 6, no.2 (2011): e16885, http://dx.doi.org/10.1371/journal.pone.0016885
326. McHugh, "Transgender Surgery isn't the Solution," op. cit.
327. McHugh P., "Transgenderism: a Pathogenic Meme," *Public Discourse*, June 10, 2015, http://www.thepublicdiscourse.com/2015/06/15145/
328. Fleming M., "Why Is Transgender An Identity But Anorexia A disorder?" *The Federalist*, June 26, 2016, http://thefederalist.com/2016/06/27/why-is-transgender-an-identity-but-anorexia-a-disorder/
329. McHugh, "Transgender Surgery isn't the Solution," op.cit.
330. Bissinger B., "Caitlyn Jenner: The Full Story," *Vanity Fair*, June 25, 2015, accessed August 20, 2016, http://www.vanityfair.com/hollywood/2015/06/caitlyn-jenner-bruce-cover-annie-leibovitz
331. McHugh, "Transgenderism: a Pathogenic Meme."
332. McHugh, "Surgical Sex," op. cit.
333. McHugh, "Transgenderism: a Pathogenic Meme," op. cit.
334. "Rupert Everett," *The Telegraph*, op.cit.
335. McHugh, "Transgender Surgery isn't the Solution," op. cit.
336. Ibid.
337. Legge, K., "Transgender children: what's behind the spike in numbers?" *The Australian*, July 18, 2015, accessed August 20, 2016, http://www.theaustralian.com.au/life/weekend-australian-magazine/transgender-children-whats-behind-the-spike-in-numbers/story-e6frg8h6-1227446188926
338. McHugh, "Transgenderism: a Pathogenic Meme," op. cit.
339. Ibid.
340. Anderssen E., "Gender identity debate swirls over CAMH psychologist, transgender program," *The Globe and Mail*, February 4, 2016, http://www.theglobeandmail.com/news/toronto/gender-identity-debate-swirls-over-camh-psychologist-transgender-program/article28758828/
341. Singal J., "How the fight over transgender kids got a leading sex-researcher fired", *New York Magazine*, February 7, 2016, http://nymag.com/scienceofus/2016/02/fight-over-trans-kids-got-a-researcher-fired.html
342. Mayer L., McHugh P., "Sexuality and Gender: Findings from the Biological, Psychological and Social Sciences," *The New Atlantis* no.50 (August 2016): 6, http://www.thenewatlantis.com/docLib/20160819_TNA50SexualityandGender.pdf

343 McHugh, "Transgenderism: a Pathogenic Meme," op. cit.

344 McHugh, "Transgender Surgery isn't the Solution," op. cit.

345 Love S., "The WHO says being transgender is a mental illness. But that could soon change," *Sydney Morning Herald*, July 29, 2016, accessed August 20, 2016, http://www.smh.com.au/world/the-who-says-being-transgender-is-a-mental-illness-but-that-could-soon-change-20160728-gqg7kv.html

346 Sax L, "How common is intersex? A Response to Anne Fausto-Sterling," *Journal of Sex Research* 39, no.3 (2002): 174-8, http://dx.doi.org/10.1080/00224490209552139

347 Safe Schools Coalition Australia, *All of Us*, 8.

348 Blackless M, Charuvastra A, Derryck A, Fausto-Sterling A, Lauzanne K, Lee E., "How sexually dimorphic are we? Review and synthesis," *American Journal of Human Biology* 12, no.2 (March 2000):151-166.

349 Sax, "How common is intersex?" op cit.

350 Hull C.L., Fausto-Sterling A., "How sexually dimorphic are we? Review and synthesis." *American Journal of Human Biology* 15, no.1. (Jan-Feb 2003):112-5; author reply 115-6.

351 Ibid.

352 "Why doesn't ISNA want to eradicate gender?" Intersex Society of North America, accessed August 1, 2016, http://www.isna.org/faq/not_eradicating_gender

353 McHugh, "Surgical Sex," op.cit.

354 Ibid.

355 "What does ISNA recommend for children with intersex?" Intersex Society of North America, accessed August 1, 2016, http://www.isna.org/faq/patient-centered

356 McHugh, "Surgical Sex," op.cit.

357 Ibid.

358 Ibid.

359 Latham M., "From reason to radicalism: gender fluidity," *Daily Telegraph*, May 31, 2016, accessed August 1, 2016, http://www.dailytelegraph.com.au/news/opinion/from-reason-to-radicalism-gender-fluidity/news-story/832eb330f1e68c0af8ab37521dc402d7

360 McHugh, "Transgenderism: a Pathogenic Meme," op.cit.

361 O'Neill, "Here's my beef with gay marriage," op. cit.

362 O'Neill, "Same-sex marriage: coercion dolled up as human rights," op. cit.

363 Somerville., "It's all about the children, not selfish adults," op.cit.

364. ibid.

365. Rennie D., "How's your 'Progenitor A'?" *The Telegraph*, March 7, 2006, accessed August 1, 2016, http://www.telegraph.co.uk/news/worldnews/europe/spain/1512344/Hows-your-Progenitor-A.html

366. Lawson K., "New gender non-specific birth certificates for the ACT," *Canberra Times*, February 16, 2016, accessed August 1, 2016, http://www.canberratimes.com.au/act-news/new-gender-nonspecific-birth-certificates-for-the-act-20160216-gmv41w.html

367. Kengor P., *Takedown: From Communists to Progressives, How the Left Has Sabotaged Family and Marriage* (Washington DC: WND Books, 2015), Kindle edition, loc. 3307.

368. Engels F., *The Origin of the Family Private Property and the State* (New York: International, 1942), 67.

369. Weikart R., "Marx, Engels, and the Abolition of the Family," *History of European Ideas* 18, no.5 (1994): 664, cited in Kengor, *Takedown*, loc. 366.

370. Pope Pius IX, "Qui Pluribus" (On Faith and Religion), Papal Encyclicals Online, November 9, 1846, http://www.papalencyclicals.net/Pius09/p9quiplu.htm

371. Pope Leo XIII, "Quod Apostolici Muneris" (On Socialism), Vatican Publishing House, December 28, 1878, http://w2.vatican.va/content/leo-xiii/en/encyclicals/documents/hf_l-xiii_enc_28121878_quod-apostolici-muneris.html

372. Pope Pius XI, "Divini Redemptoris" (On Atheistic Communism), Vatican Publishing House, March 19, 1937, https://w2.vatican.va/content/pius-xi/en/encyclicals/documents/hf_p-xi_enc_19370319_divini-redemptoris.html

373. Kengor, *Takedown*, loc. 576.

374. Kengor, *Takedown*, loc. 667, 686.

375. McKay H., "Critics slam MSNBC host's claim that kids belong to community, not parents," *Fox News*, April 9, 2013, accessed August 1, 2016, http://www.foxnews.com/entertainment/2013/04/09/critics-slam-msnbc-hosts-claim-that-kids-belong-to-community-not-parents/

376. *Time* magazine cover, August 31, 1970, http://content.time.com/time/covers/0,16641,19700831,00.html

377. Millett K., *Sexual Politics* (Urbana and Chicago: University of Illinois Press, 1969), 62.

378. Millett M., "Marxist Feminism's Ruined lives," *Front Page Magazine*, September 2, 2014, http://www.frontpagemag.com/fpm/240037/marxist-feminisms-ruined-lives-mallory-millett, Altman, interview by Annette Shun Wah, *Radio National*, op. cit.

379. Altman D, Sydney Writers' Festival 2012, Radio National http://www.abc.net.au/radionational/programs/lifematters/why-get-married/4058506

380 Kengor, *Takedown*, loc. 1642.

381 Escoffier J., "Marcuse, Herbert (1898-1979)," *GLBTQ Encyclopedia*, 2004, http://www.glbtqarchive.com/ssh/marcuse_h_S.pdf

382 de Toledano R., *Cry Havoc! The Great American Bring-down and How it Happened* (Washington DC: Anthem, 2006), 48.

383 Altman D., quoted in Escoffier, "Marcuse, Herbert (1898-1979)," *GLBTQ Encyclopedia*, 2004, http://www.glbtqarchive.com/ssh/marcuse_h_S.pdf

384 Reich W., *The function of the orgasm* (New York: Farrar, Straus & Giroux, 1973), 8.

385 O'Brien S., "Toddlers to be taught about cross-dressing in controversial sex ed program," *Herald Sun*, March 6, 2016, accessed September 3, 2016, http://www.heraldsun.com.au/news/toddlers-to-be-taught-about-crossdressing-in-controversial-sex-ed-program/news-story/7b935bb2e1573c1b2e748755d0f18986

386 Roz Ward quoted in Bita N., "Safe School Coalition: Sexual politics in the classroom," *The Australian*, February 13, 2016, accessed August 1, 2016, http://www.theaustralian.com.au/news/inquirer/safe-schools-coalition-sexual-politics-in-the-classroom/news-story/bf58ff141ba0b08bf165e3d53cc8a055

387 Roz Ward quoted in Donnelly K., "Marxist view of Australia a long way from the truth," *Herald Sun*, May 30, 2016 http://www.heraldsun.com.au/news/opinion/marxist-view-of-australia-a-long-way-from-the-truth/news-story/0b0c618ba7d13d6b98360c1d87a04905

388 Kengor, *Takedown*, loc. 168.

389 Kengor, *Takedown*, loc. 3268.

390 "'Values in Western Civilisation' – the Hon. John Howard," Campion College graduation address, December 2011, http://www.campion.edu.au/values-in-western-civilisation-the-hon-john-howard/

391 *Wikipedia*, "Chai Feldblum," last updated May 23, 2016, https://en.wikipedia.org/wiki/Chai_Feldblum

392 Reno R., "The Selma Analogy", *First Things*, May 2012, https://www.firstthings.com/article/2012/05/the-selma-analogy

393 Ibid.

394 Australian Catholic Bishops Conference, *Don't Mess With Marriage* (2015), http://sydneycatholic.org/pdf/DMM-booklet_web.pdf

395 "Media Release: Church school marriage booklet likely violates anti-bias law," Australian Marriage Equality, June 24, 2015, accessed August 1, 2016, http://www.australianmarriageequality.org/2015/06/24/media-release-church-school-marriage-booklet-likely-violates-anti-bias-law/

396. Shanahan A., "Gay marriage leaves Catholic schools under threat," *The Australian*, July 4, 2015, accessed August 1, 2016, http://www.theaustralian.com.au/opinion/columnists/angela-shanahan/gay-marriage-leaves-catholic-schools-under-threat/news-story/c13f232f45b5cf15e196d288ccc500ec

397. van Gend D. and Croome R., interviewed by Melanie Tait, *ABC Hobart*, radio, August 31, 2015, https://soundcloud.com/936-abc-hobart/for-and-against-the-same-sex-marriage-debate, audio at 32.35.

398. Puplick C, "Catholic Church must stop vilifying same-sex marriage advocates," *The Australian*, December 5, 2015, accessed August 1, 2016, http://www.theaustralian.com.au/opinion/catholic-church-must-stop-vilifying-samesex-marriage-opponents/news-story/8926038b4ff158a35a59496ba0321401

399. *Catechism of the Catholic Church*, 2nd. ed. (Washington, DC: United States Catholic Conference, 2000), [2357]; see also the Congregation on the Doctrine of the Faith, "Considerations regarding proposals to give legal recognition to unions between homosexual persons," http://www.vatican.va/roman_curia/congregations/cfaith/documents/rc_con_cfaith_doc_20030731_homosexual-unions_en.html, Section 1, Part 4.

400. van Gend and Croome, ABC audio at 31.40

401. Ibid., 32.35

402. Drummond A., "Transgender activist Martine Delaney drops complaint over Catholic Church's marriage booklet," *The Mercury*, May 5, 2016, http://www.themercury.com.au/news/tasmania/transgender-rights-activist-martine-delaney-drops-complaint-over-catholic-churchs-marriage-booklet/news-story/d8d9079bf932526b27e5f094e57dbe84

403. Hiini R., "Anti-discrimination proceedings dropped but Archbishop Porteous disappointed," *The Catholic Weekly*, May 7, 2016, https://www.catholicweekly.com.au/anti-discrimination-proceedings-dropped-but-archbishop-porteous-disappointed/

404. Mehta D., "Trinity University loses appeal at Ontario's top court," *Toronto Metro*, June 30, 2016, accessed August 1, 2016, http://www.metronews.ca/news/canada/2016/06/29/private-christian-university-loses-appeal-at-ontario-s-top-court.html

405. Johns G., "Leftist politics and damned outcomes on matters of principle," *The Australian*, July 28, 2016, accessed August 20, 2016, http://www.theaustralian.com.au/opinion/columnists/gary-johns/leftist-politics-and-damned-outcomes-on-matters-of-principle/news-story/ff73798276afdfdcff69a35e04d0bcb9

406. Supreme Court of the USA, Obergefell v Hodges, March 2015 at http://www.supremecourt.gov/opinions/14pdf/14-556_3204.pdf

407. Ibid.

408 Ibid.

409 Ibid.

410 Australian Catholic Bishops, *Don't Mess With Marriage*, op.cit.

411 Bingham J., "MP: use anti-terror powers on Christian teachers who say gay marriage is 'wrong'," *The Telegraph*, August 3, 2015, accessed August 1 2016, http://www.telegraph.co.uk/news/politics/11780517/MP-use-anti-terror-powers-on-Christian-teachers-who-say-gay-marriage-is-wrong.html

412 San Martin I., "If Spanish cardinal is homophobic, defenders suggest so is Pope Francis," *Crux*, June 1, 2016, accessed August 1, 2016, https://cruxnow.com/global-church/2016/06/01/spanish-cardinal-homophobic-defenders-suggest-pope-francis/

413 Sheridan G., "Presbyterians 'will cut state ties' over gay marriage," *The Australian*, June 3, 2016, accessed August 1, 2016, http://www.theaustralian.com.au/national-affairs/presbyterians-will-cut-state-ties-over-gay-marriage/news-story/304106057da65c419a0c9e08b36b1667

414 Humanum YouTube Channel, https://www.youtube.com/user/humanumit, speeches published in *Not just Good but Beautiful: the complementary relationship between man and woman* (New York: Plough Publishing House, 2015).

415 Australian Catholic Bishops Conference, *Don't Mess With Marriage* (2015), http://sydneycatholic.org/pdf/DMM-booklet_web.pdf

416 Pope Francis, *Amoris Laetitia*, (Vatican Press, 2016), https://w2.vatican.va/content/dam/francesco/pdf/apost_exhortations/documents/papa-francesco_esortazione-ap_20160319_amoris-laetitia_en.pdf

417 Prader D., "Judaism, Homosexuality and Civilisation," *Ultimate Issues* 6, No. 2 (1990), 2.

418 Satinover J, *Homosexuality and the Politics of Truth* (Baker Books, Grand Rapids MI, 1996), 147, 244.

419 Ibid. 148.

420 Ibid. 176.

421 Ibid. 17.

422 Ibid. 250.

423 Yeats W, *The Second Coming* (1920; Wikisource, 2012), accessed August 1, 2016, https://en.wikisource.org/wiki/The_Second_Coming_(Yeats)

424 "Pro-traditional marriage doctor cops vandalism spray," *ABC Southern Queensland*, June 2, 2015, http://www.abc.net.au/local/stories/2015/06/02/4246975.htm

425 Post on Twitter by Bernard Keane, May 23, 2015, accessed August 20, 2016,

https://twitter.com/BernardKeane/status/602092692181524480

426 Bochenski N., "Vandals strike at anti-gay marriage doctor," *The Sydney Morning Herald*, June 3, 2015, accessed August 1, 2016, http://www.smh.com.au/queensland/vandals-strike-at-anti-gay-marriage-doctor-20150602-ghexcf

427 Post on Australian Marriage Forum Inc. Facebook page, June 2, 2015, accessed August 1, 2016, https://www.facebook.com/australianmarriageforum/photos/a.642826785816888.1073741828.617438041689096/642825969150303/?type=1&theater

428 O'Neill B., "Same-sex marriage: coercion dolled up as human rights," op. cit.

429 Barry P., "Media equality on marriage equality?" *ABC Media Watch*, transcript of Episode 29, August 17, 2015, http://www.abc.net.au/mediawatch/transcripts/s4295137.htm

430 "TV AD # 1: "MARRIAGE EQUALITY? WHAT ABOUT EQUALITY FOR THE CHILD?" Australian Marriage Forum, accessed August 1, 2016, http://australianmarriage.org/tv-ad-1-marriage-equality-what-about-equality-for-the-child/

431 Backlash after anti-marriage equality ad debuts on Mardi Gras night, SMH, 5/3/15 http://www.smh.com.au/entertainment/tv-and-radio/backlash-after-antimarriage-equality-ad-debuts-on-mardi-gras-night-20150308-13y8yi.html

432 Support for free speech on the AMF TV ad: Wilson T., "Australian Marriage Forum ad might be distasteful but it should have been screened," *The Sydney Morning Herald*, March 12, 2015, accessed August 1, 2016, http://www.smh.com.au/comment/australian-marriage-forum-ad-might-be-distasteful-but-it-should-have-been-screened-20150310-140q3w.html ; Knott M., "Mardi Gras: SBS wrong to dump ad opposing same sex marriage, say MPs Dean Smith and David Leyonhjelm," *The Sydney Morning Herald*, March 9, 2015, accessed August 1, 2016, http://www.smh.com.au/federal-politics/political-news/mardi-gras-sbs-wrong-to-dump-ad-opposing-same-sex-marriage-say-mps-dean-smith-and-david-leyonhjelm-20150309-13yw0z.html ; McLean S., "SBS should have run this offensive ad," *ABC The Drum*, March 13, 2015, accessed August 1, 2016, http://www.abc.net.au/news/2015-03-13/mclean-sbs-shouldn't-censor-anti-gay-marriage-ad/6314748

433 "MEDIA HIGHLIGHTS SINCE OUR LAUNCH: OVER HALF A MILLION VIEWS!" Australian Marriage Forum, March 13, 2015, http://australianmarriage.org/media-highlights-since-our-launch-over-half-a-million-views/

434 Canavan M., "SBS 'Biased Against Traditional Marriage'," Media Release, May 28, 2015, http://www.mattcanavan.com.au/sbs_biased_against_traditional_marriage

435 Milton J., *Areopagitica* (1644; Project Gutenberg, 2013), http://www.gutenberg.

org/files/608/608-h/608-h.htm

[436] Steyn M., "A Difference of Degree," *National Review*, April 2, 2011, http://www.nationalreview.com/corner/263716/difference-degree-mark-steyn

[437] *Queensland Anti-Discrimination Act 1991*, section 124A: "Vilification on grounds of race, religion, sexuality or gender identity unlawful: A person must not, by a public act, incite hatred towards, serious contempt for, or severe ridicule of, a person or group of persons on the ground of the race, religion, sexuality or gender identity of the person or members of the group." https://www.legislation.qld.gov.au/LEGISLTN/CURRENT/A/AntiDiscrimA91.pdf

[438] Brooks K. and van Gend D., "Gay marriage – the case for and against," *The Courier Mail*, June 29, 2011, accessed August 1, 2016, http://www.couriermail.com.au/news/labor-will-create-a-gay-stolen-generation-of-children-forcibly-deprived-of-a-mum-says-dr-david-van-gend/story-e6frerdf-1226083757106

[439] Boswell R., Parliament of Australia, *Senate Hansard*, October 12, 2011, http://parlinfo.aph.gov.au/parlInfo/search/display/display.w3p;db=CHAMBER;id=chamber%2Fhansards%2Fe95e40a0-18cf-4b68-ab20-b45a9f514412%2F0045;query=Id%3A%22chamber%2Fhansards%2Fe95e40a0-18cf-4b68-ab20-b45-a9f514412%2F0000%22

[440] Harkness K., "State Says Bakers Should Pay $135,000 for Refusing to Bake Cake for Same-Sex Wedding," *The Daily Signal*, April 24, 2015, accessed August 12, 2016, http://dailysignal.com/2015/04/24/state-says-bakers-should-pay-135000-for-refusing-to-bake-cake-for-same-sex-wedding/

[441] "Gay marriage debate: Penny Wong vs Cory Bernardi," YouTube video, op. cit.

[442] Karp P., "Shorten: Labor won't change discrimination laws to please same-sex marriage opponents," *The Guardian*, March 31, 2016, https://www.theguardian.com/australia-news/2016/mar/31/shorten-labor-wont-change-discrimination-laws-to-please-gay-marriage-opponents

[443] "Ashers: The story so far," YouTube video, Asher's bakery case as of July 1, 2016, posted by "The Christian Institute," July 1, 2016, https://youtu.be/p3Z1gyhyz_Y

[444] "Final day of Ashers appeal: 'It's the cake not the customer'," The Christian Institute, May 12, 2016, accessed August 12, 2016, http://www.christian.org.uk/news/final-day-of-ashers-appeal-its-the-cake-not-the-customer/

[445] The Associated Press, "Court: Lakewood baker who refused gay wedding cake can't cite beliefs," *The Denver Post*, August 13, 2015, accessed August 12, 2016, http://www.denverpost.com/2015/08/13/court-lakewood-baker-who-refused-gay-wedding-cake-cant-cite-beliefs/

[446] "The Barronelle Stutzman Story," YouTube video, posted by "Alliance Defending Freedom," March 16, 2014, https://youtu.be/MDETkcCw63c

447 "State of Washington v. Arlene's Flowers | Ingersoll v. Arlene's Flowers," Alliance Defending Freedom, accessed August 12, 2016, http://www.adflegal.org/detailspages/case-details/state-of-washington-v.-arlene-s-flowers-inc.-and-barronelle-stutzman

448 Anderson R.T., "Same-Sex Marriage Trumps Religious Liberty in New Mexico," *Daily Signal*, August 22, 2013, accessed August 1, 2016, http://dailysignal.com/2013/08/22/same-sex-marriage-trumps-religious-liberty-in-new-mexico/

449 Harkness, K., "Fearing Another Lawsuit, Christian Business Owners Stopped Hosting All Weddings. Now Their Business Is Dead," *Daily Signal*, June 19, 2015, accessed August 1, 2016, http://dailysignal.com/2015/06/19/fearing-another-lawsuit-christian-business-owners-stopped-hosting-all-weddings-now-their-business-is-dead/

450 *Wikipedia*, "Brendan Eich," last updated August 5, 2016, https://en.wikipedia.org/wiki/Brendan_Eich

451 Sullivan, A., "The Hounding of a Heretic," *The Dish*, April 3, 2014, accessed August 1, 2016, http://dish.andrewsullivan.com/2014/04/03/the-hounding-of-brendan-eich/

452 Friedersdorf, C., "Mozilla's gay-marriage litmus test violates liberal values," *The Atlantic*, April 4, 2014, accessed August 1, 2016, http://www.theatlantic.com/politics/archive/2014/04/mozillas-gay-marriage-litmus-test-violates-liberal-values/360156/

453 O'Neill B., "Same-sex marriage: coercion dolled up as human rights," *Spiked*, April 30, 2014, accessed August 1, 2016, http://www.spiked-online.com/newsite/article/same-sex-marriage-coercion-dolled-up-as-civil-rights/14967#.V3mEQSN96Cc

454 Satinover, *Homosexuality and the Politics of Truth*, op. cit., 21.

455 Kelly P., "Race, gender: the risk of identity politics," *The Australian*, August 6, 2016, accessed August 12, 2016, http://www.theaustralian.com.au/opinion/columnists/paul-kelly/race-gender-the-risk-of-identity-politics/news-story/ee7e4ef3f632b6475ba215be60322908

456 "I'm gay and I'm voting No. Here's why," YouTube video, Paddy Manning and Keith Mills Irish referendum video, posted by "Mothers and Fathers Matter," May 16, 2015, https://youtu.be/Q6HD8KLQBvA

457 Stark J., "David van Gend from The Australian Marriage Forum responds to questions on marriage equality," *The Sydney Morning Herald*, May 20, 2016, accessed July 1, 2016, http://www.smh.com.au/national/lyle-shelton-from-the-australian-christian-lobby-responds-to-questions-on-marriage-equality-20160520-gozr7a.html

458 Anthony, "Sex in Australia" op.cit.

459 Spitzer R.L., quoted in Ronald Bayer, *Homosexuality and American Psychiatry: the Politics of Diagnosis* (Princeton University Press, 1981), 128 and Afterword (1987 edition).

460 "Homosexuality is immoral, say almost 3 in 10 Coalition voters," Roy Morgan Research, June 30, 2016, accessed August 1, 2016, http://www.roymorgan.com/findings/6872-plebiscite-voters-who-say-homosexuality-is-immoral-march-2016-201606301142

461 *Catechism of the Catholic Church,* 2nd. ed. (Washington, DC: United States Catholic Conference, 2000), [2357, 2358].

462 Willingham R., "Same-sex marriage: Premier Andrews tells Turnbull Victorians against plebiscite," *The Age,* July 25, 2016, accessed August 1, 2016, http://www.theage.com.au/victoria/samesex-marriage-plebiscite-premier-daniel-andrews-attacks-malcolm-turnbull-20160724-gqcu45.html

463 "Rowena Allen is Victoria's First Gender and Sexuality Commissioner," Media Release by Premier of Victoria, July 15, 2015, accessed August 1, 2016, http://www.premier.vic.gov.au/rowena-allen-is-victorias-first-gender-and-sexuality-commissioner/